Analyzing Building Structures

An Exercise and Solutions Manual

By Nawari O. Nawari

University of Florida

Bassim Hamadeh, CEO and Publisher
Christopher Foster, General Vice President
Michael Simpson, Vice President of Acquisitions
Jessica Knott, Managing Editor
Kevin Fahey, Cognella Marketing Manager
Jess Busch, Senior Graphic Designer
Zina Craft, Acquisitions Editor
Jamie Giganti, Project Editor
Brian Fahey, Licensing Associate
Kate McKellar, Interior Designer

First published in the United States of America in 2013 by Cognella, Inc.

Printed in the United States of America

ISBN: 978-1-60927-581-5 (pbk) / 978-1-60927-582-2 (pf)

www.cognella.com 800.200.3908

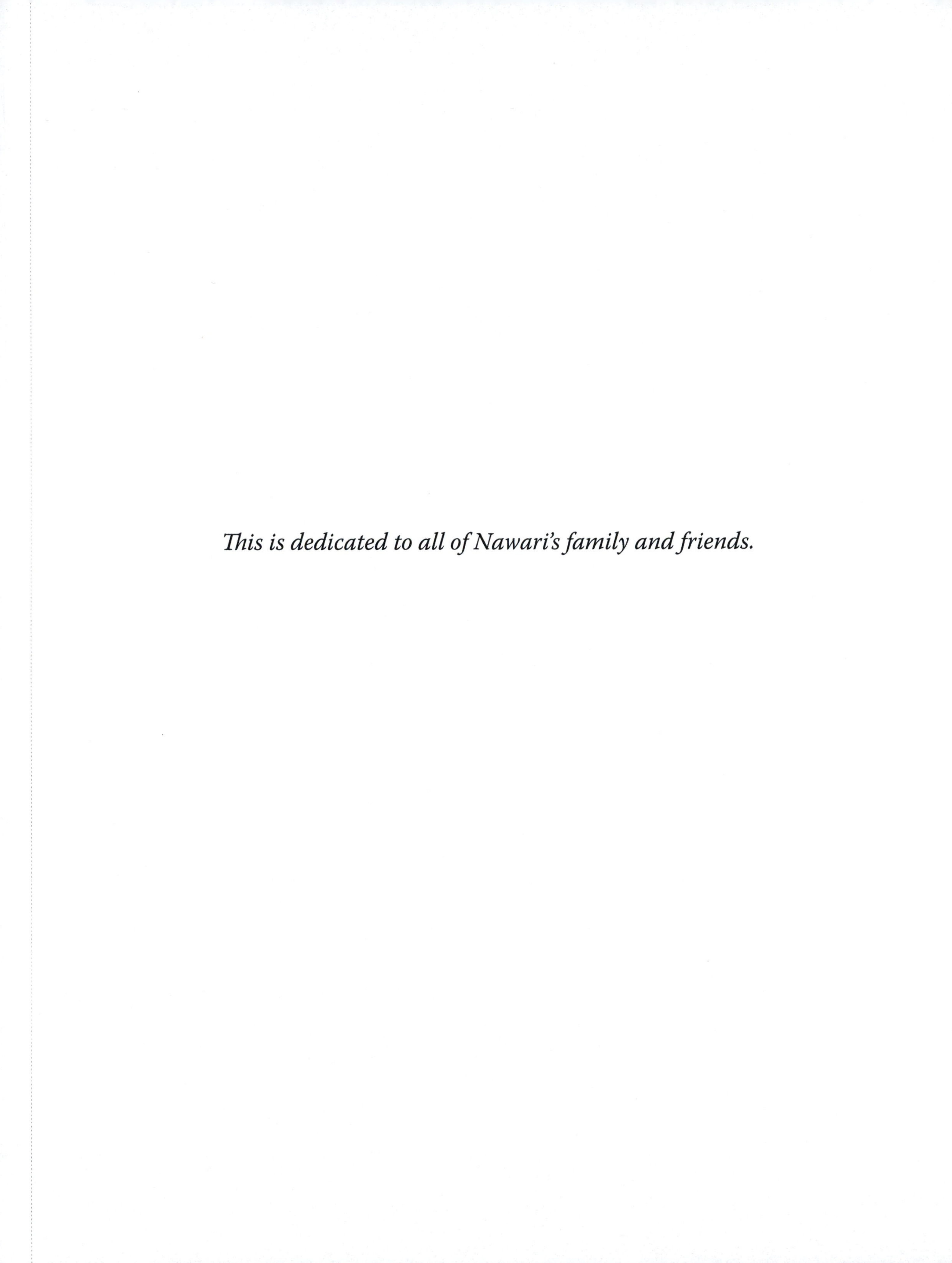

This is dedicated to all of Nawari's family and friends.

CONTENTS

ACKNOWLEDGMENTS

I WOULD LIKE to express my deep gratitude to many students who have assisted in bringing this book into publication. They are too numerous to be mentioned individually, but special thanks are due to the following: Stanley NG and Azhar Khan for their hard work in reviewing solutions and illustrations, Ran Li and Luis Delfin for their excellent drawings, and Jennifer Szilagyi for her helpful suggestions and feedback.

I would also like to sincerely thank the faculty and staff of the School of Architecture at the University of Florida for the many helpful discussions, particularly Prof. Michael Kuenstle, Prof. Martin Gold, and Prof. Wolfgang Schueller.

Finally, I should especially like to thank my family for their patience, encouragement, and support.

N. Nawari

Gainesville, Florida
2011

PREFACE

THIS BOOK has been written to help students learn about the fundamentals of building structures by involving them in the kinds of work that building design professionals—architects, engineers, and builders—encounter in the course of designing building structures and getting them constructed.

Students will find that these exercises make it easier to learn the essential information in the accompanying book "Building Structures: Fundamentals of Crossover Design." Students will also discover that they will give them a good start toward becoming proficient in many different phases of building activity.

As you work through these exercises, try to keep the text "Building Structures: Fundamentals of Crossover Design" close by since these problems are immediately related to different sections of the book. Each problem will have suggestions for a solution outline to help students get starting solving these assignments. Nearly everything you need to know to solve the problems is in the textbook, and in most cases you will be given explicit directions about where to look for it. Most of the answers for the numerical problems are given as well to assist students in revising and correcting their solutions.

The numbering system following in the problems is such that the first digit refers to the chapter in your text book "Building Structures: Fundamentals of Crossover Design" and the second part of the problem designates the sequential number of the question. For example problem 3.15 refers to the 15th question in Chapter 3. Here is a glance at what's in each chapter:

- Chapter 1: **Introduction** This is a general introduction to foster a deeper understanding of what building structures really are and how they can be assessed within the context of buildings and architectural design strategies.
- Chapter 2: **Forces on Buildings** This chapter introduces the type and nature of loading conditions a structure may be exposed to, their effects, and their mathematical modeling.
- Chapter 3: **Equilibrium of Building** This chapter explores the meaning of static equilibrium of forces and its application in analyzing building forces and stability.

- Chapter 4: **Load Path—Vertical Forces** In this chapter vertical load paths are introduced along with the framing systems and the nature of the structural support systems that define vertical load paths.
- Chapter 5: **Load Path—Lateral Forces** Covers the second part of the load paths in building structures and their resisting system and how they relate to stability of buildings.
- Chapter 6: **Structural Elements—Cables** This chapter introduces the basic behavior and analysis of cables along with their practical applications such as relation to form and components of cable-supported structures.
- Chapter 7: **Structural Elements—Arches** In this chapter the fundamental behaviors of arches are explained as well as their analysis and design criteria.
- Chapter 8: **Structural Elements—Trusses** This chapter deals with truss structures configuration, behavior, analysis and their applications in buildings.
- Chapter 9: **Shape Factors—Properties of Sections** Describes the geometric characteristics of structural members and explains their importance and application in building design.
- Chapter 10: **Structural Materials—Strength and Behavior** In this chapter the fundamental characteristics of structural materials are introduced along with identifying relationships between external loads on structural members and the induced stresses and deformation.
- Chapter 11: **Structural Elements—Beams** This chapter describes and identifies beam types and explains their behavior and roles in building structures. It also introduces beam analysis and design.
- Chapter 12: **Structural Elements—Columns** This chapter focuses on understanding column behavior and functions in building structures, and designing simple columns.

On your first attempt at solving these problems it is recommended that you block out the solution outline and refer to it only if you are in doubt about the next step in the solution. Try to use sketches to illustrate your answer when appropriate. You may draw freehand or with the aid of CAD or any drafting board and instruments, as you prefer or as directed by your instructor. In either case, only minimal use of an architect's scale is required.

When you are satisfied that you have included all necessary details in your solution, you can examine the solution outline and the final answers. You may find some of these exercises difficult at first, but if you follow the recommended procedures, they will become easier and more enjoyable as you acquire experience and gain confidence in your growing abilities.

N. Nawari

Gainesville, Florida
2011

PROBLEMS

PROBLEM 1.1

Use the library, internet or your own sources to find photographs of a series of buildings that represent each of the primary structural types such as trusses, frames, arches, cables, shells and plates, and space frames. For example, identify one that uses trusses as the primary supporting structures. Clearly mark and label the truss structure. Repeat for other structural systems. Also include information about the building name, location, architect, and any relevant information. Upload your photos to the course website.

1.2 PROBLEM

Find three natural structures that have a clear relationship to man-made structures. Provide images or hand drawings and identify similarities.

PROBLEM 1.3

Define the term "Crossover Design" in building structures and illustrate your answer with a diagram.

1.4 PROBLEM

Give a list of the main structural system categories and subcategories.

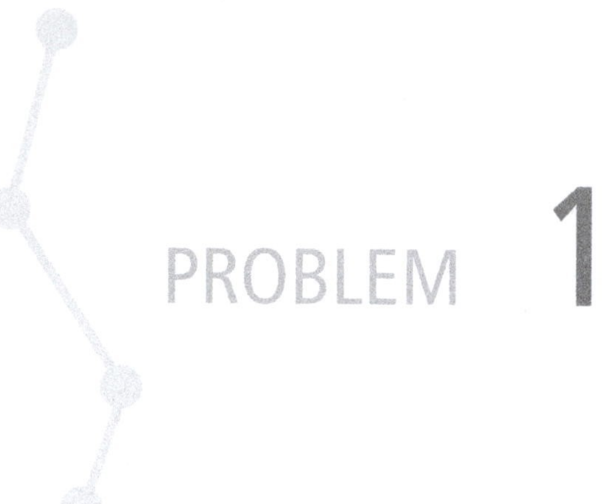

PROBLEM 1.5

Define the term "Substructure." What is the main purpose of substructure? Give three examples of substructural elements.

1.6 PROBLEM

The composition and orchestration of the structural systems influences building design in various ways. Name the four fundamental ways in which structures impact architectural design and give a contemporary example for each.

PROBLEM 1.7

Use the library, internet or your own sources to find photographs of a series of buildings that are characterized mainly by the following architectural orchestration:

i. Exposed structural systems
ii. Partially exposed structural systems
iii. Concealed structural systems
iv. Celebrated structural systems

For each example, identify the type of primary supporting structures. Clearly mark and label drawings and photos. Also include information about the building name, location, architect, and any relevant information. Upload your photos and drawings to the course website.

2.1 PROBLEM

Give an example (including units of measurement) of the following in a typical building structure:

i. Point load
ii. 2D-uniformly distributed load (area load)
iii. 2D-non-uniformly distributed load
iv. 1D-uniformly distributed load (lineal load)

PROBLEM 2.2

Distinguish between external and internal forces (use sketches to support your answer).

2.3 PROBLEM

Given:

Determine the resultant of the two forces shown (magnitude and direction) acting on the pin shown below.

Scale: 1" = 100 lb

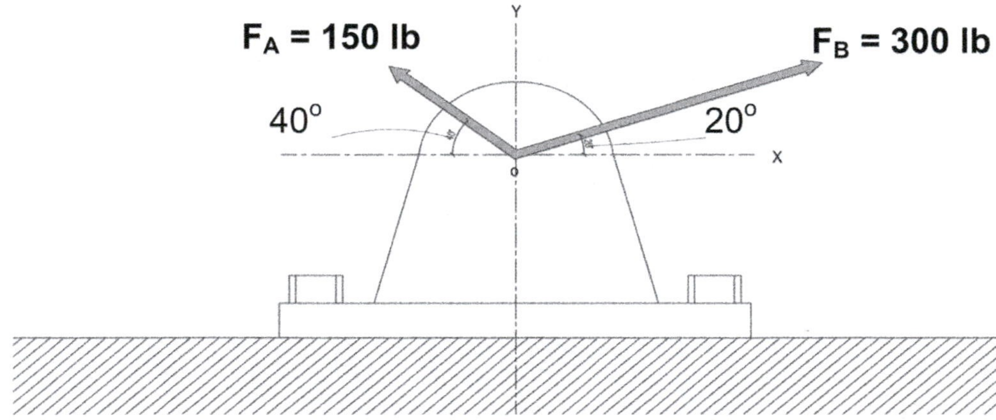

Required:

Resultant magnitude, $R = ?$
Resultant direction, $\theta = ?$

PROBLEM 2.4

Given:

Three members at Joint *A* of the truss shown in figure 2.4a are carrying the forces illustrated in figure 2.4b below. All forces can be assumed to intersect at a common point as shown in figure 2.4b. Determine the resultant member force at Joint *A*, magnitude and direction.

F_1 = 5 kips, $\alpha = 45°$
F_2 = 10 kips, $\beta = 10°$
F_3 = 5 kips, $\delta = 45°$

Scale: 1 in = 2000 lb

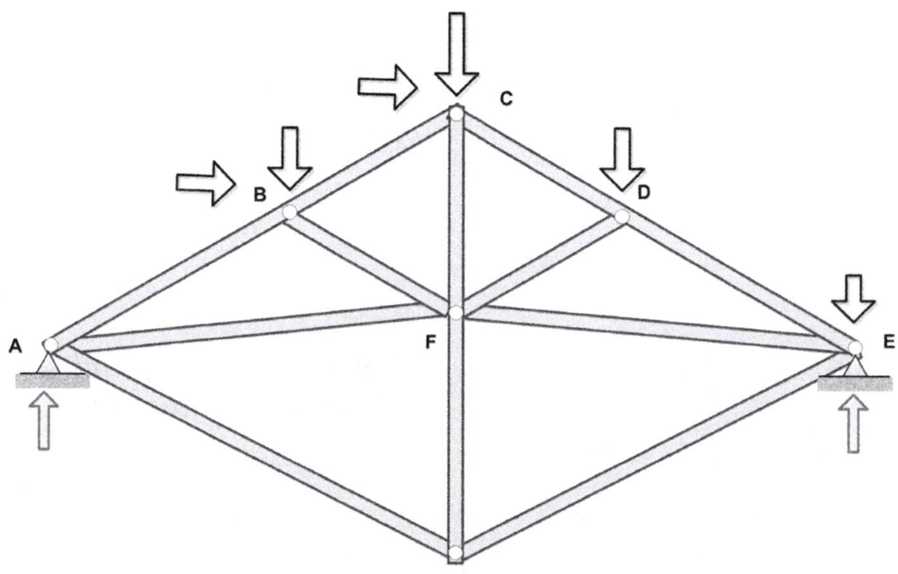

Figure 2.4a

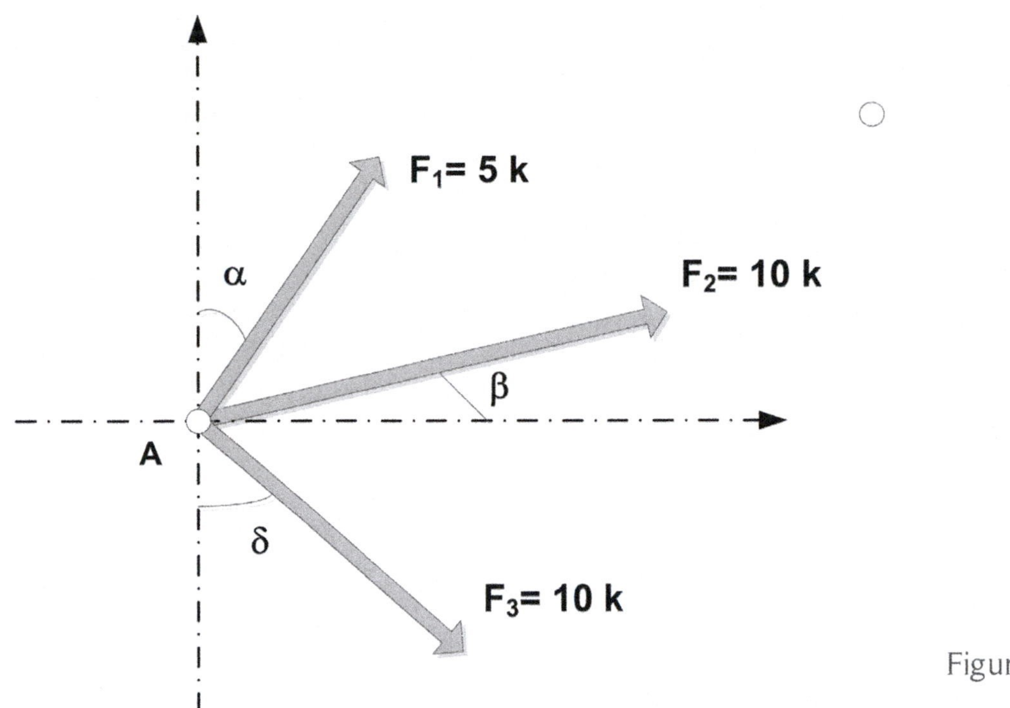

Figure 2.4b

Required:

Resultant magnitude, $R = ?$
Resultant direction, $\theta = ?$

PROBLEM 2.5

Given:

Determine the tension force *F* required to stabilize the 500 lb tension so that the resultant force acts vertically down the supporting column.

$F_{Given} = 500$ lb, $\theta = 45°$ from the x-axis
F, $\alpha = 30°$ from the y-axis
Scale: 1" = 250 lb

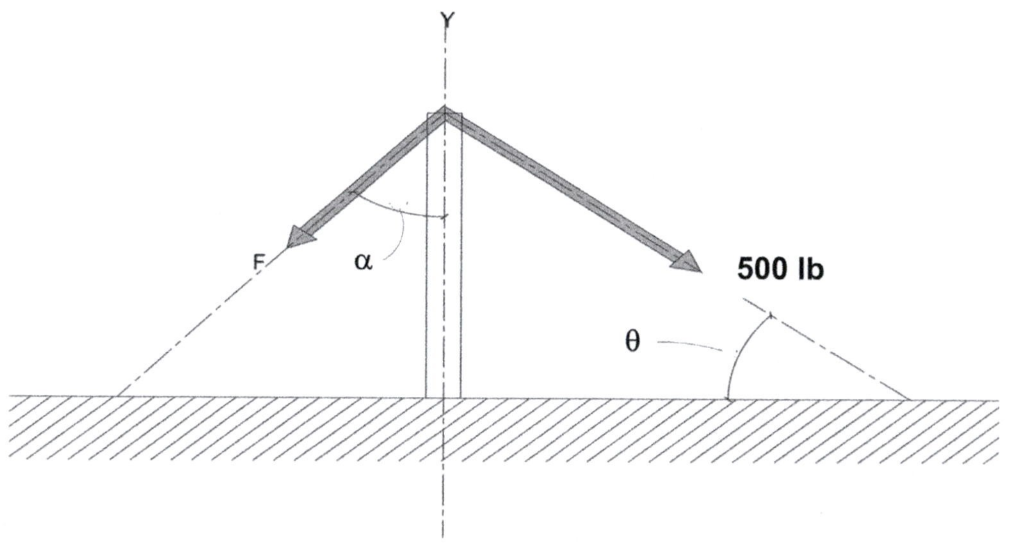

Required:

$F = ?$

2.6 PROBLEM

Given:

i. Determine the components (F_x and F_y) of the forces shown below.

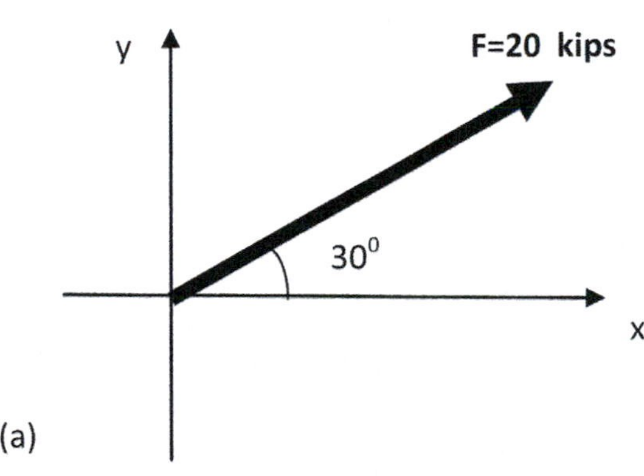

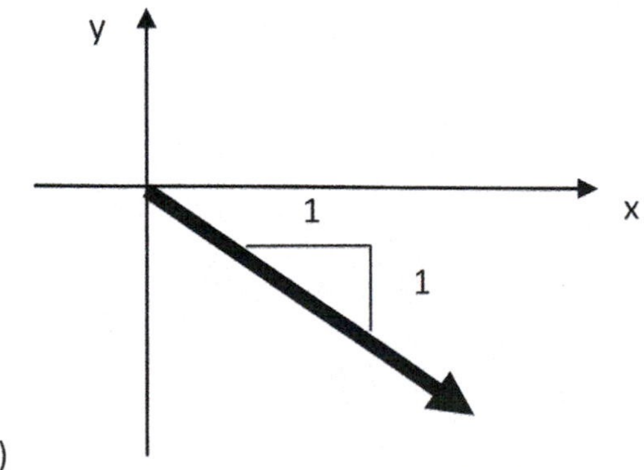

ii. Three members of a truss are framing into a steel gusset plate as shown in figure 2.6c. All forces are concurrent at point *C*. Determine the resultant of the three forces that must be carried by the gusset plate.

$F_1 = 15\ k$ at 45° from the y-axis
$F_2 = 12\ k$ horizontally towards point *C*
$F_3 = 20\ k$ with at 45° from the x-axis

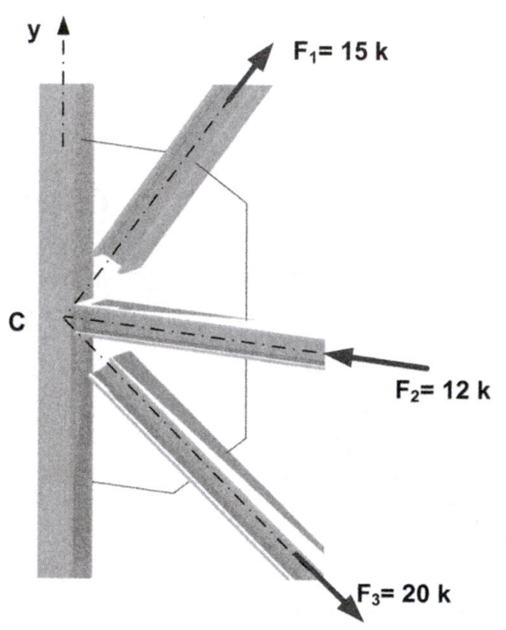

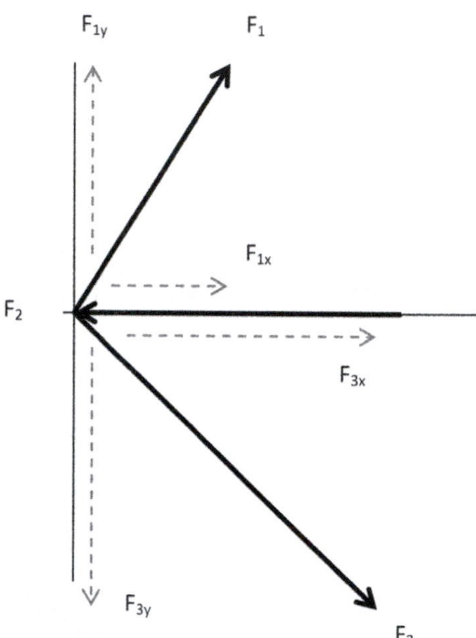

Figure 2.6c

Required:

$F_{Resultant} = ?$

2.7 PROBLEM

Given:

Consider one end of a timber roof truss that is supported on a masonry wall. The reaction at the masonry wall must be only vertical. Assuming that the maximum capacity of either the inclined or horizontal member is 10 kips, determine the maximum magnitudes of F_1 and F_2 so that their resultant is vertical through the masonry wall.

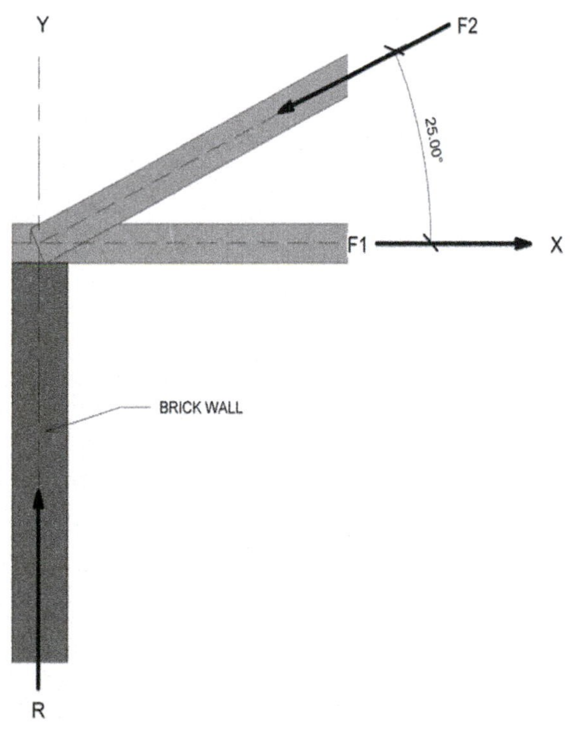

Required:

$F_1 = ?$
$F_2 = ?$

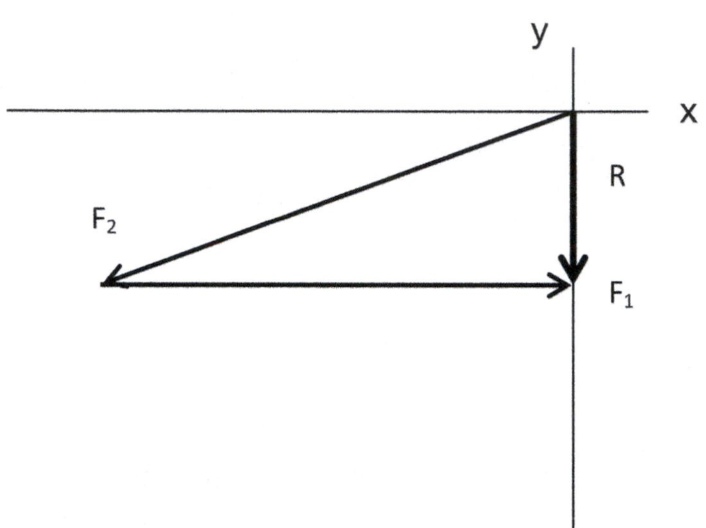

3.1 PROBLEM

Given:

A concrete footing for cable anchorage is shown below. The total weight of the concrete foundation is 80 kips (assumed concentrated at its center of gravity). The cable force is acting horizontally (*F*) equal to 100 k. What is the resultant moment about point *A*? Does the concrete foundation tip over?

$F = 100$ kips

$W = 80$ kips

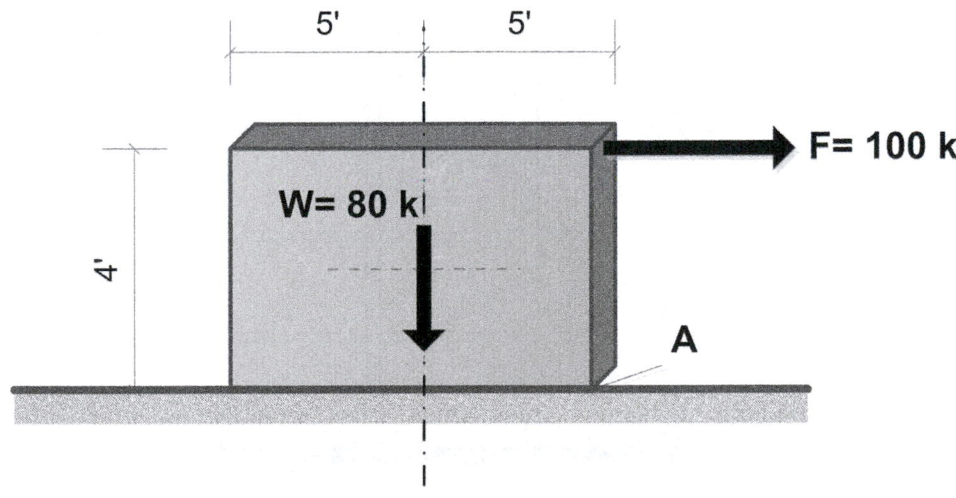

Required:

$M_A = ?$

PROBLEM 3.2

Given:

The figure below shows the forces exerted by wind on each floor of a six-story steel frame building. Determine the resultant overturning moment at the base of the building at *O*.

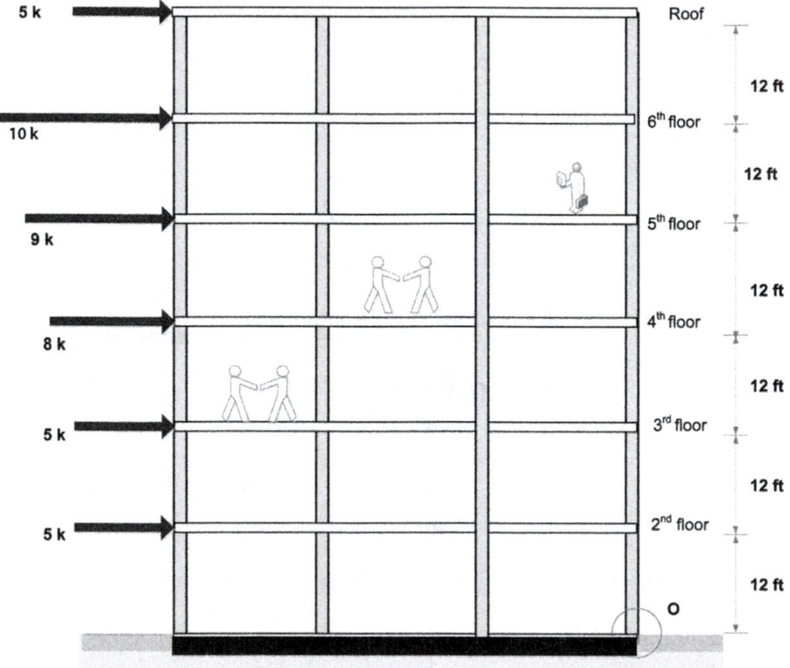

Required:

$M_O = ?$

3.3 PROBLEM

Given:

A roof truss is subjected to wind loads as shown in the figure below. Determine the moment of the 2 kips force applied at truss joint *D* about points *B* and *C*.

$F = 2$ kips with slope $\dfrac{5}{12}$

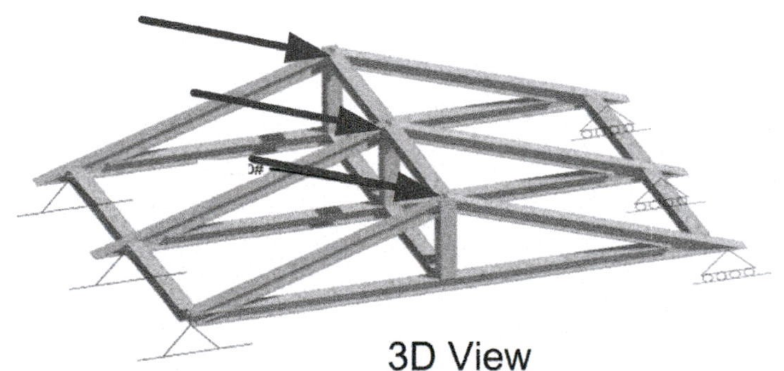

3D View

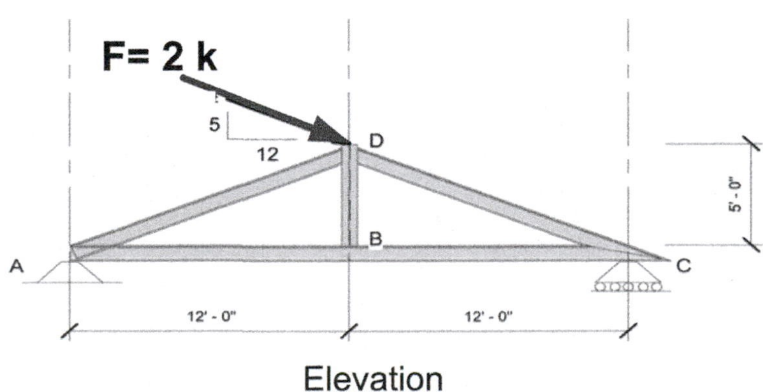

Elevation

Required:

$$M_B = ?$$
$$M_C = ?$$

3.4 PROBLEM

Given:

Consider the cantilever steel truss depicted below. Determine the resultant moment at support points *A* and *B* due to the forces acting on the truss as shown. Assume that the 8 kips forces are acting perpendicular to the truss slope.

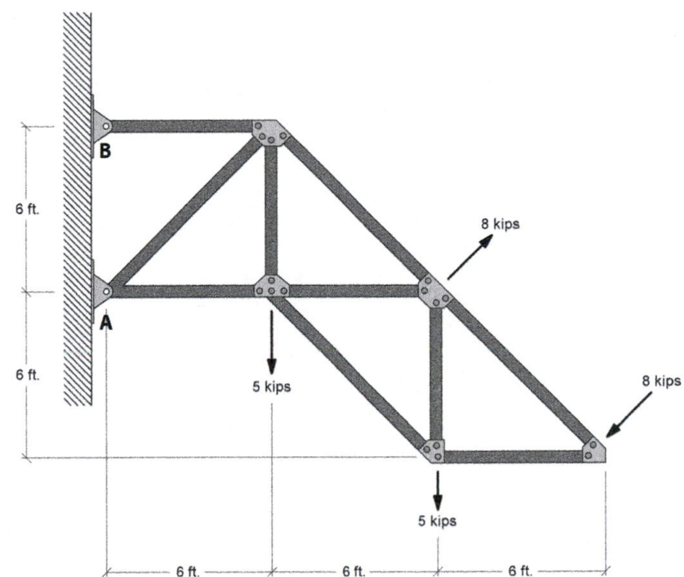

Required:

$M_A = ?$
$M_B = ?$

PROBLEM 3.5

Given:

Consider a ladder used by a construction worker as shown below. The worker's weight plus his tools is estimated to be 200 lb at mid-height. The ladder is supported at points *A* and *B*, developing reactions as shown in the free-body diagram. Assuming that reaction forces R_{A_x} and R_{B_x} develop magnitudes of 50 lb each and R_{A_y} = 200 lb, determine M_A, M_B and M_C.

$$R_{A_x} = 50lb \;;\; R_{B_x} = 50lb \;;\; R_{A_y} = 200lb \;;\; W = 200lb$$

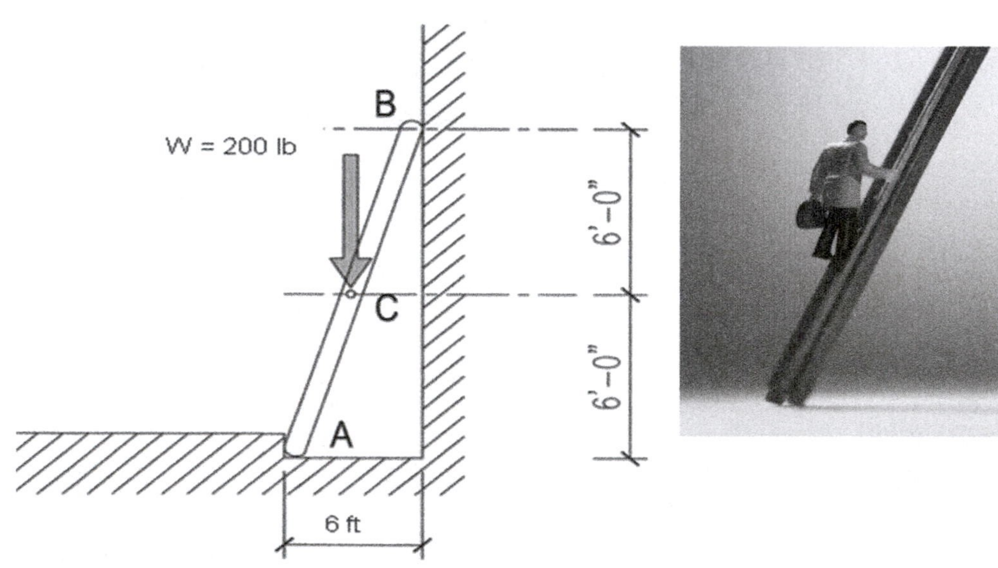

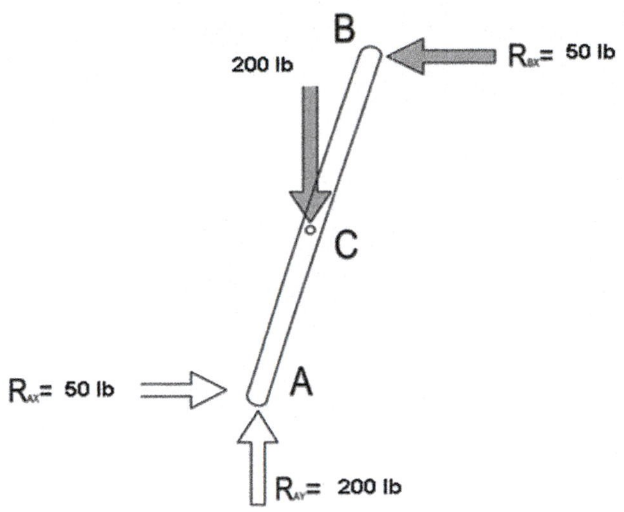

Required:

$M_A = ?$
$M_B = ?$
$M_C = ?$

PROBLEM 3.6

Given:

Replace the 10 kips beam load with an equivalent force-couple system through the column centerline.

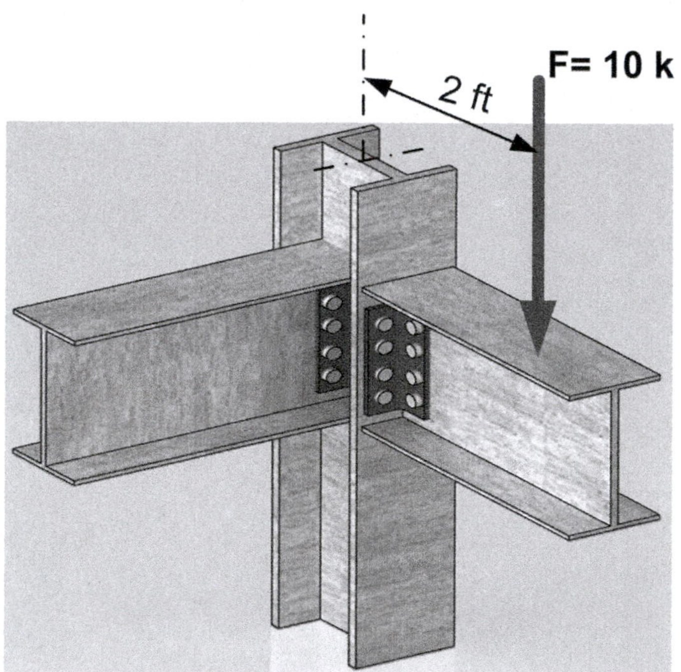

Required:

A force and M_{Couple} = ?

3.7 PROBLEM

Given:

Consider the cantilever beam *ABC* shown below. A 100 lb force is applied to the end of the cantilever as shown. Determine an equivalent force-couple system (a) at *A* and (b) at *B*.

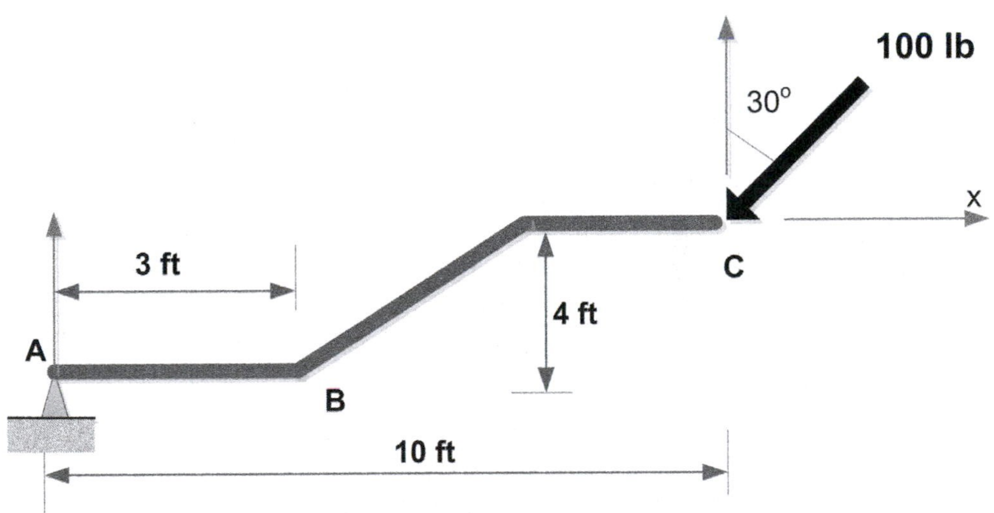

Required:

Force and M_A = ?
Force and M_B = ?

PROBLEM 3.8

Given:

Inclined column *AC* supports cable *BA* and an additional vertical load of 800 lb at *A*. Determine the forces in cable *BA* and the column *AC* using the analytical method. Assume that a condition of equilibrium exists at *A*.

$$\text{Slope}_{AB} = \frac{5}{12}$$

AC is 60° from the y-axis

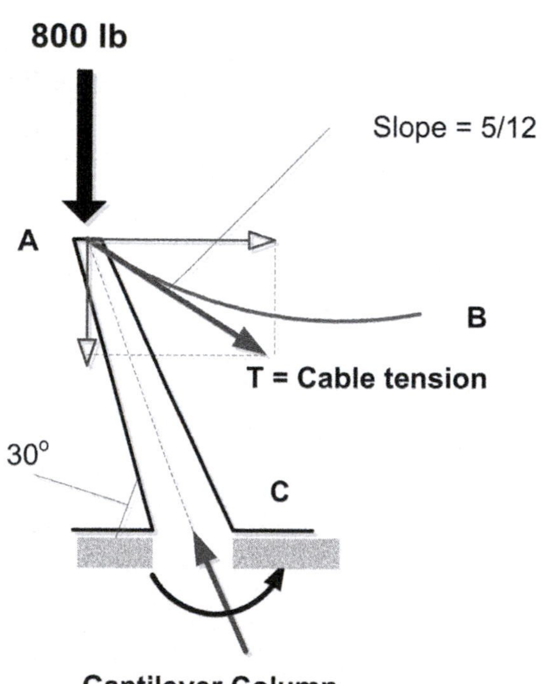

Required:

Tension force F_{AB} = ?
Compression force F_{CA} = ?

PROBLEM 3.9

For the cable support structure shown below, determine the weight W required if the maximum tensile force in cable AB cannot exceed 2,000 lb. Also, determine the forces in column BE, and cables BC and CD.

$AB = 2{,}000$ lb with slope $-\dfrac{5}{12}$

BC with slope $\dfrac{3}{4}$

CD at 45° below x-axis with slope -1

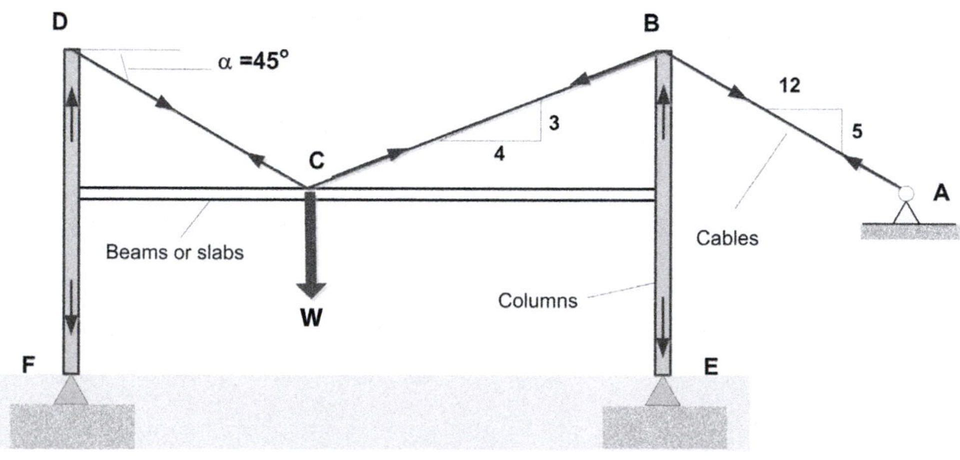

Required:

Forces
$W = ?$
$BC = ?$
$BE = ?$
$CD = ?$

PROBLEM 3.10

For the connections shown below determine the idealized (analytical) connection type for the analytical model.

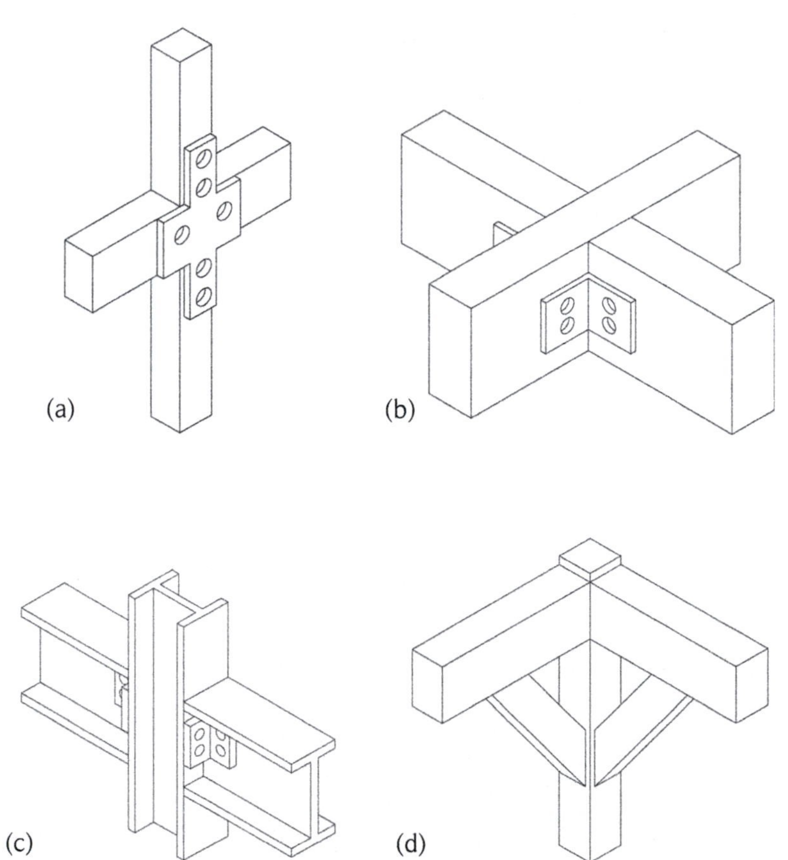

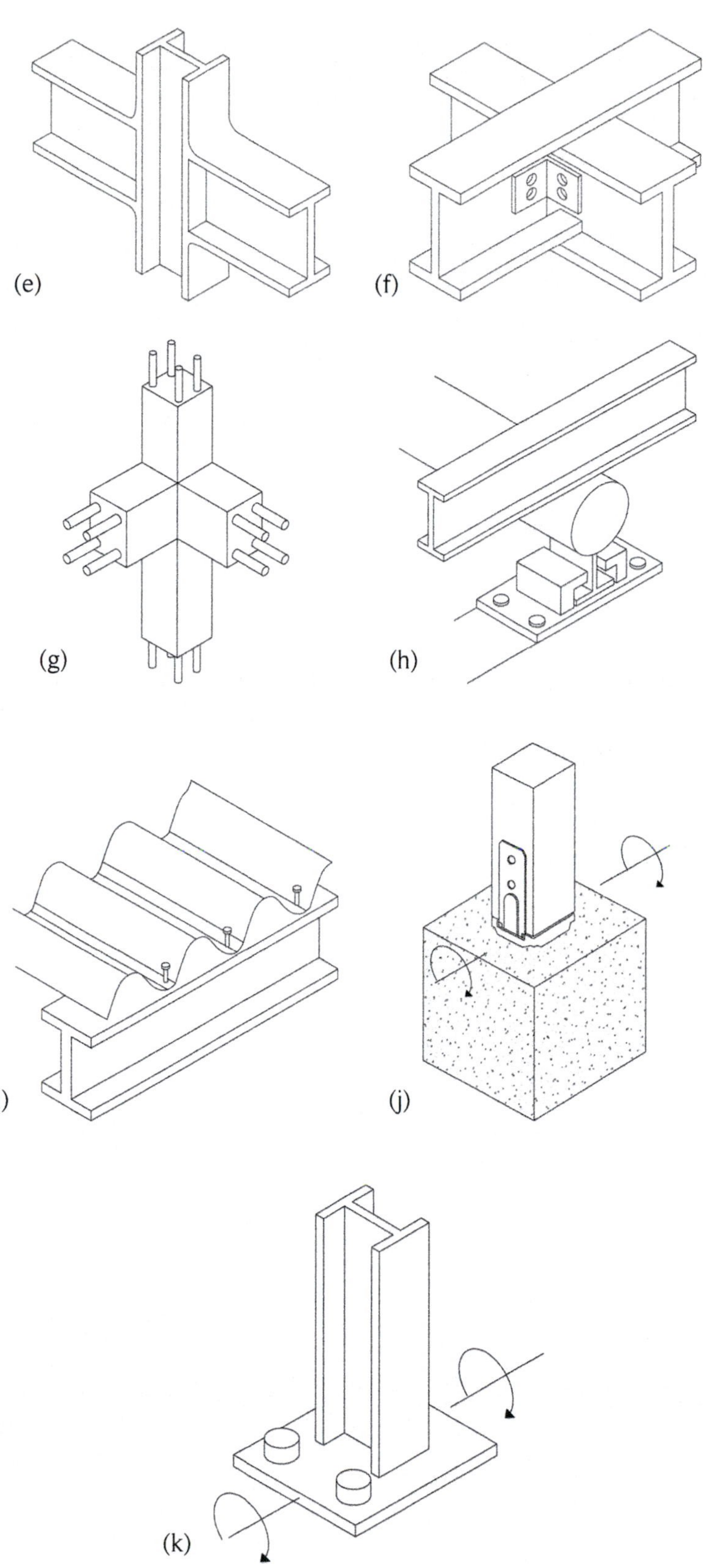
(e)
(f)
(g)
(h)
(i)
(j)
(k)

PROBLEM 3.11

Given:

A simple wood frame is supported as shown in figure 3.11a. The structure must carry a vertical load of 1 kip at point *B*. Find the reactions R_A and R_C.

AB at 60° from x-axis
BC at 45° from x-axis
W = 1 kip

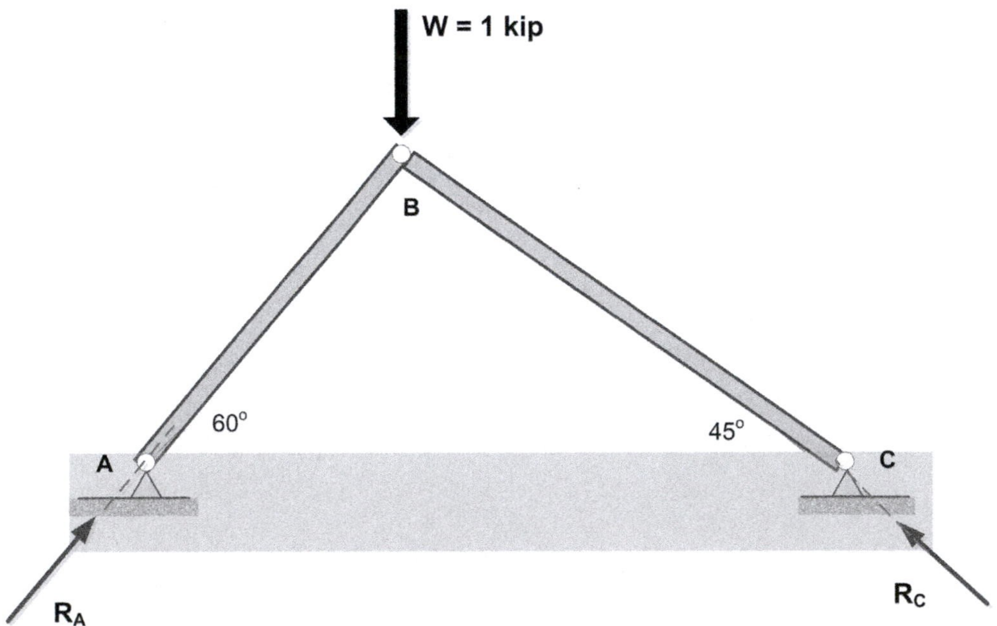

Figure 3.11a

Required:

Reaction R_A = ?
Reaction R_C = ?

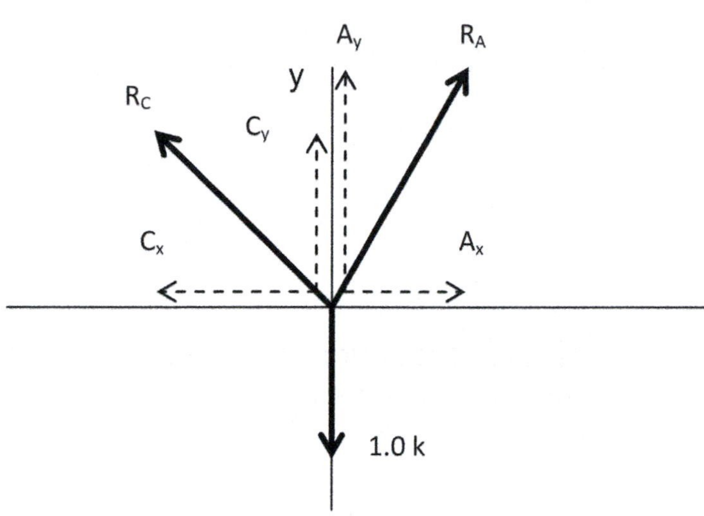

Figure 3.11b

PROBLEM 3.12

Compute the magnitude of reactions on the beam shown in figure 3.12, using the loads as indicated.

$$\Sigma M = 0$$
$$\Sigma F_V = 0$$
$$\Sigma F_H = 0$$

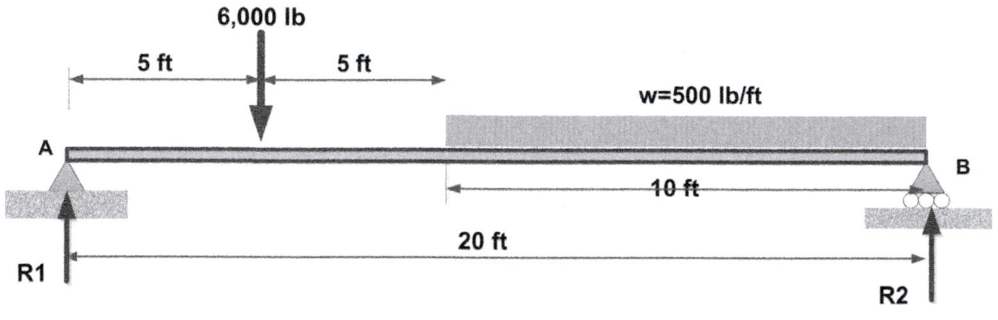

$$0 = 0$$

Sign convention:

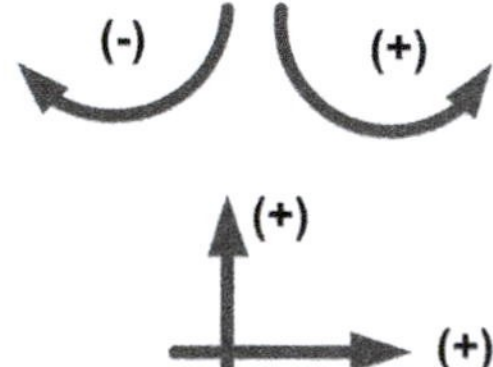

3.13 PROBLEM

Given:

The overhanging beam shown is subjected to point loads and a uniform load as depicted in figure 3.13. Determine the reactions $R1$ and $R2$.

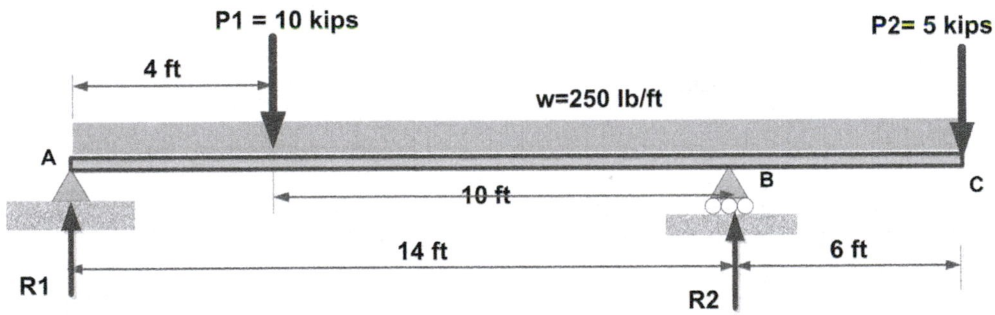

Required:

$R1 = ?\,;\qquad R2 = ?$

Sign convention:

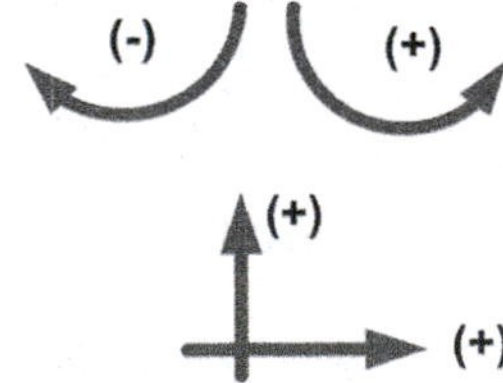

PROBLEM 3.14

Given:

An overhanging floor beam is subjected to loads as depicted in figure 3.14 Find the reactions *R*1 and *R*2.

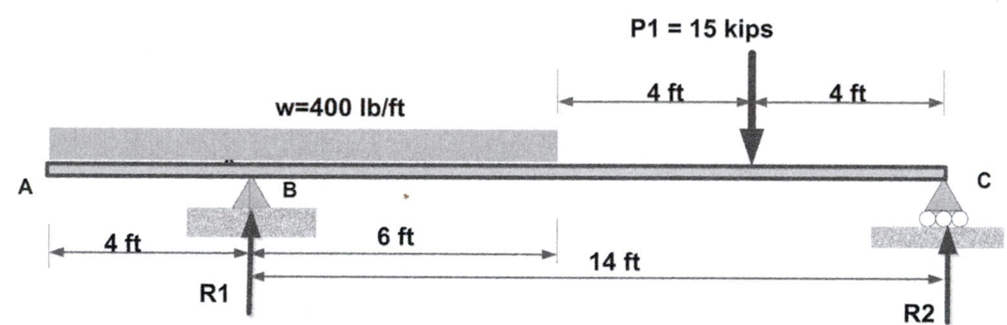

Required:

*R*1 = ? ; *R*2 = ?

Sign convention:

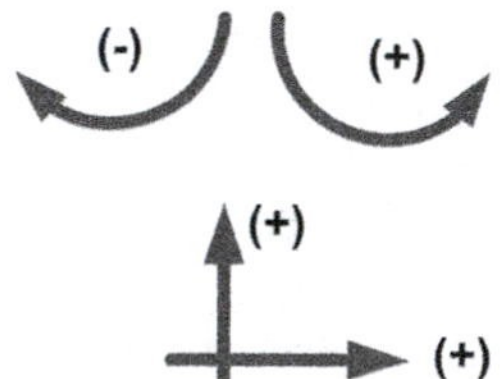

3.15 PROBLEM

Given:

A floor beam subjected to point loads as well as a uniformly distributed load over a part of the beam (see figure 3.15). Determine the reactions *R*1 and *R*2

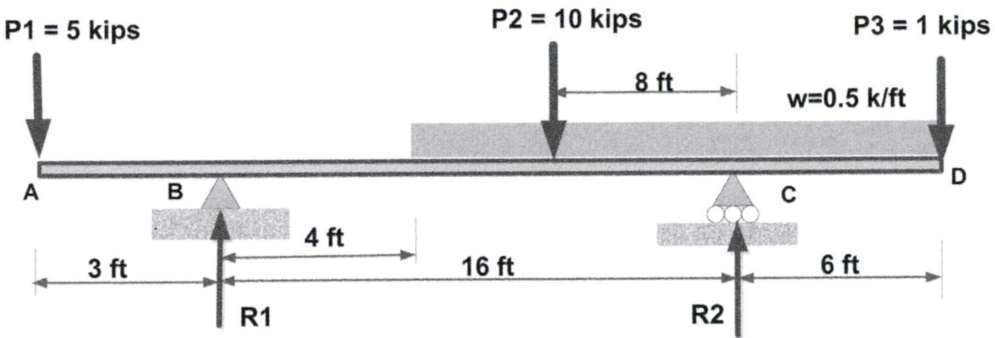

Required:

*R*1 = ? ;   *R*2 = ?

Sign convention:

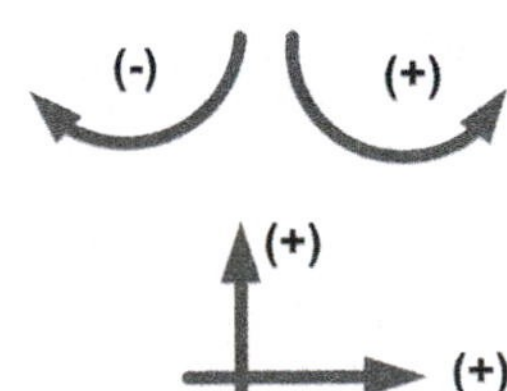

PROBLEM 3.16

Given:

A structural L-frame is subjected to a lateral load of 5 kips as illustrated in figure 3.16. Determine the reactions at the supports *A* and *B*.

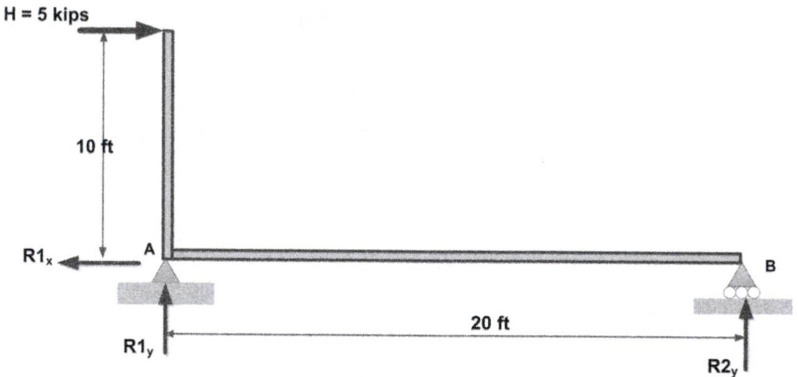

Figure 3.16

Required:

$R1_x = ?$; $R1_y = ?$; $R2_y = ?$

Sign convention:

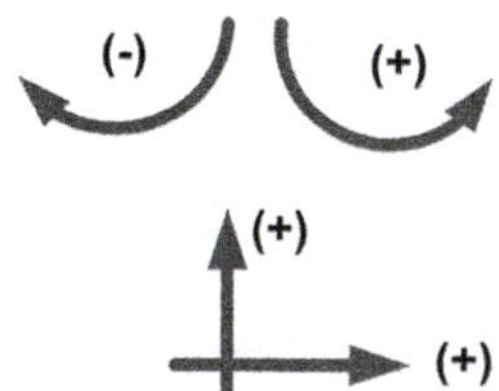

3.17 PROBLEM

For the structural L-frame shown below, find the reactions developed at *A* and *B*.

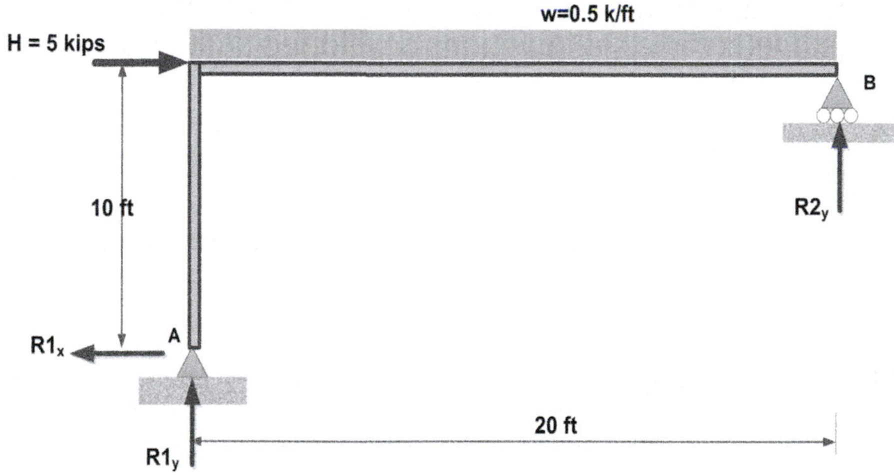

Required:

$R1_x = ?\ ;\quad R1_y = ?\ ;\quad R2_y = ?$

Sign convention:

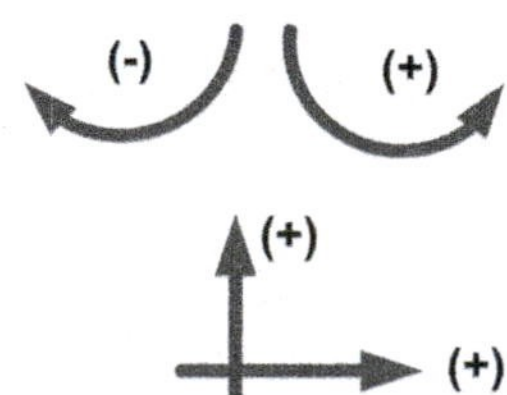

PROBLEM 3.18

Given:

The L-frame shown below is supporting a wind pressure of 0.5 k/ft as indicated in figure 3.18 plus a gravity point load of 5 kips at mid-span. Determine the reactions developed at support *A* and *B*.

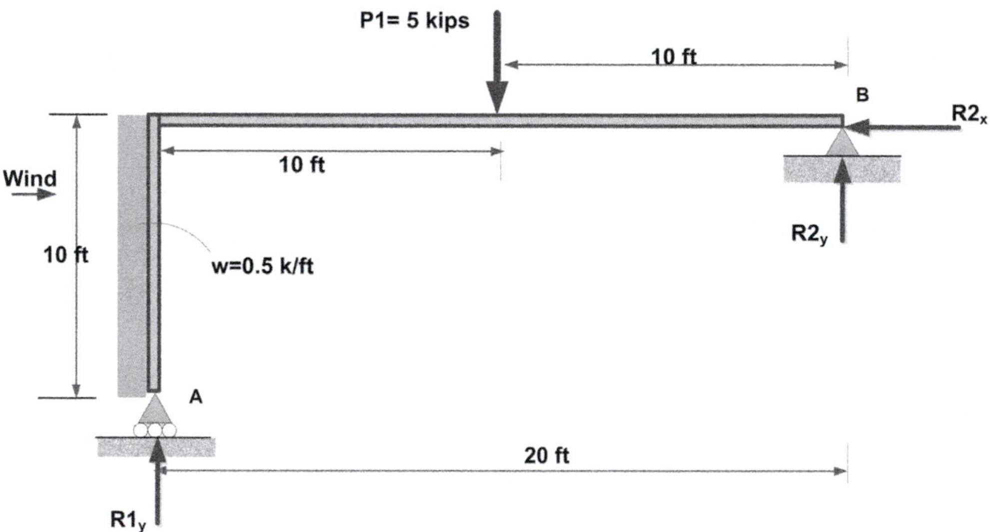

Figure 3.18

Required:

$R1_x = ?$; $R1_y = ?$; $R2_y = ?$

Sign convention:

(-) (+)

(+)

(+)

PROBLEM 3.19

Given:

A weight $W = 400$ lb is supported by a cable system as shown in figure 3.19. Determine all cable forces and the force in the vertical column *BC*.

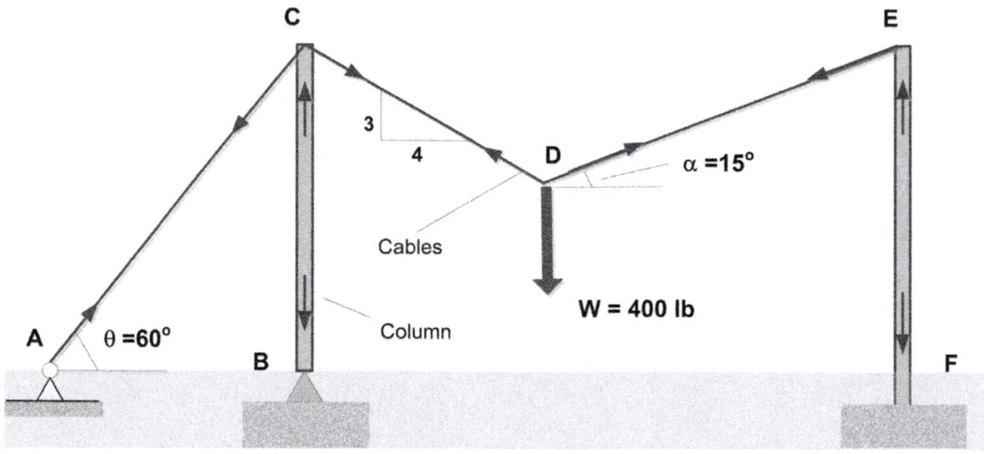

Required:

Figure 3.19

AC = ?
BC = ?
CD = ?
DE = ?

3.20 PROBLEM

Given:

A steel erection worker is positioning a steel beam, weighing 1,000 lb, by pulling on a rope attached to the crane cable at *A*. The angle of the cable is 10° off vertical when the worker pulls with a force of *P* at a 30° angle from the horizontal. Determine the force *P* and the cable tension *AB*.

W = 1,000 lb
P at 30° below x-axis
AB at 10° from y-axis

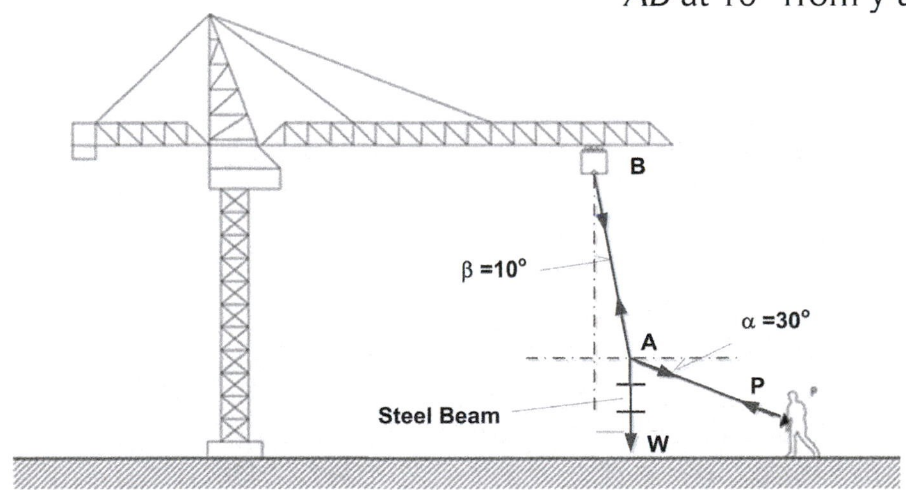

Required: Forces

P = ?
AB = ?

PROBLEM 3.21

Given:

A part of the steel frame for a building is shown in figure 3.21a. The partial framing plan (figure 3.21b) depicts a girder supported by columns at *A* and *B*. Two smaller beams push downward on the girder with a force of 20 kips at *C*, and two other beams push downward with a force of 25 kips at *D*. Find the reactions at *A* and *B*.

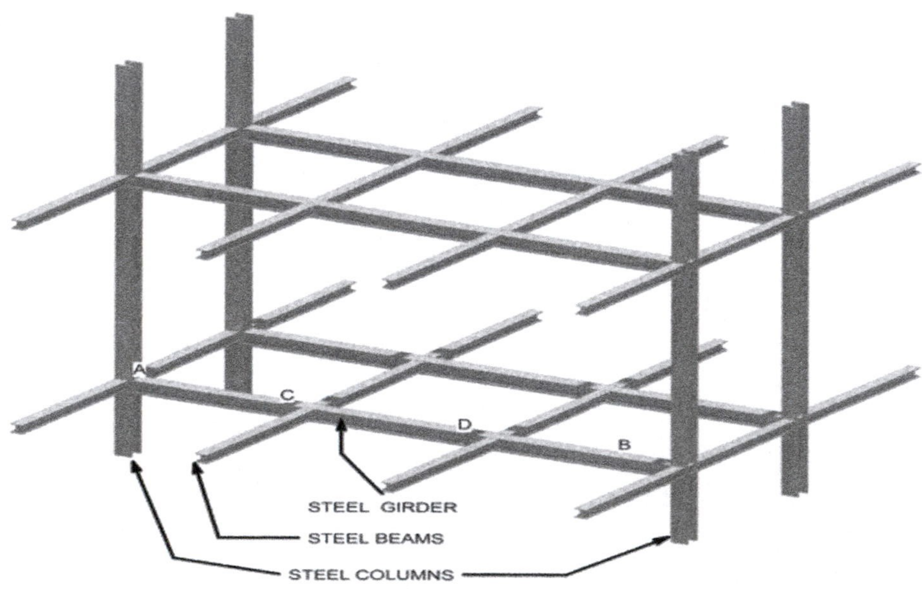

Figure 3.21a

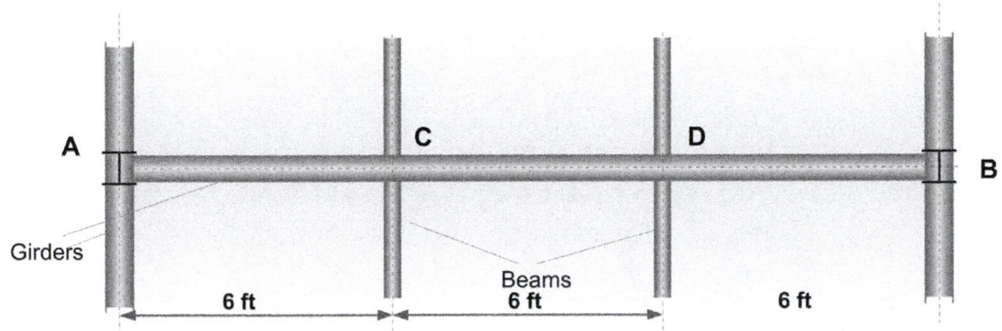

Figure 3.21b

Required:

$A_y = ?$
$B_y = ?$

PROBLEM 3.22

Given:

A bridge over a river is loaded at three panel points as indicated in figure 3.22. Determine the support reactions at *A* and *B*.

$F_1 = 2.5$ k
$F_2 = 5$ k
$F_3 = 7$ k

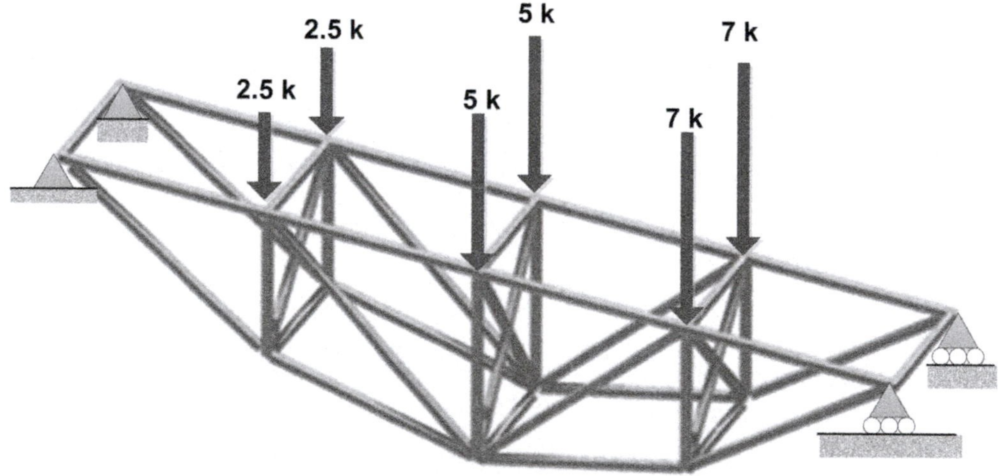

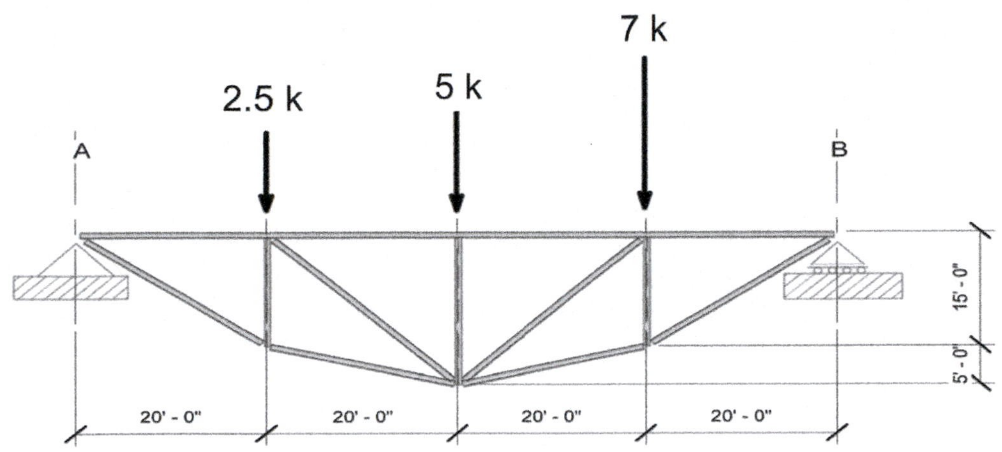

Required:

Reactions
$A_y = ?$
$B_y = ?$

PROBLEM 3.23

Given:

A part of a wood structural framing elevation is shown in figure 3.23. The beam supports a roof that weighs 250 pounds per square foot and supports a concentrated load of 1,200 pounds at the overhang ends. Determine the support reactions at the support points *A* and *B*.

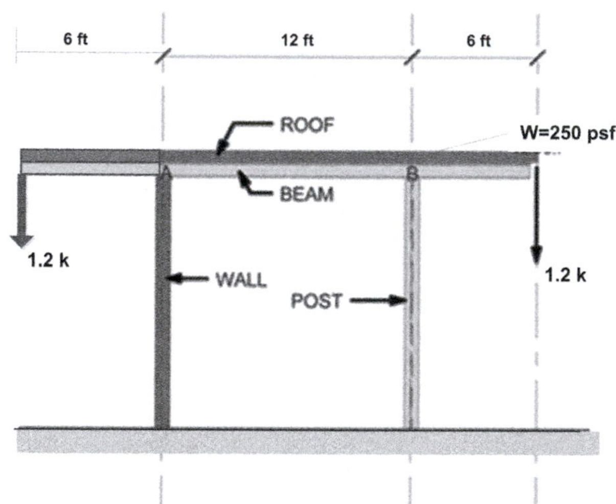

Figure 3.23

Required:

Reactions at
A = ?
B = ?

3.24 PROBLEM

Given:

For the structural wood frame depicted in figure 3.24, solve for the support reactions at *A* and *B*.

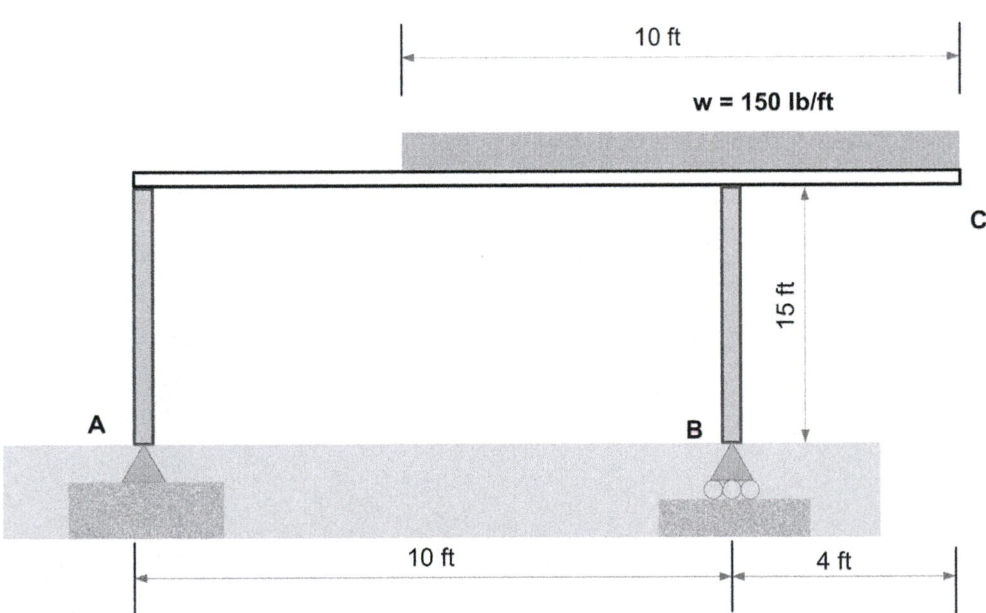

Figure 3.24

Required:

Reaction forces
$A = ?$
$B = ?$

PROBLEM 3.25

Given:

Construct the appropriate FBDs and solve for the support reactions at *A* and *C*.

$F_1 = 2$ kN
$F_2 = 3$ kN

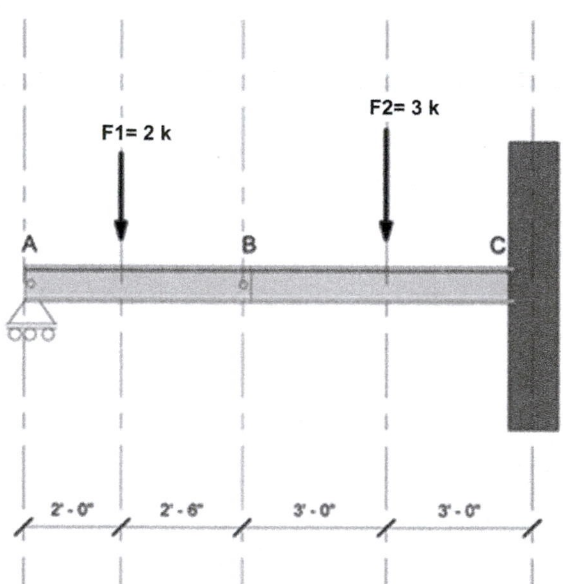

Required:

Reactions
$A_y = ?$

3.26 PROBLEM

Given:

A bridge truss spans across a river carrying the loads shown. Determine the support reactions at *A* and *B*.

$F_1 = 2k$
$F_2 = 3k$
$F_3 = 2k$
$F_4 = 5k$

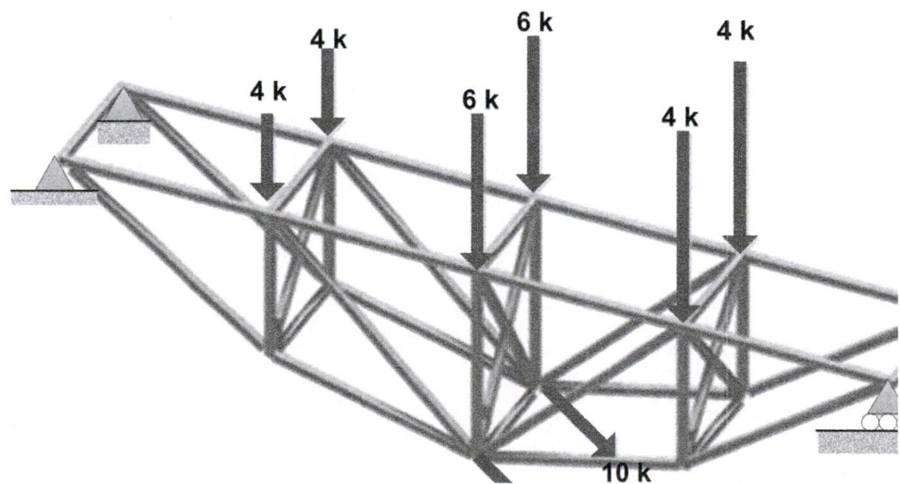

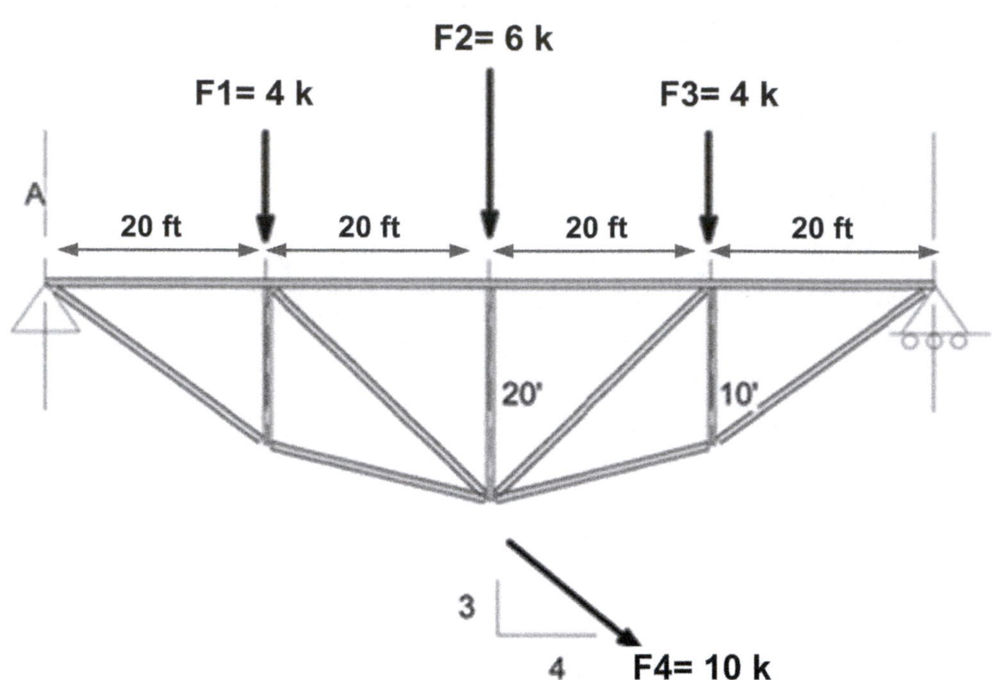

Required:

$A_x = ?$
$A_y = ?$
$B_y = ?$

3.27 PROBLEM

Given:

A steel frame is subjected to loads as illustrated in figure 3.27. Calculate the beam reactions at supports *A*, *C*, and *D*. Draw all appropriate FBDs.

$F_1 = 400$ lb
$F_2 = 200$ lb
$F_3 = 100$ lb

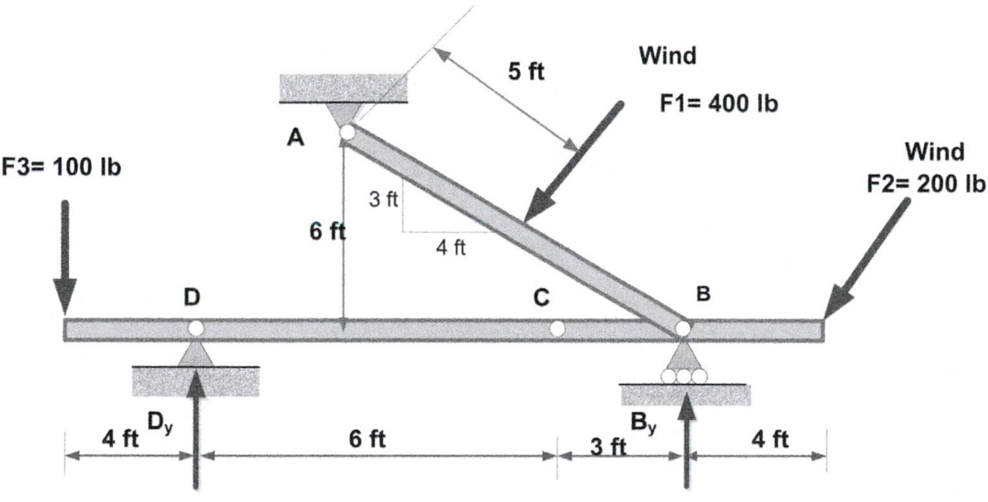

Figure 3.27

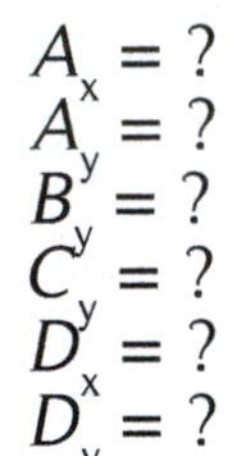

Required: Reactions

$A_x = ?$
$A_y = ?$
$B_y = ?$
$C_y = ?$
$D_x = ?$
$D_y = ?$

3.28 PROBLEM

Given:

Analyze the reinforced concrete stairway and landing shown by considering a 1-ft-wide strip of the structure. Concrete (dead load) weighs 150 pounds per cubic foot, and the live load (occupancy) is equal to about 100 psf.

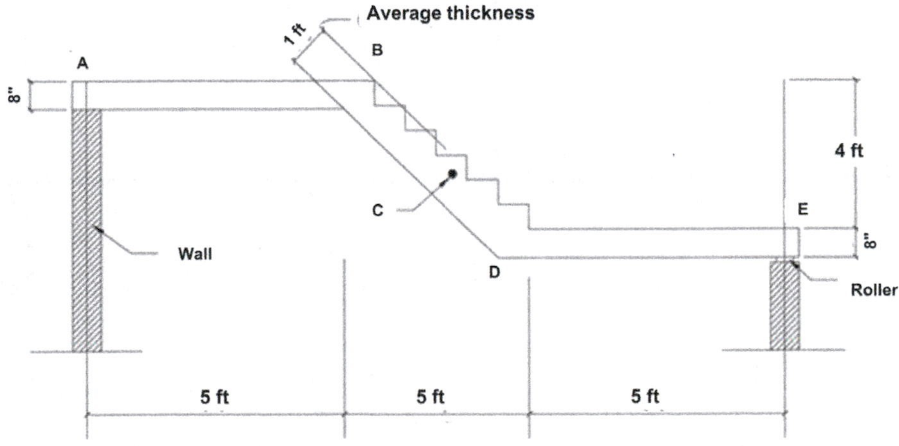

Required: Reaction forces at

$E = ?$
$A = ?$

PROBLEM 4.1

A steel framing plan for a commercial building is depicted in 4.1 below. The diaphragm spanning directions are indicated by arrows in the middle of each bay. Draw the FBD of the beams *B*1, *B*4, and *B*2 assuming a constant load of *w* psf.

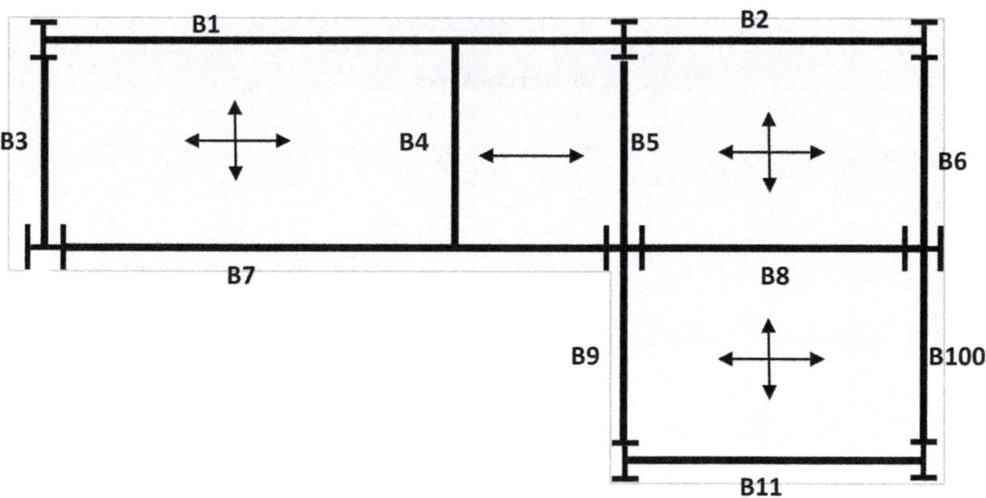

Figure 4.1

4.2 PROBLEM

Given:

A part of steel structural framing for a residential building is shown in figure 4.2a. Assume the following loading conditions:

DL (decking, flooring, etc.) = 15 psf
LL (occupancy) = 40 psf
Total = 55 psf

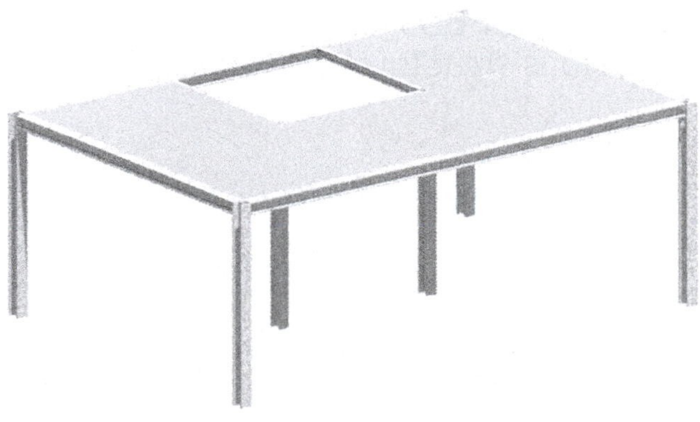

Figure 4.2a

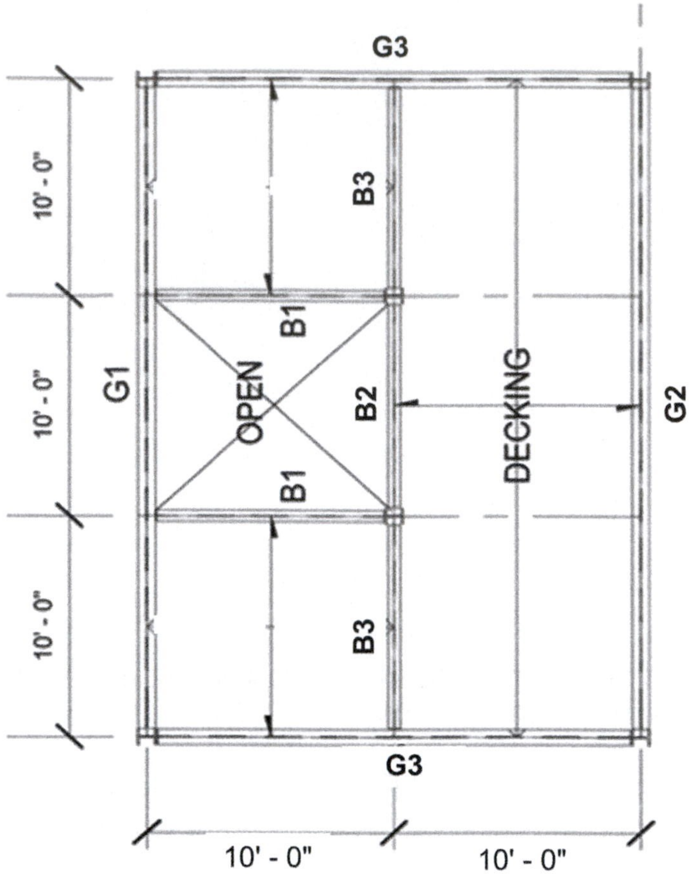

Required:

Figure 4.2a

Construct a series of FBDs and show the propagation of loads through the various structural elements.

4.3 PROBLEM

Early in the design phase an initial assumption has to be made by the designer about the path across which building forces must travel as they move throughout the structural system. For example, a load path can be created from a single-level, double-level, or triple-level framing. Explain these concepts. Use hand sketches to support your answer.

PROBLEM 4.4

For the structural frame depicted in figure 4.4, calculate and show the reactions in a load diagram for each of the joists and frames. Assume Dead Load = 5 psf, Live Load = 25 psf. Ignore self-weight of members.

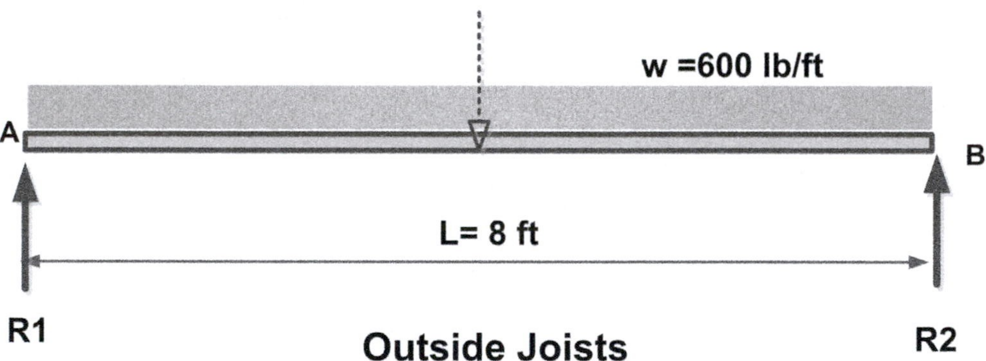

Figure 4.4a

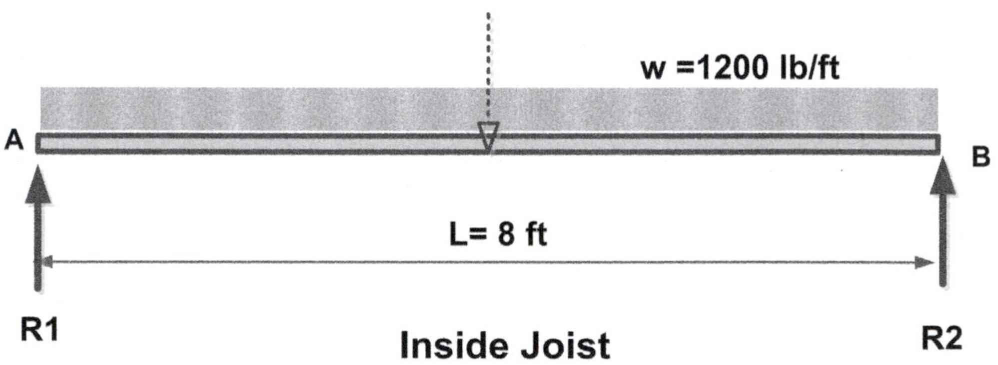

Figure 4.4b

4.5 PROBLEM

For the wood framing shown below, calculate and show the reactions in a load diagram for each of the joists, beams, and columns necessary for determining the loads transferred to the footings. Assume Dead Load = 12 psf, Live Load = 68 psf. Ignore self-weight of members.

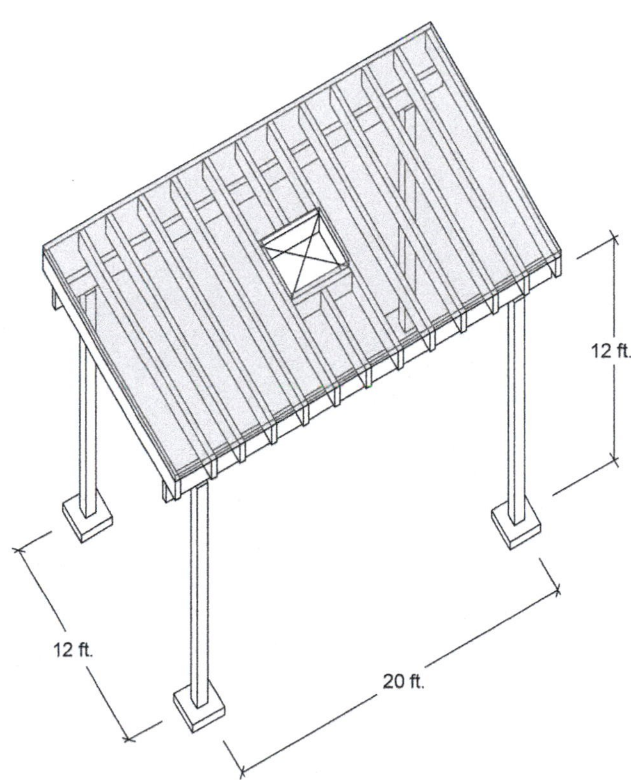

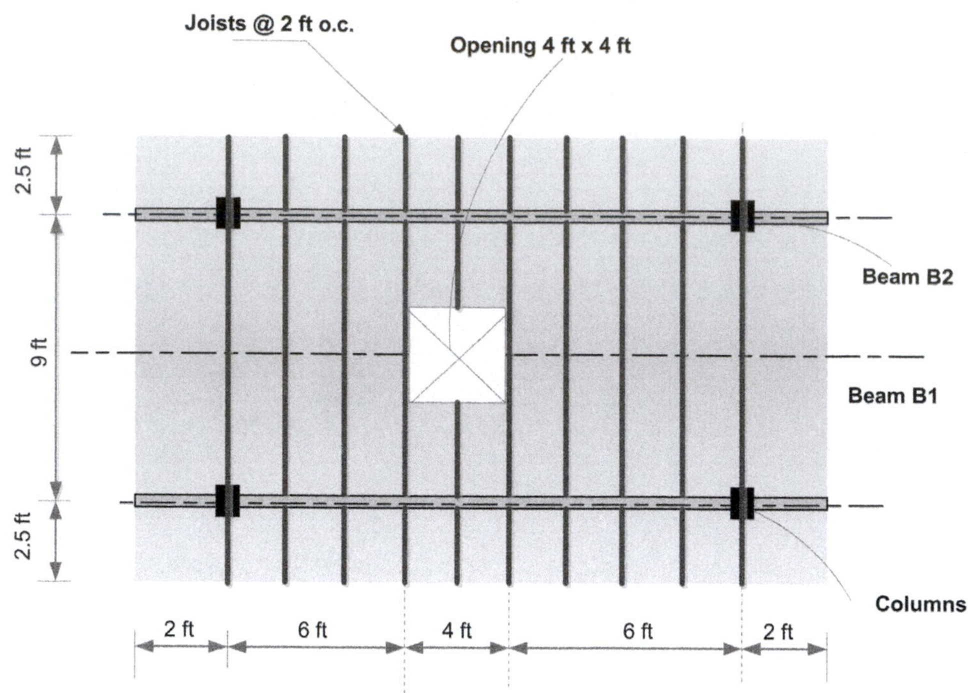
Joists @ 2 ft o.c.
Opening 4 ft x 4 ft
2.5 ft
9 ft
2.5 ft
Beam B2
Beam B1
Columns
2 ft
6 ft
4 ft
6 ft
2 ft

4.6 PROBLEM

The steel framing shown below (figure 4.6) is supported by a reinforced concrete wall at one side and two columns on the other end. The total floor load is 65 psf and the total roof load is estimated as 50 psf. Calculate and show the reactions in a load diagram for each of the joists (*J*), beams (*B*), girders (*G*), and columns necessary for determining the loads transferred.

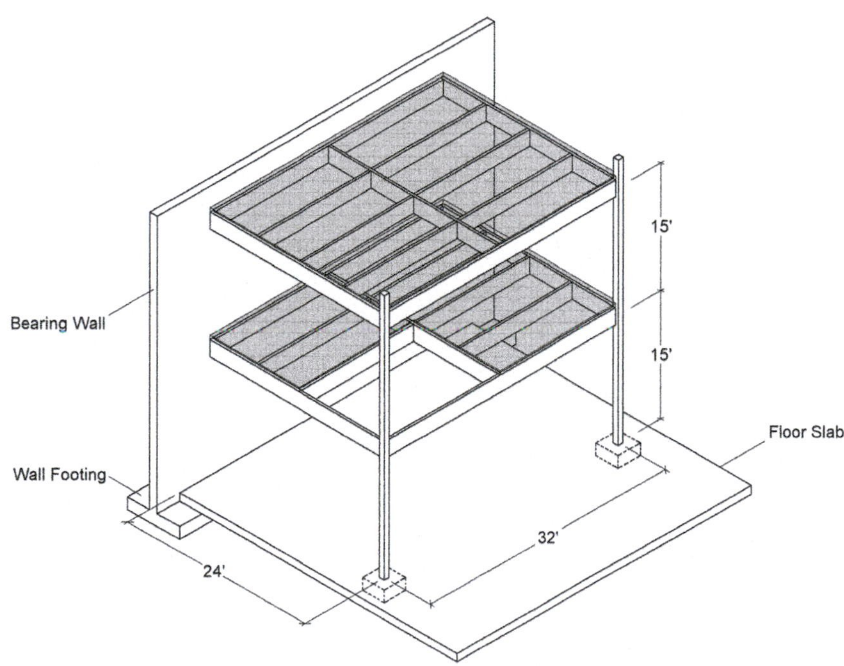

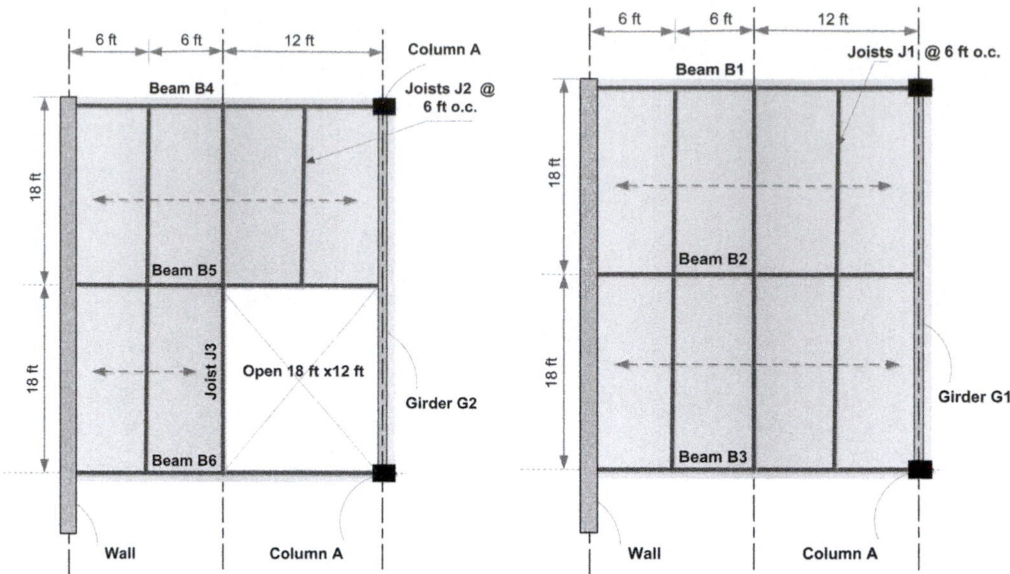
6 ft
6 ft
12 ft
Column A
Beam B4
Joists J2 @ 6 ft o.c.
18 ft
Beam B5
18 ft
Joist J3
Open 18 ft x12 ft
Girder G2
Beam B6
Wall
Column A
6 ft
6 ft
12 ft
Beam B1
Joists J1 @ 6 ft o.c.
18 ft
Beam B2
18 ft
Girder G1
Beam B3
Wall
Column A

Figure 4.6

4.7 PROBLEM

Calculate and show the reactions in a load diagram for each of the joists (*J*), beams (*B*), and columns (*C*) necessary for determining the loads transferred to the footings.
$R_1 = R_2 = 3675 \text{ lb} / 2 = 1837.5 \text{ lb}$

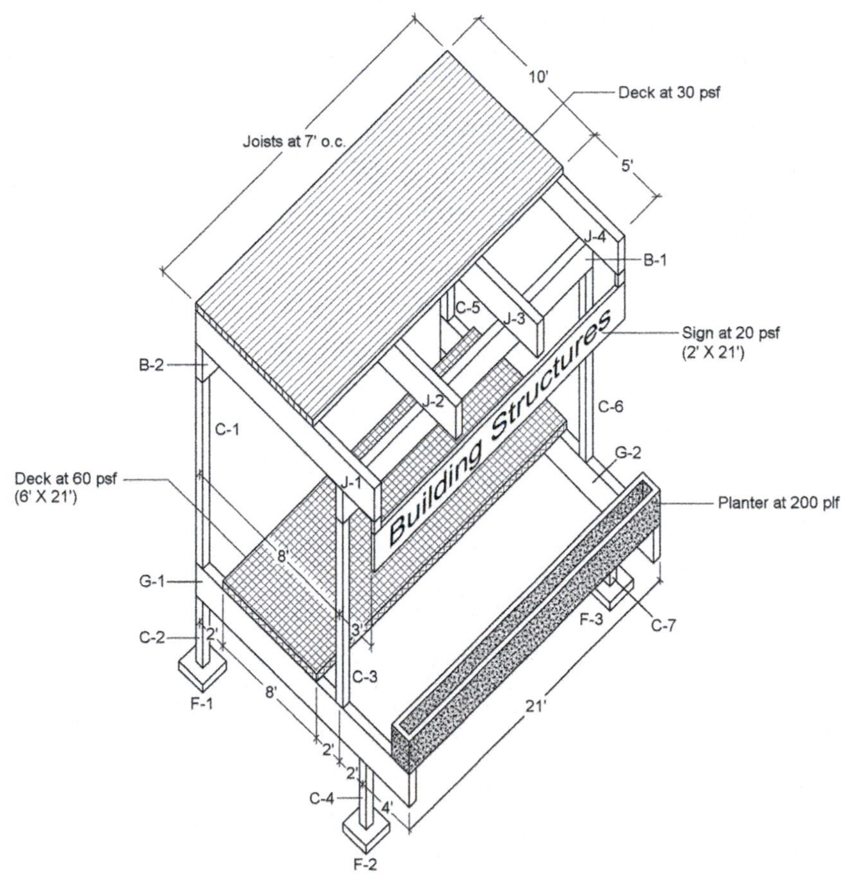

PROBLEM 5.1

According to the International Building Code, which statement regarding wind pressure for the design of a building is incorrect and why?

A. Wind pressure acts either inward or outward on walls, but not in both directions at the same time.
B. Wind pressure is greater at the corners than in the middle of the wall.
C. Wind pressure is decreased when there are significant surface irregularities of the ground in the vicinity of the site.
D. Wind pressure does not take into account the effect of tornadoes.

5.2 PROBLEM

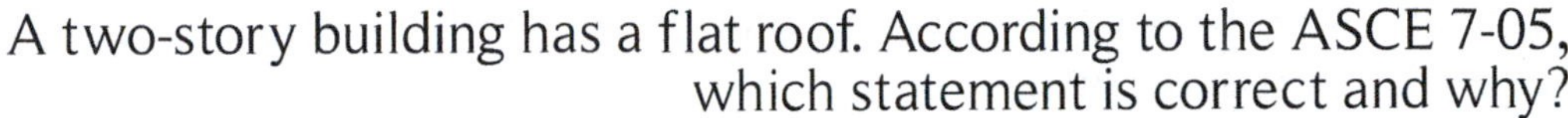
A two-story building has a flat roof. According to the ASCE 7-05, which statement is correct and why?

A. The wind force is zero on the roof and causes a positive pressure on the windward side.
B. The wind force acts downward on the roof.
C. The wind force acts upward on the roof and causes a positive pressure on the windward side and a negative pressure on the leeward side.
D. The wind force acts upward or downward depending on the value of directionality coefficient C_q.

PROBLEM 5.3

Describe the effects of wind loads on buildings. Support your answers with sketches.

5.4 PROBLEM

The following illustration shows a two-story rigid frame structure subjected to lateral loadings. Sketch the deformed shape and determine the type of stresses (tension or compression) developed in each side of the members (use C = compression, T = tension).

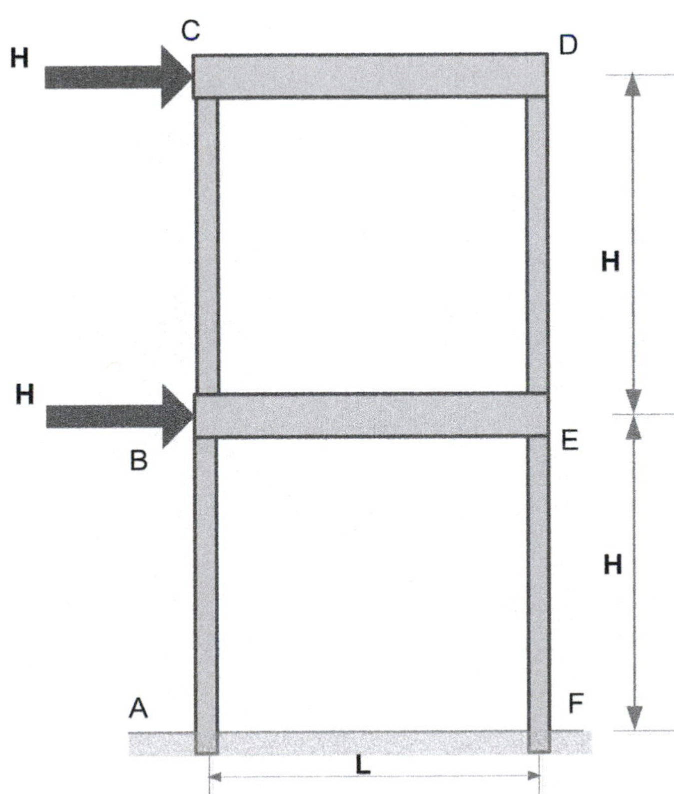

PROBLEM 5.5

A one-story building is 50 ft x 150 ft. The 150-foot dimension is in the east–west direction. The building is constructed with plywood shear walls and diaphragms. Only the east, north, and south walls are shear walls. If a lateral force of 20 kips is applied to the building in the north–south direction, what is the rotational lateral shear force on the north and south shear walls?

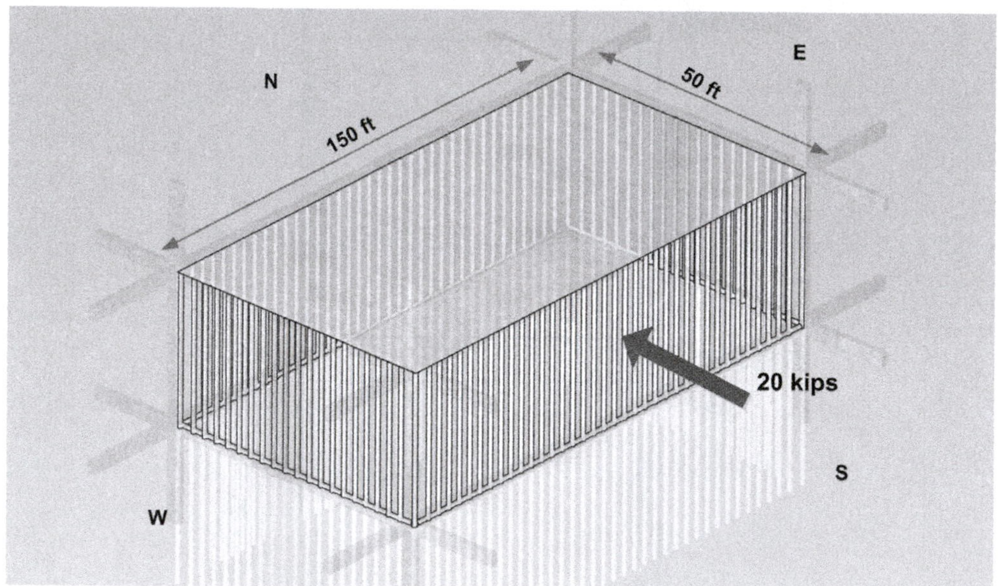

5.6 PROBLEM

For the advertisement sign shown below, determine the average wind pressure acting on the sign using the approximate method and then estimate the overturning moment at the ground caused by wind forces. Assume a wind design speed of 110 mph.

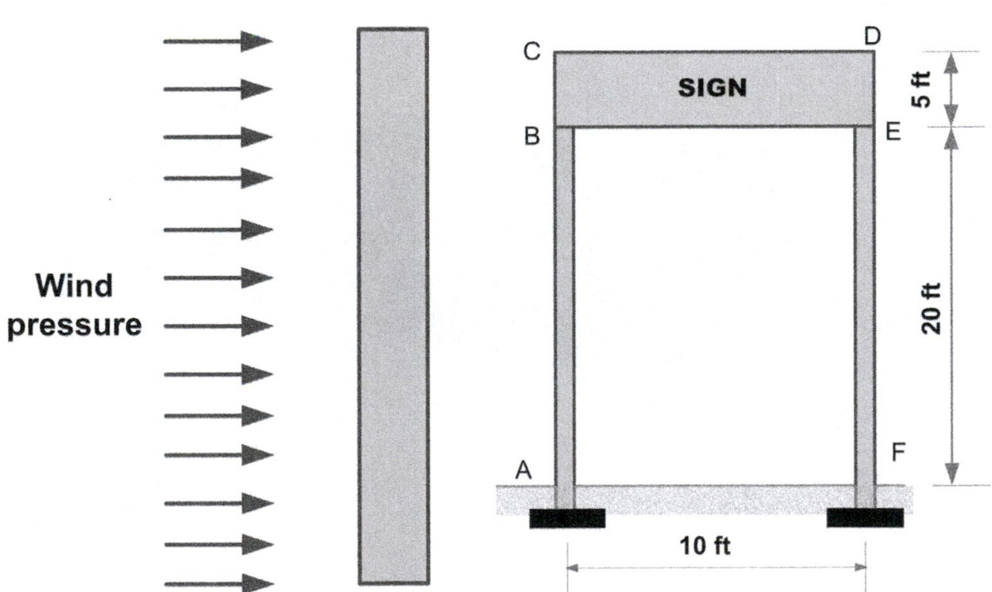

PROBLEM 5.7

The photovoltaic (PV) panels shown below are supported by a steel frame. The 3D view and the framing section are depicted in figure 5.7a and 5.7b respectively. The PV system is installed on the roof of a residential building at 30 ft in height. Determine the average wind pressure acting on the panel using the approximate method and estimate the resulting overturning moment at point *C*. Assume wind speed of 100 mph.

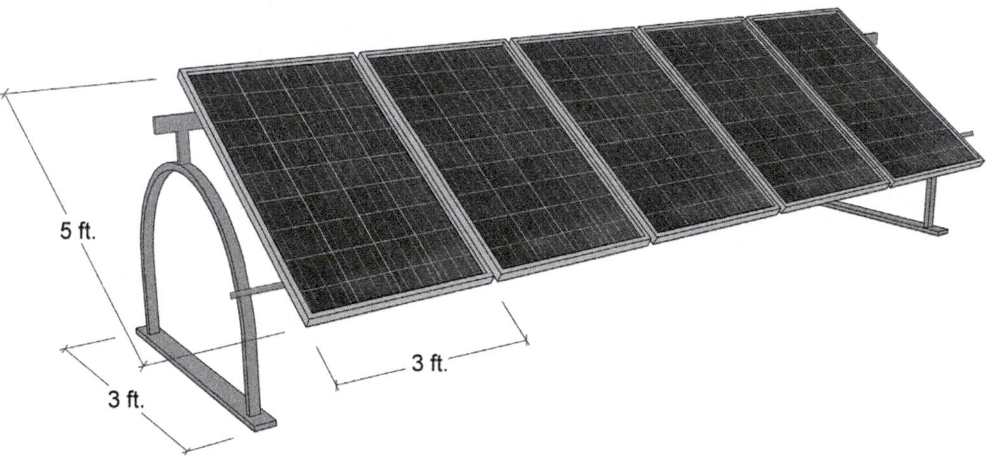

Figure 5.7a

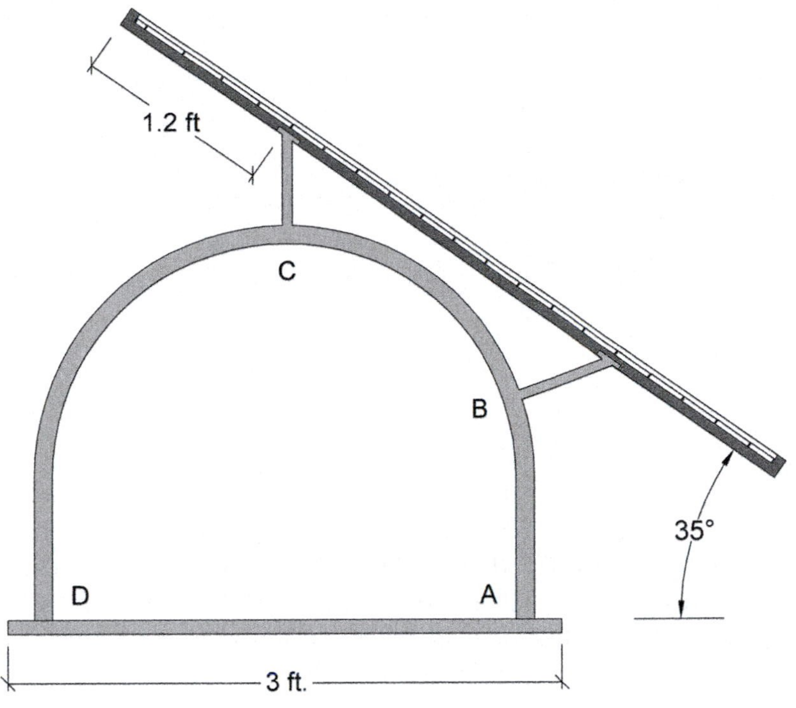

Figure 5.7b

PROBLEM 5.8

Define the term "fundamental period of a building." What is the most important consideration when estimating the fundamental period of a structure? Give an approximate value of the fundamental period of your school building.

5.9 PROBLEM

A one-story commercial building 120 ft x 45 ft is subjected to wind and seismic forces. The structure consists of 8-in masonry bearing walls that act as shear walls to resist lateral forces (see figure 5.9). The roof structure consists of wood framing with joists supported on girders, which in turn are resting on walls. The wind speed can be assumed to be 100 mph. The following seismic parameters can be assumed as well:

$R = 6$; $S_{D1} = 0.4g$ and $S_{D1} = 1.0g$ for a building supported on rock foundation, where g is the gravitational acceleration. The loads on the building are as follows:

Felt, three-ply with gravel =	5.0 psf
0.5-in plywood sheathing =	2.0 psf
Joists =	3.5 psf
Girders =	4.5 psf
Insulation, electric, misc. =	5.0 psf
Suspended ceiling =	4.0 psf
Masonry walls =	90.0 psf
Live Load =	20.0 psf

Determine the maximum wind and seismic forces at the roof level and indicate which one controls the design.

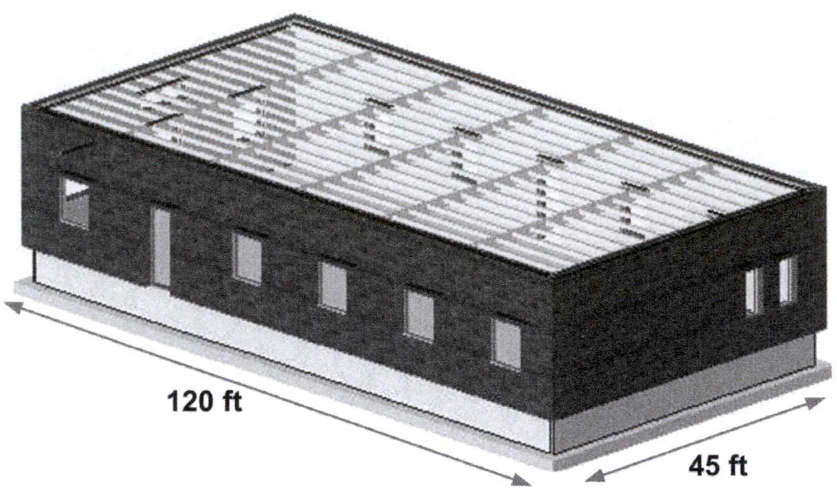

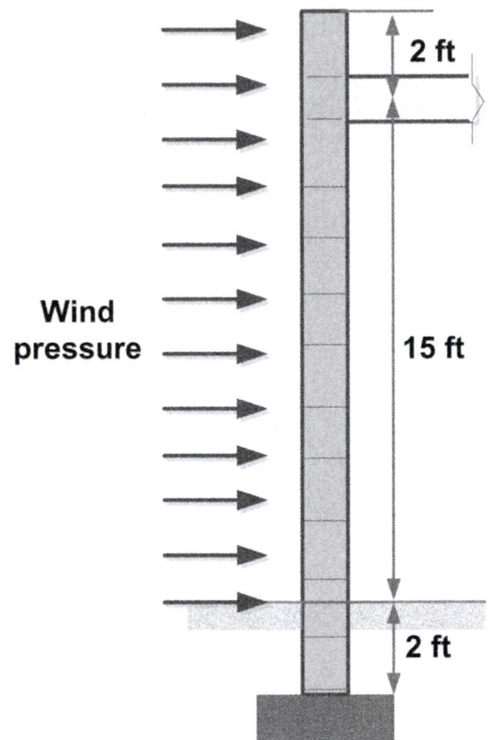

Figure 5.9

5.10 PROBLEM

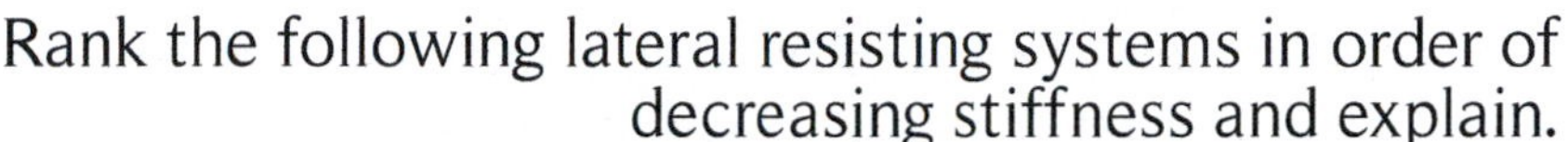

Rank the following lateral resisting systems in order of decreasing stiffness and explain.

i. shear wall
ii. braced frame
iii. moment-resisting frame

A. I, II, III
B. I, III, II
C. II, III, I
D. III, II, I

PROBLEM 5.11

Distinguish between flexible and rigid diaphragm actions. Support your answers with illustrations.

5.12 PROBLEM

i. The following diagrams show possible joint locations in buildings. What are the main purposes of these joints?

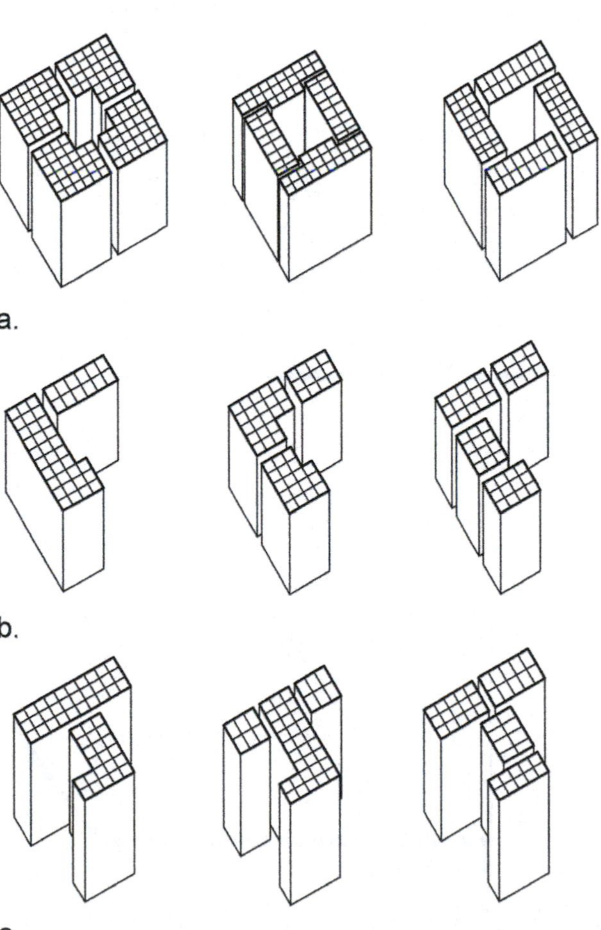

ii What criteria should be followed when locating these joints?

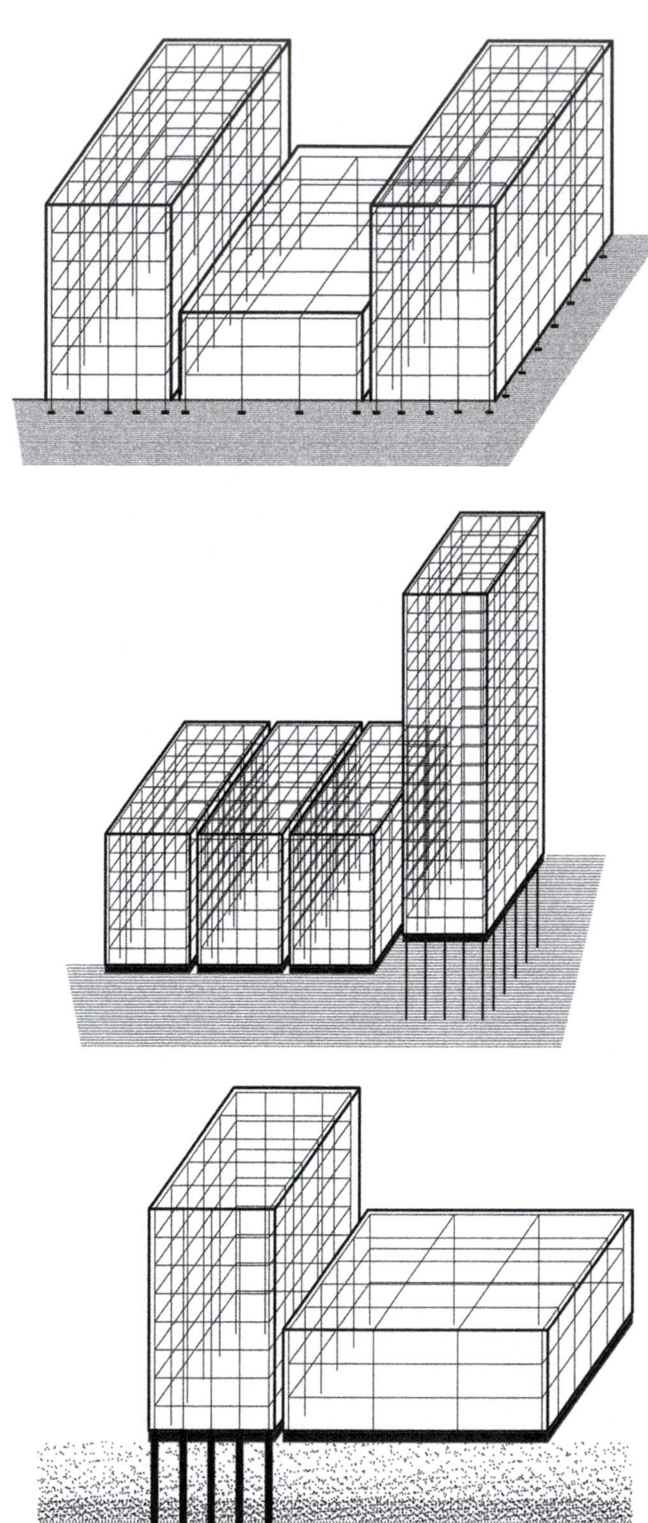

5.13 PROBLEM

Answer each of the following questions with True or False and explain why.

i. Slow, shaking motions of an earthquake are particularly damaging to tall buildings.
ii. Surface ruptures due to seismic activities cause more damage than ground shaking.
iii. During an earthquake heavy damage occurs at locations where alluvial soils meet stiff, solid rocks.
iv. Generally speaking, wood frame buildings perform relatively better than concrete or steel structures when subjected to seismic forces.

PROBLEM 5.14

The lateral resisting system of a building consists of shear walls arranged as shown in figure 5.14. A total wind pressure of 20 psf is acting perpendicular to the façades of the building and must be resisted by the shear walls. For this condition, determine the shear force in each wall. Remember that the wall assemblage is not considered as a single channel-shaped unit but as discrete, independent elements.

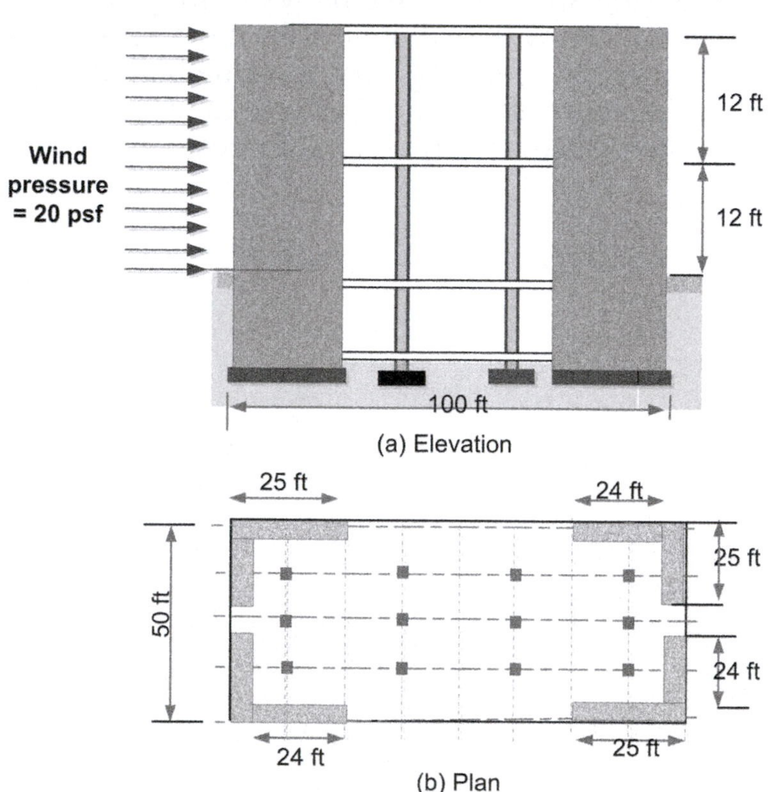

5.15 PROBLEM

Two office buildings are constructed next to each other, constructed nearly from the same building materials. Building *A* has a fundamental period of vibration calculated to be one second. Building *B*'s fundamental period of vibration is calculated to be 1.9 seconds. If all the other factors are equal, which statement is correct and why?

i. The two buildings have equal seismic forces.
ii. Building *A* has a larger seismic force.
iii. Building *A* has a smaller seismic force.
iv. There is insufficient data to determine seismic forces.

PROBLEM 5.16

An industrial building with a plan dimension of 25' x 45' and a height of 15' is subjected to a wind load of 5 kips as shown in figure 5.16. Two braced exterior walls parallel to the wind direction are used to resist the horizontal diaphragm force in the roof. Assuming horizontal reactions at *A* and *B* are equal, determine the magnitude of force developed in each brace member.

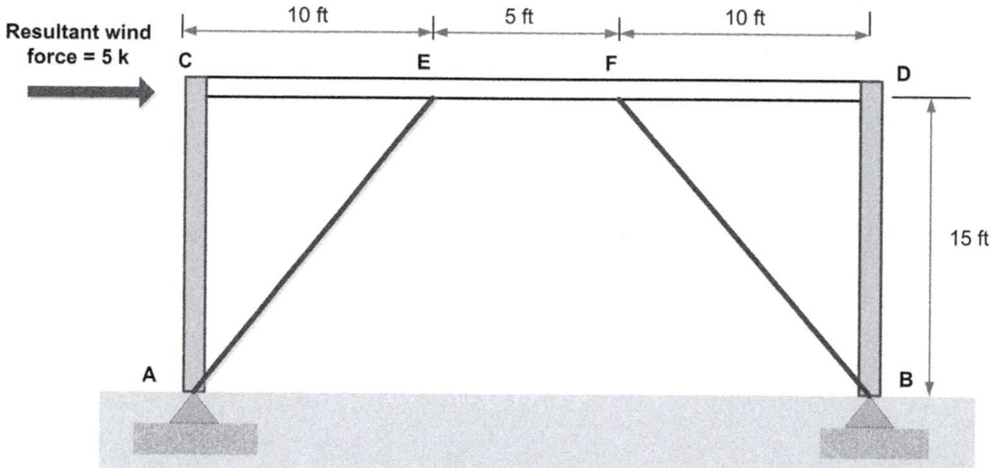

PROBLEM 6.1

i. In reference to cable supported structures explain the meaning of the term "fluttering." Use sketches to support your answers.

ii. Various methods can be employed to stabilize cable structures. Describe five methods normally used to stabilize cable structures against instability.

6.2 PROBLEM

Given:

Three equal loads are suspended from the cable as shown. If $H_B = H_D = 5$ ft, determine the support reaction components at E and the sag at point C.

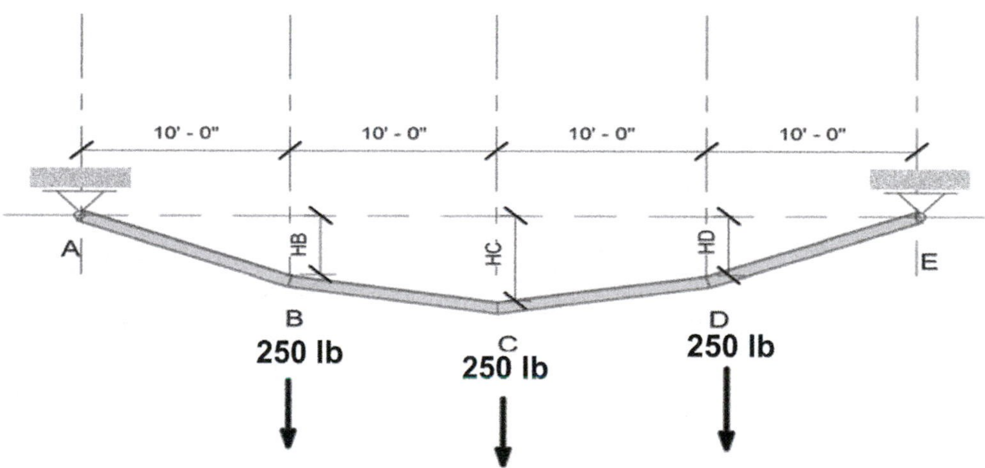

Required:

$E = ?$
$E_x = ?$
$E_y = ?$
$H_c = ?$

PROBLEM 6.3

For the cable structure shown in figure 6.3, determine the cable tension between each force, and determine the required length of the cable for the system shown. Assume the sag at C as h_c = 10 ft.

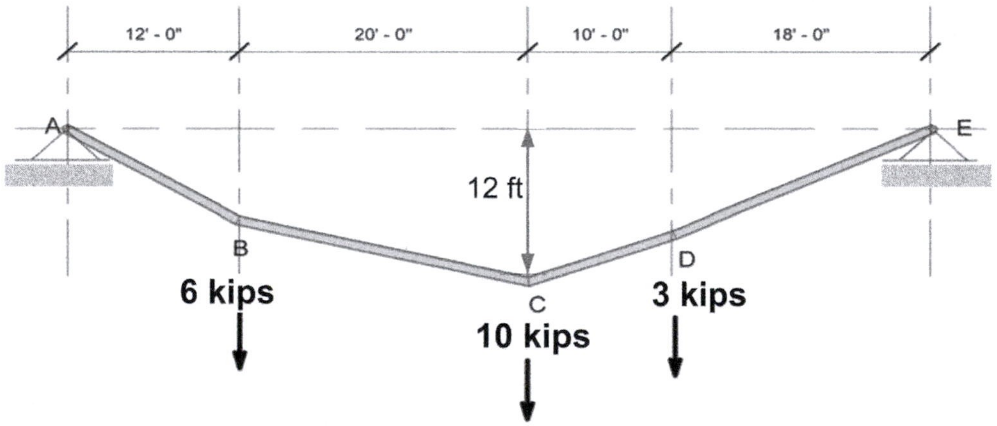

Required:

Figure 6.3

AB, A_x, A_y, CB, CD, ED, E_y, E_x

6.4 PROBLEM

The cable structure shown in figure 6.4 is used to support a roof for outdoor activities. Determine the maximum horizontal component of the cable tension force in terms of *w*, *L*, and *h* as defined in figure 6.4. Assume the load is "*w*," uniformly distributed over the horizontal projection.

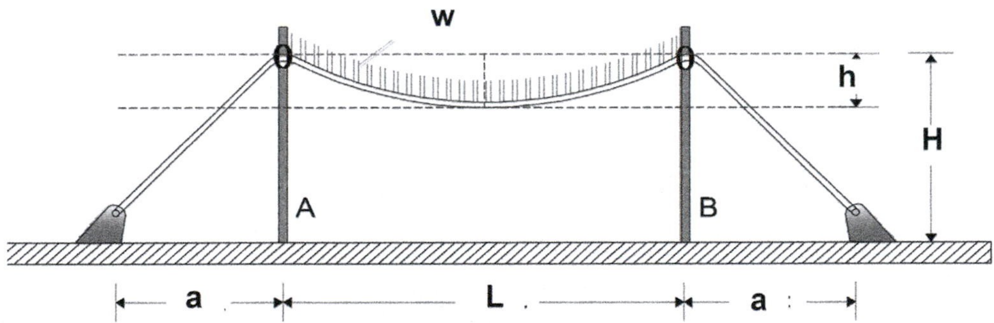

Figure 6.4

PROBLEM 7.1

(i). Describe one of the most famous arch vaults of the ancient world. Give information about name, time, and location of the arch vault along with any details, photos, and sketches.
(ii). Give a detailed structural description of the Pont Du Gard, Nîmes, 150 A.D., and explain how stone was used to its full advantage.

7.2 PROBLEM

An interesting example of contemporary arches can be seen in the roof structure of the Cowboys Stadium, Texas. Describe the main structural features of this roof along with the support systems used. Provide drawings and photos to support your answer.

PROBLEM 7.3

Compare the behavior of fixed-arches, two-hinged arches, and three-hinged arches with respect to applied forces and thermal stresses. Support your answers with sketches.

7.4 PROBLEM

Given:

A three-hinged trussed arch is subjected to two forces as depicted in figure 7.4 below

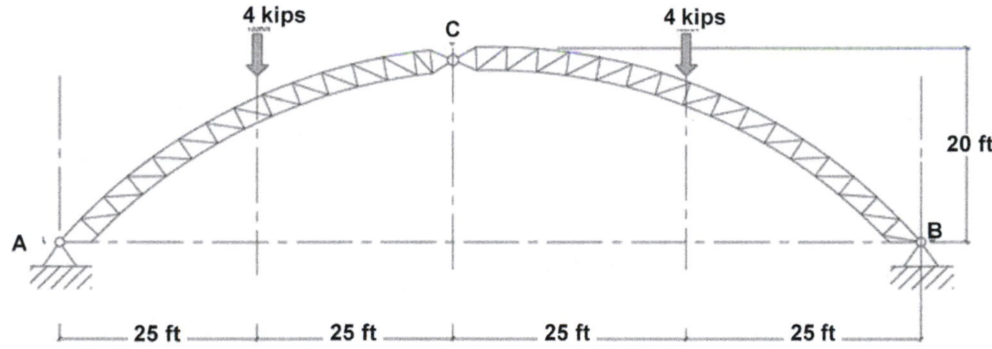

Required:

Determine all support and pin forces for the arch member.

PROBLEM 7.5

The arch shown below is loaded over its entire span. Determine the total compressive force acting on the arch in terms of *w*, *L*, and *h*. Ignore self-weight of the arch members.

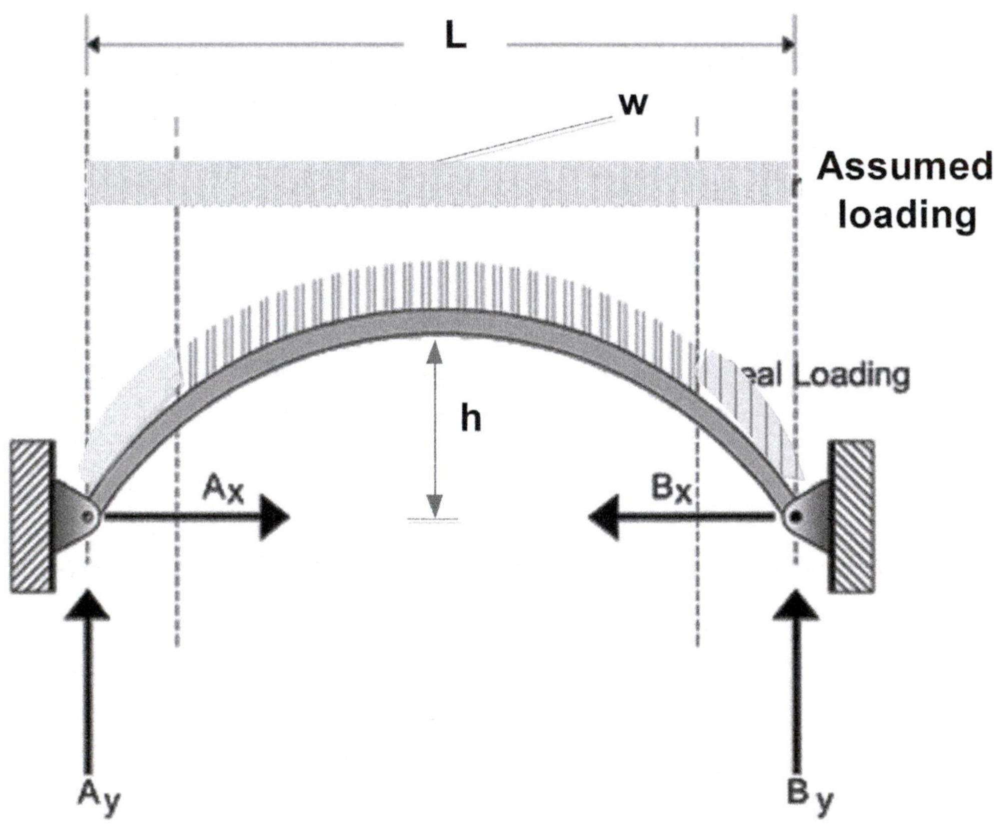

8.1 PROBLEM

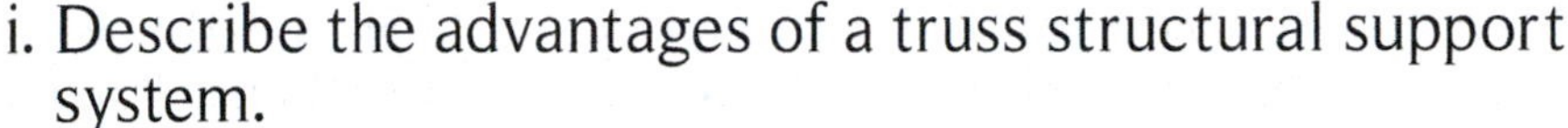

i. Describe the advantages of a truss structural support system.

ii. Distinguish between simple truss and Vierendeel truss systems. Draw an example of each.

PROBLEM 8.2

The simple truss depicted in figure 8.2 is subjected to a point load at point *B*. Determine which member of the truss is in tension or compression. The numerical values of the internal forces are NOT required.

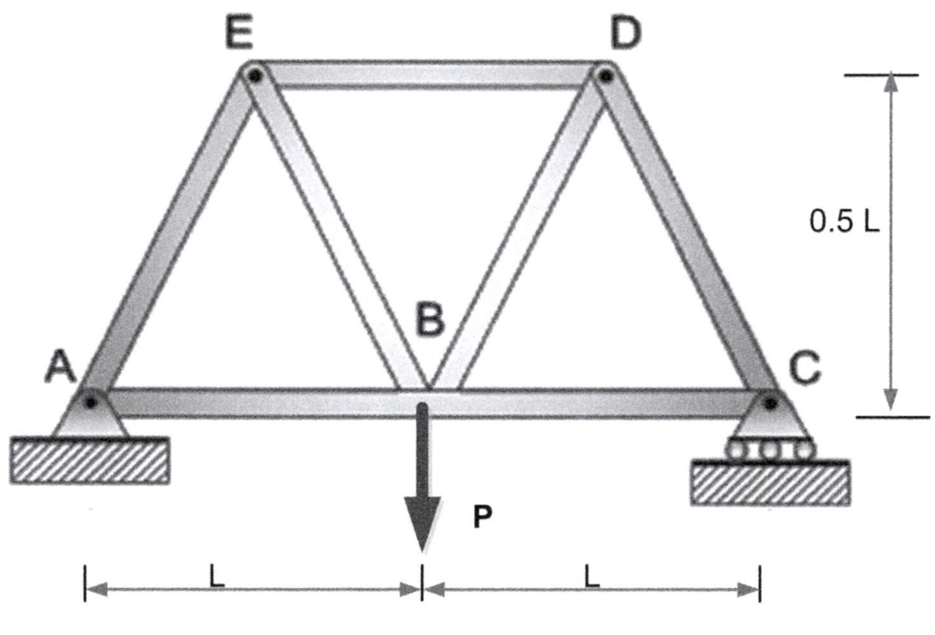

Figure 8.2

8.3 PROBLEM

The simple truss shown in figure 8.3a is subjected to a point load at point *C*. Determine which member of the truss is in tension or compression. The numerical values of the internal forces are NOT required.

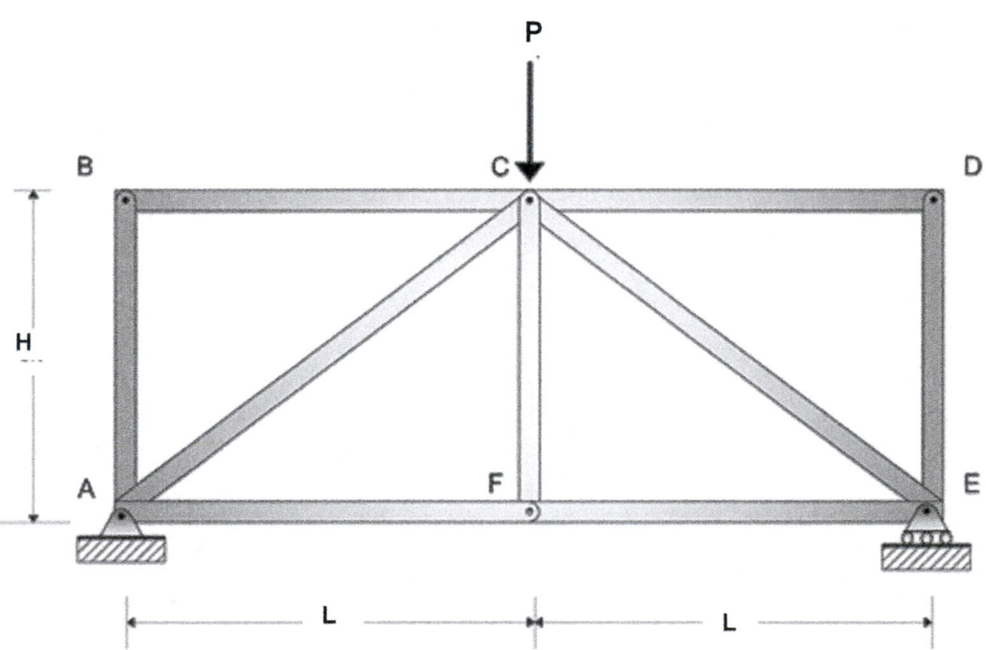

Figure 8.3a

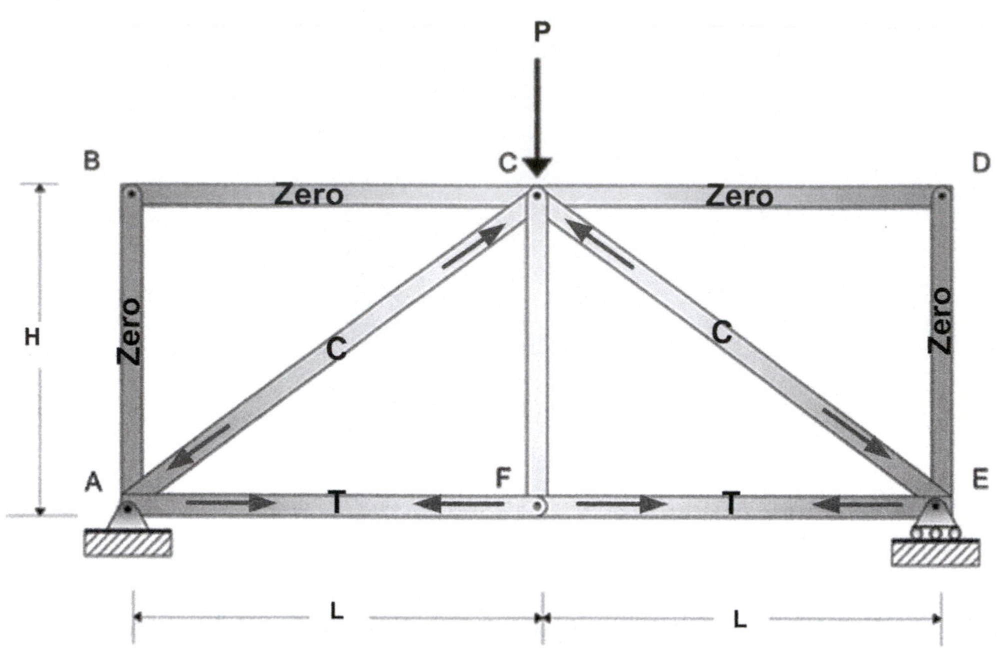

Figure 8.3b

8.4 PROBLEM

The cantilever truss shown below is used to support an entrance canopy. Using the method of joints, determine the force in each member of the truss shown. Summarize the results on a force summation diagram and indicate whether each member is in tension or compression.

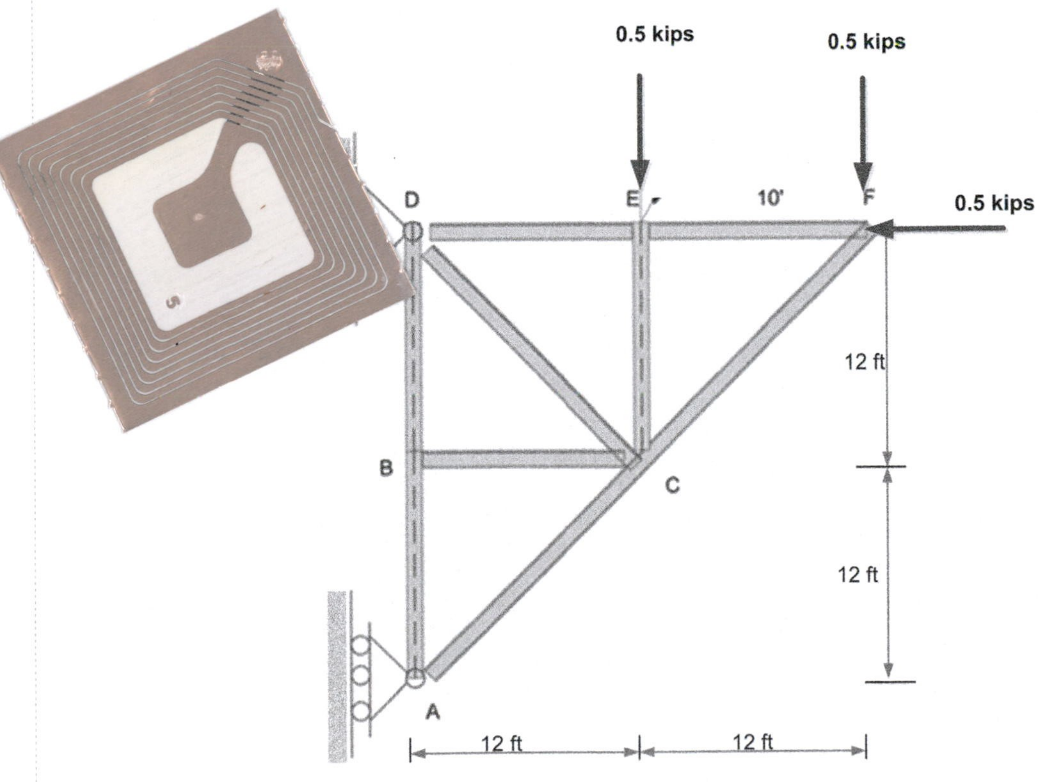

PROBLEM 8.5

Under certain loading conditions, some truss members may not develop an internal force. Such elements are called zero-force members. Also, these special loading conditions will help to minimize the number of unknown forces at those joints. Describe these loading cases.

8.6 PROBLEM

For the roof truss depicted in figure 8.6 identify zero-force members.

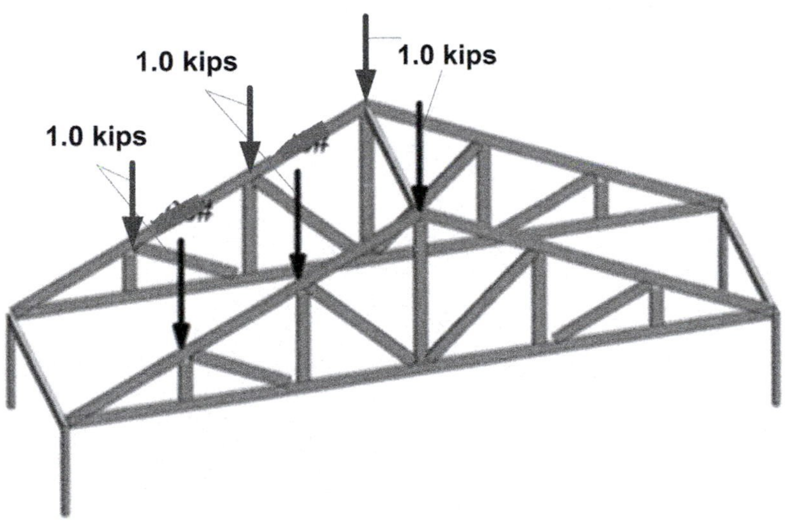

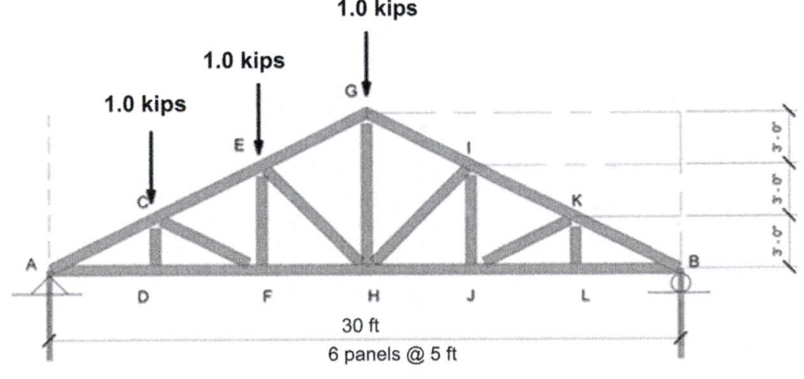

Figure 8.6

PROBLEM 8.7

The truss depicted in figure 8.7a below is used to support an outdoor roofing structure. Using the method of joints, determine the forces in each member. Show your final answers in the truss diagram by specifying magnitude and sense of the force.

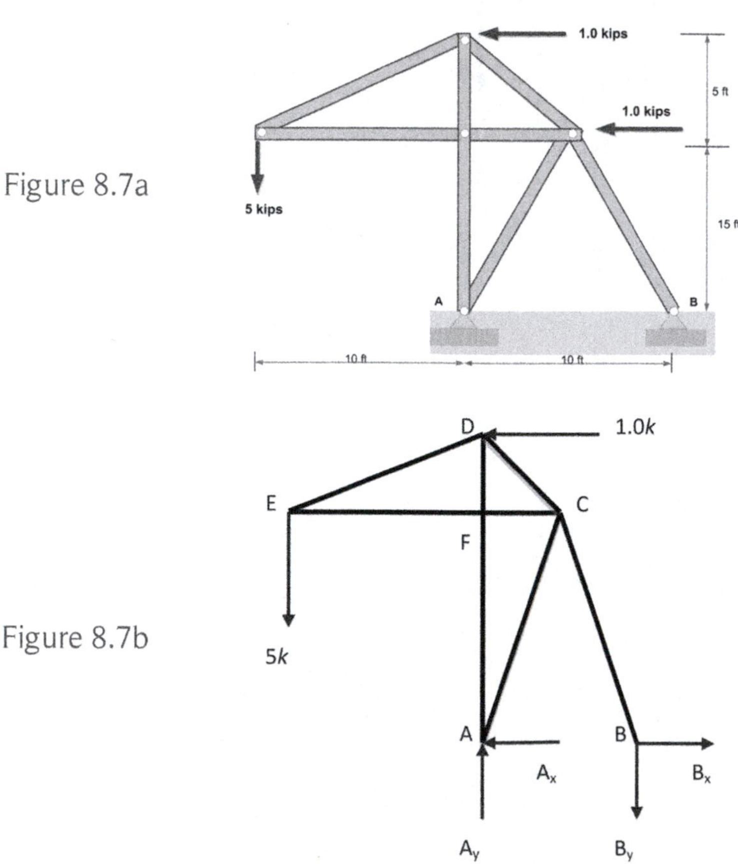

Figure 8.7a

Figure 8.7b

8.8 PROBLEM

For the truss shown in figure 8.8, the vertical and horizontal members are equal in length (L). Determine the zero-force members and identify the nature of the force in each member of the truss.

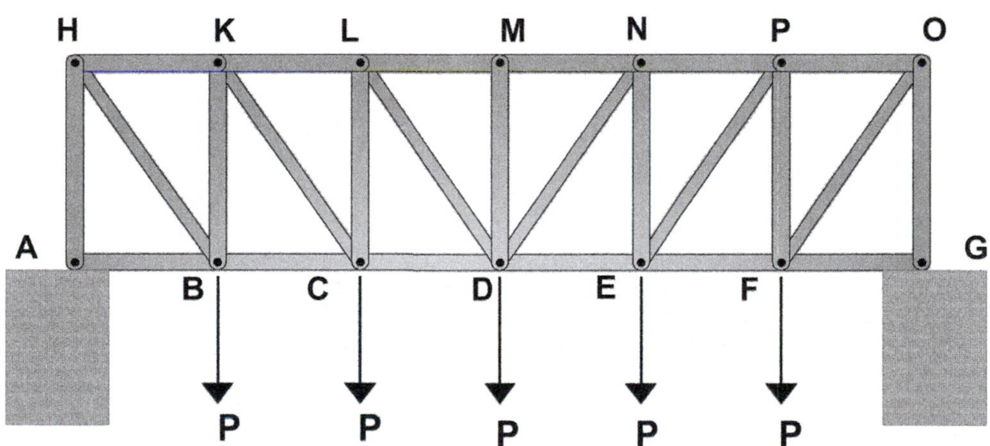

Figure 8.8

PROBLEM 8.9

The cantilever truss shown below is a part of the shading support structure. Using the method of section determine the forces in members *AC*, *BC*, and *BD*. (Hint: Pass only one section and then use the right side part of your section.)

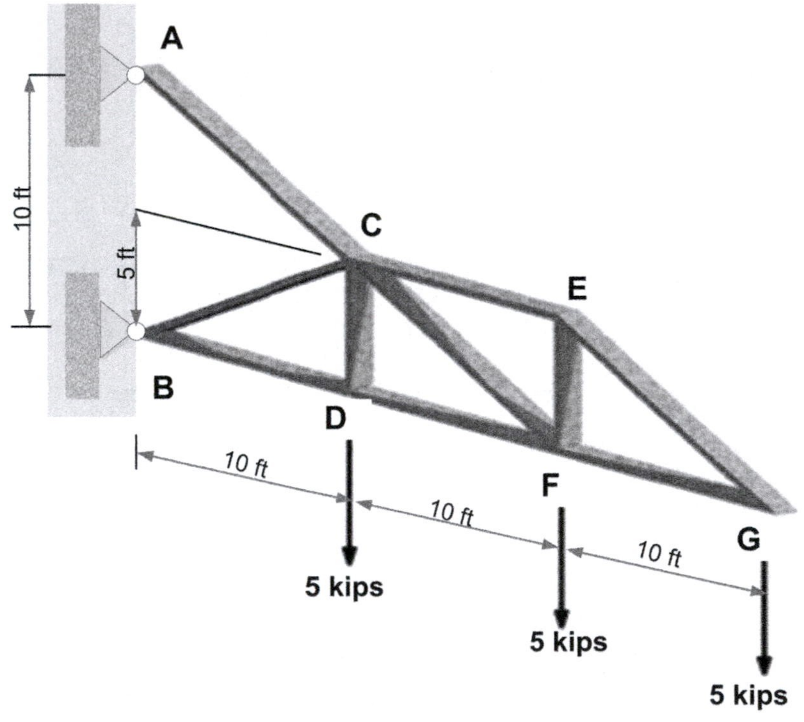

8.10 PROBLEM

The bridge truss shown in figure 8.10 below is carrying a maximum resultant force of 100 kips at mid-span. Solve for the member forces *AB*, *BH*, and *HG* using the method of section.

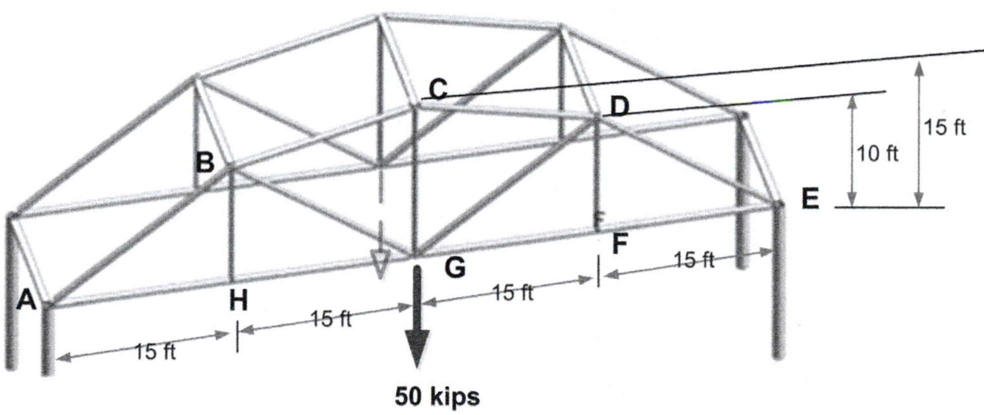

Figure 8.10

PROBLEM 8.11

A power transmission tower is subjected to wind loads as depicted in figure 8.11a. Using the method of section, determine the force in members *IJ*.

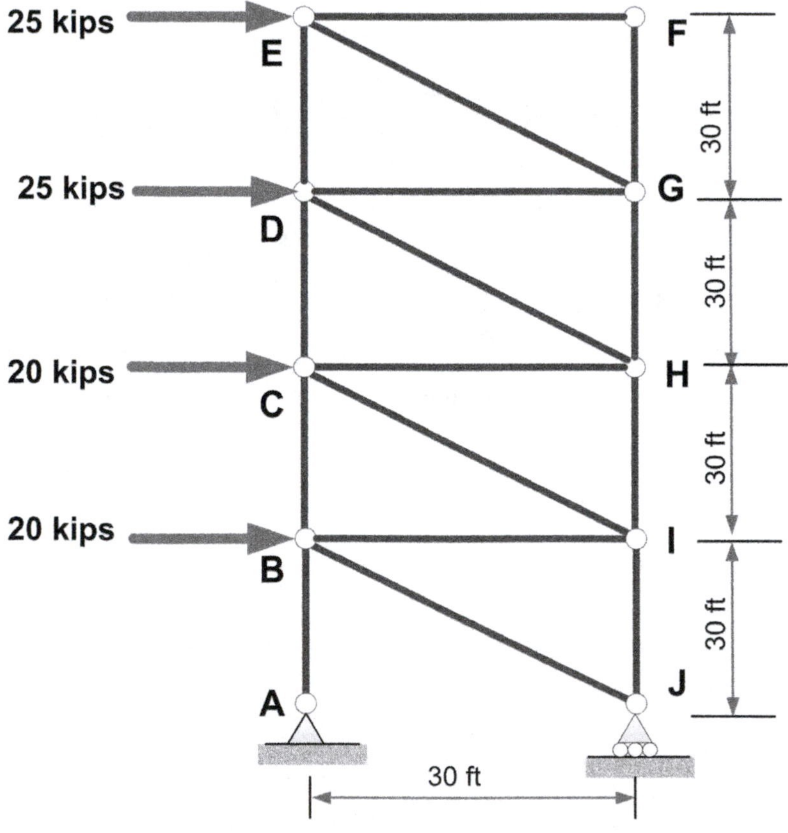

Figure 8.11a

8.12 PROBLEM

The roof truss in figure 8.12 is subjected to gravity and wind loads as depicted. Determine the effective tension counters and their respective magnitudes.

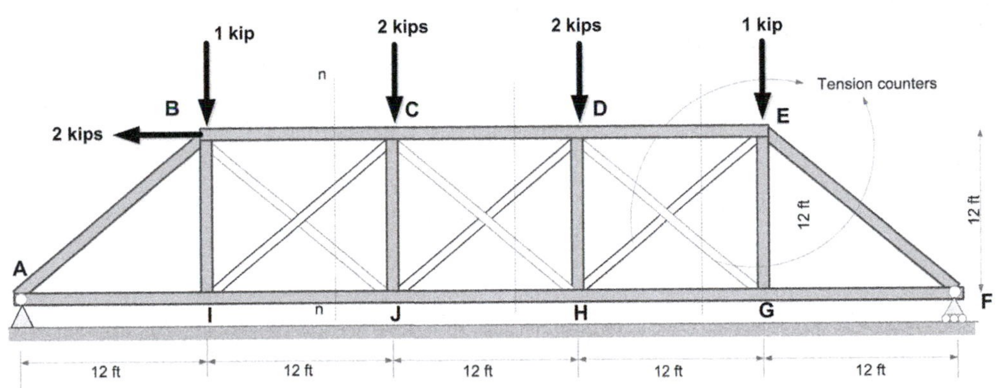

Figure 8.12

PROBLEM 9.1

Define the following terms:

(a) Centroids of an area
(b) Neutral axis
(c) Moment of inertia
(d) Radius of gyration
(e) Section modulus

9.2 PROBLEM

For the structural members cross-sections shown below determine the moment of inertia about the x- and y-axis along with the respective values for the radii of gyration.

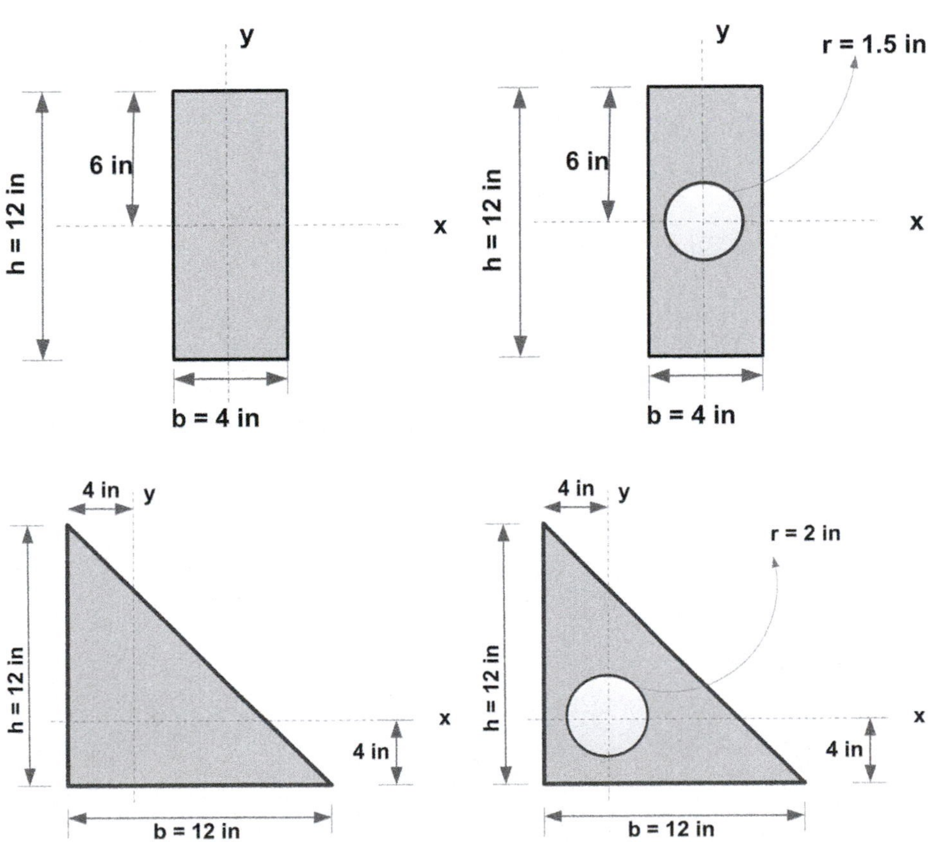

PROBLEM 10.1

Distinguish between normal stress and bearing stress. Use examples and sketches to support your answer.

10.2 PROBLEM

In the stress-strain diagram shown in figure 10.2 below, identify the missing labels.

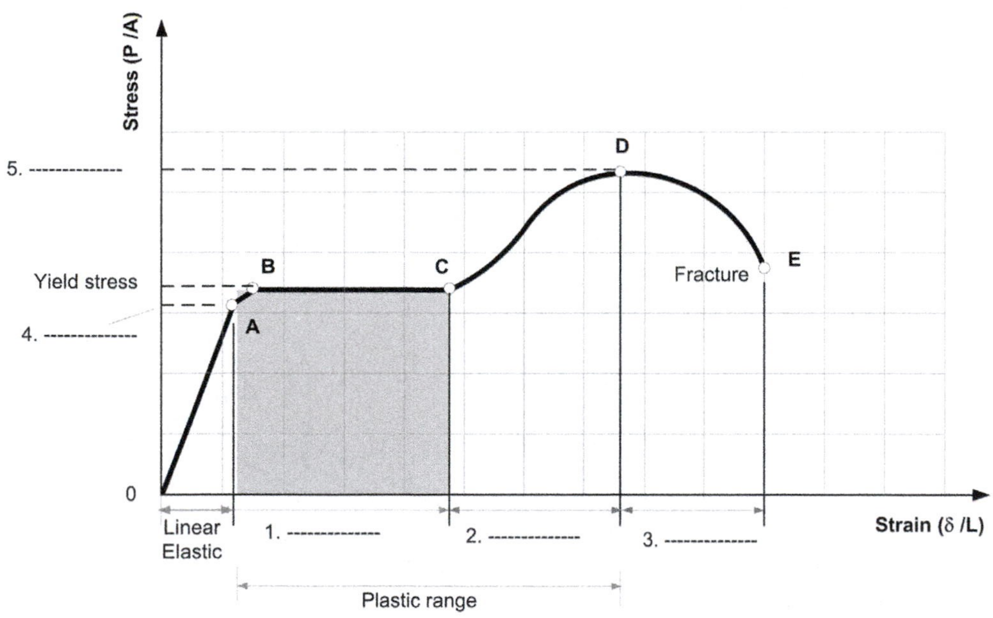

Figure 10.2

PROBLEM 10.3

Three pieces of wood are glued together to form an assembly (shown in figure 10.3 below) that can be used to test the shear strength of a glued joint. A load *P* of 10 kips is applied. Compute the average shear stress in each joint.

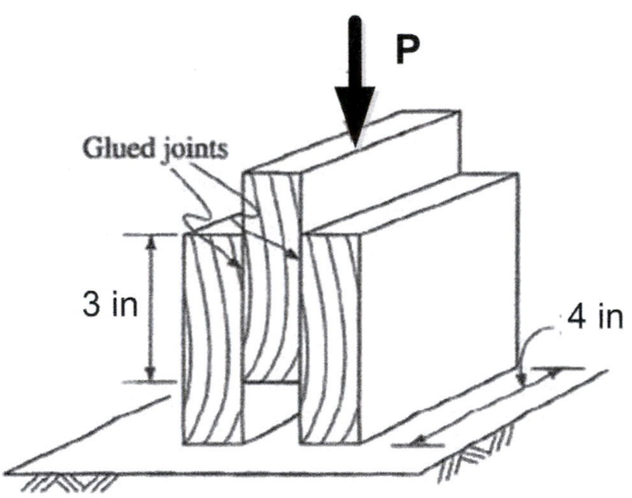

Figure 10.3

10.4 PROBLEM

Determine the magnitude and nature of the stress developed in the truss member *CD* due to the loadings given in figure 10.4. The size of member *CD* is $\frac{1}{2}$" thick by 2" wide.

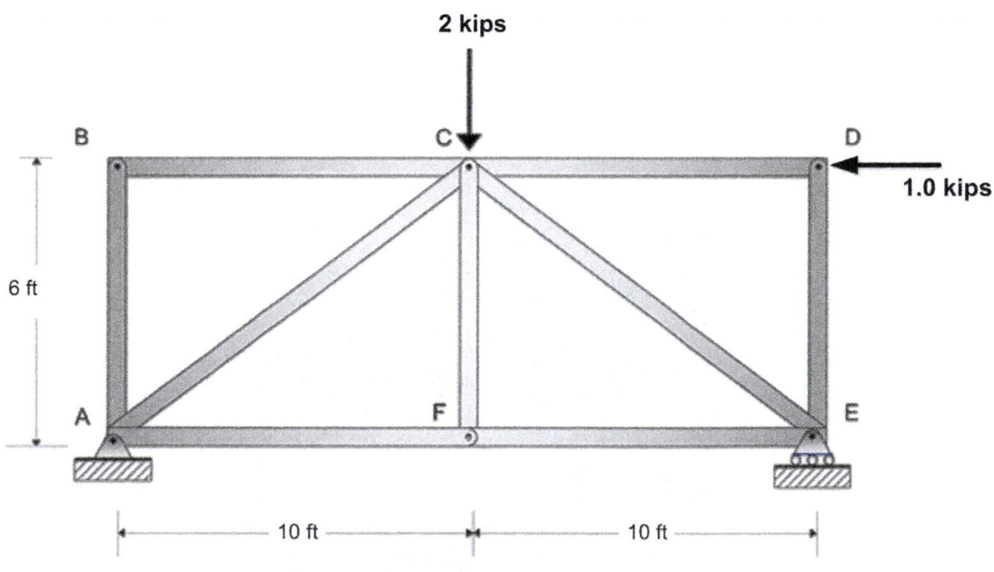

Figure 10.4

PROBLEM 10.5

A 12 ft x 24 ft commercial building marquee hangs from two steel rods inclined at an angle of 35°. The combined effects of dead load and wind load on the marquee add up to 150 psf. Design the two rods out of steel that has an allowable tensile stress F_t = 24 ksi (allowable stress).

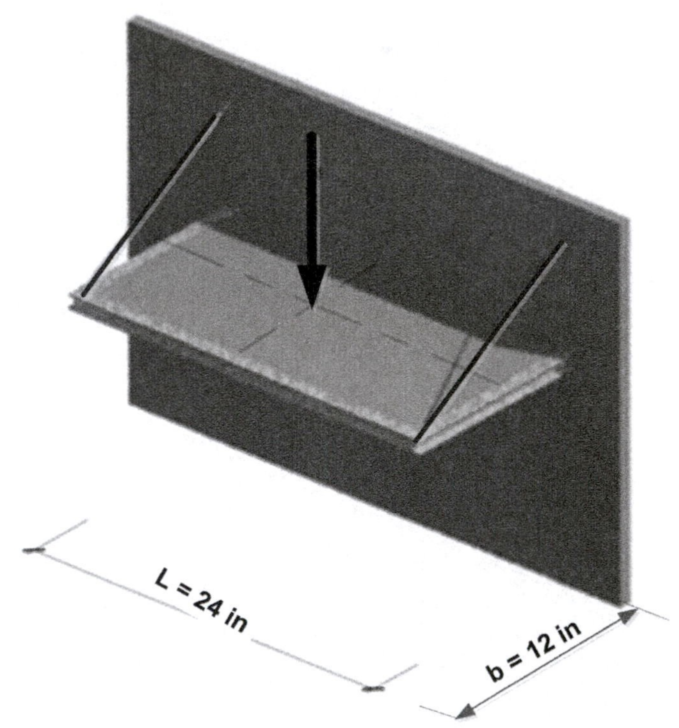

10.6 PROBLEM

During the test of a specimen in a tensile testing machine, it is found that the specimen elongates 0.0036 inches between two punch marks that are initially 3 inches apart. Evaluate the strain.

PROBLEM 10.7

A concrete wall has a density of 145 lb/ft^3. Determine the maximum height of this concrete wall if the allowable compressive stress is limited to 0.15 ksi and the wall is

i. 5" wide and
ii. 8" wide.

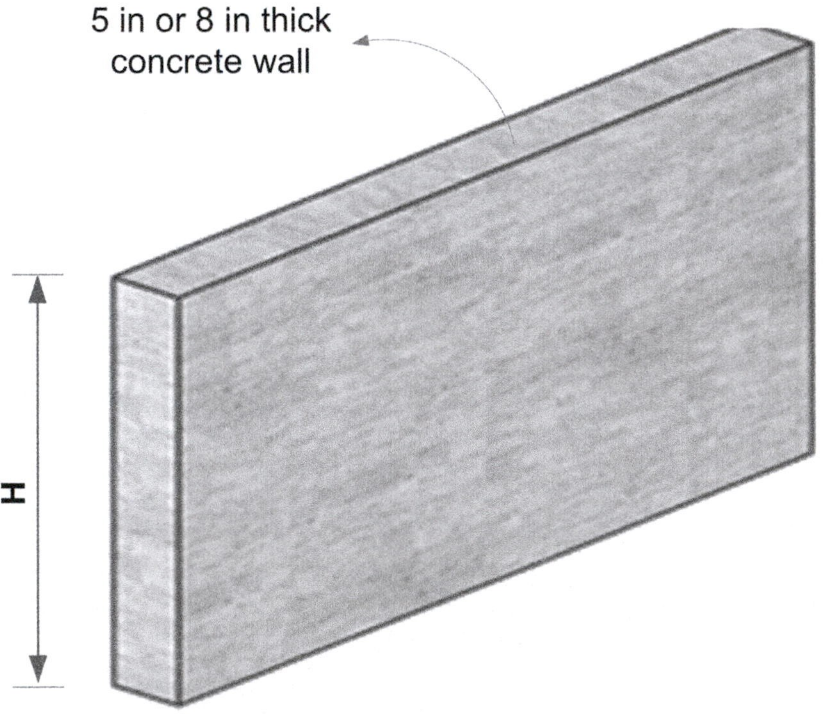

10.8 PROBLEM

A steel wire 500 ft long and $\frac{1}{8}$" in diameter weighs 0.040 lb/ft. If the wire is suspended vertically from its upper end, calculate (a) the maximum tensile stress due to its own weight and (b) the maximum weight W that can be safely supported assuming a safety factor of 2.5 and an ultimate tensile stress of 65 ksi.

PROBLEM 10.9

A concrete test cylinder 12" tall and 6" in diameter is subjected to a compressive load that results in a strain of 0.003 in/in. Determine the shortening that develops as a result of this loading.

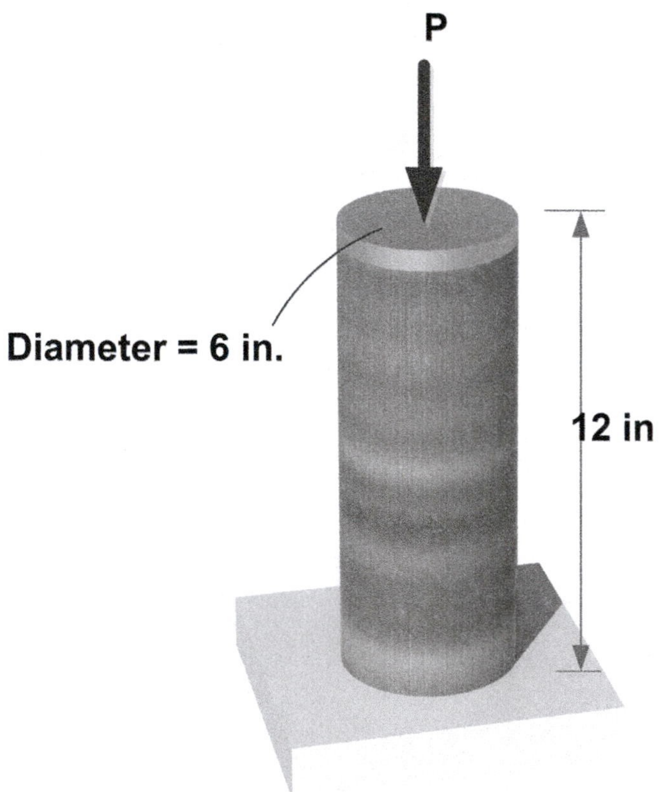

10.10 PROBLEM

A garage roof slab is supported by two 6"-wide by 10 ft-high concrete masonry walls (figure 10.10). The roof weighs 100 psf and carries a wind load of 30 psf. Check the compressive stress at the base of the wall, assuming the masonry unit has a capacity of 150 psi. Concrete masonry unit weight is estimated to be 145 lb/ft^3.

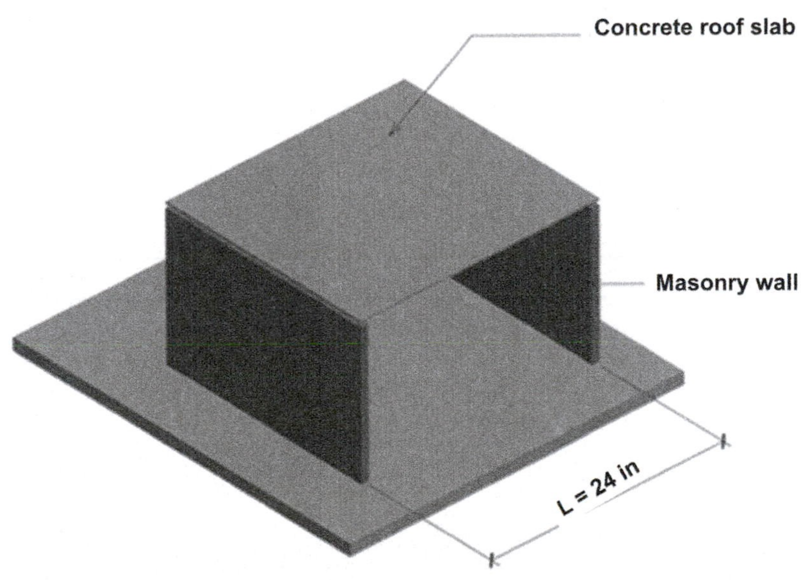

Figure 10.10

PROBLEM 10.11

The reinforced concrete beam shown below is used in a parking support structure. (i)–Determine the width of the expansion joint that must be provided for the temperature conditions: the temperature gradient from summer to winter time is ΔT = 80 °F, and the linear thermal expansion coefficient is $a = 5.5(10^{-6})$ °F^{-1}. (ii)–Secondly, how much thermal bending stresses will develop if no thermal expansion joint is provided and both ends are fully restrained? Assume modulus of elasticity for concrete E = 3,800 ksi.

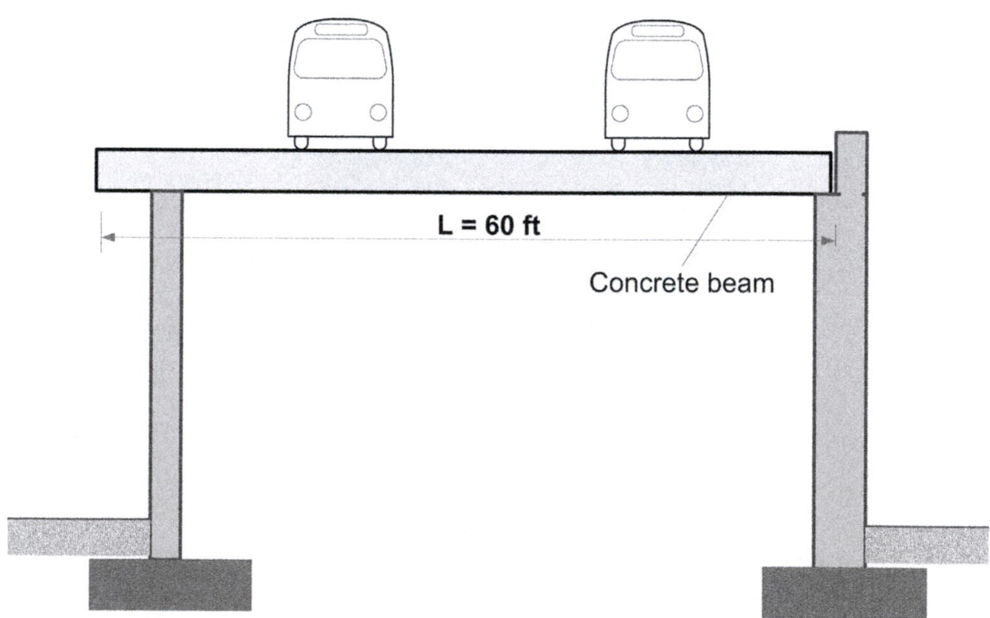

10.12 PROBLEM

An office building has exposed steel framing of 100 ft high (see figure 10.12). The south side of the building is subjected to direct sun and reaches a temperature of 60 °F while the north side remains at 5 °F. Determine the overall change in length of columns under this condition. Assume the thermal expansion coefficient of steel as $a = 7.3(10^{-6})$ °F^{-1}

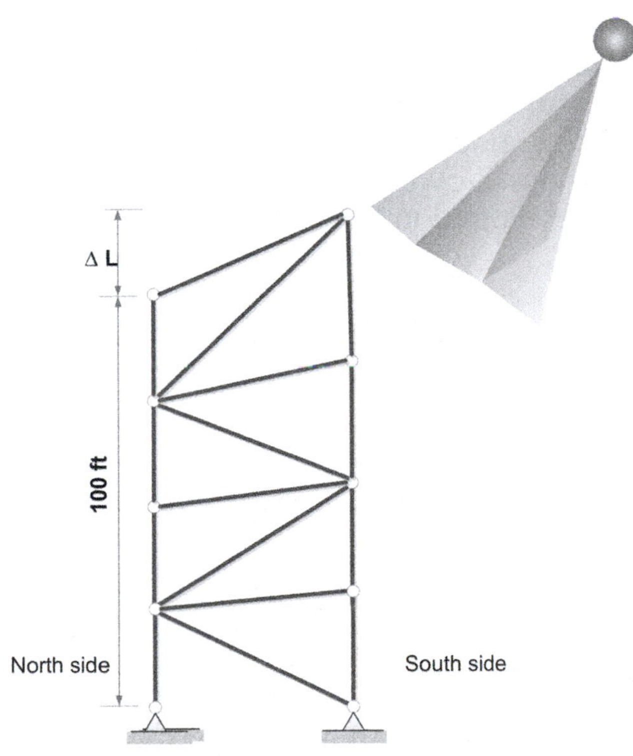

PROBLEM 10.13

A curtain wall shown in figure 10.13 was connected to a concrete structural framing system when the temperature was 30 °F. The curtain wall is made of metal mullions that are attached to the concrete frame. During a sunny day in the winter the temperature of the curtain wall reached 75 °F. Because of the insulation the temperature of the concrete supporting frame reached only 45 °F. Determine structural issues for the curtain wall that are related to this thermal change if no provision is made for an expansion joint. Assume the thermal expansion coefficient of metal to be $a = 13.5(10^{-6})\ °F^{-1}$ and for concrete to be $a = 5.5(10^{-6})\ °F^{-1}$, modulus of elasticity of metal to be $E = 10 \times 10^6$, and maximum allowable stress of $F_a = 5$ ksi. Ignore the tensile stresses developed in the concrete frame.

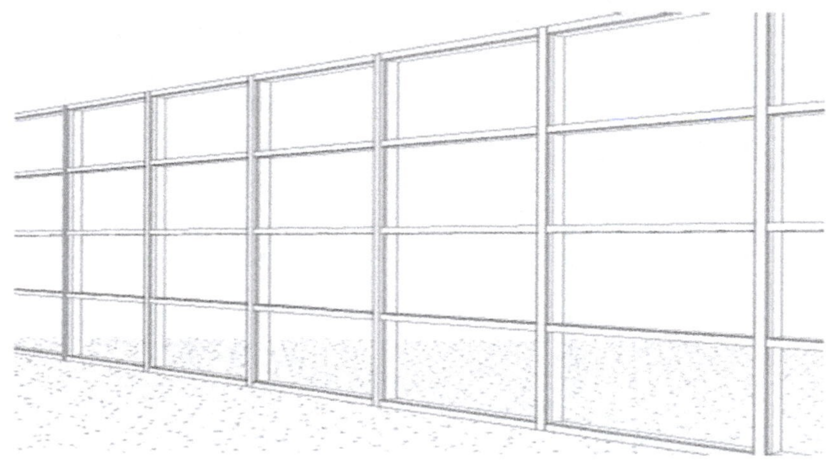

Figure 10.13

PROBLEM 11.1

Given:

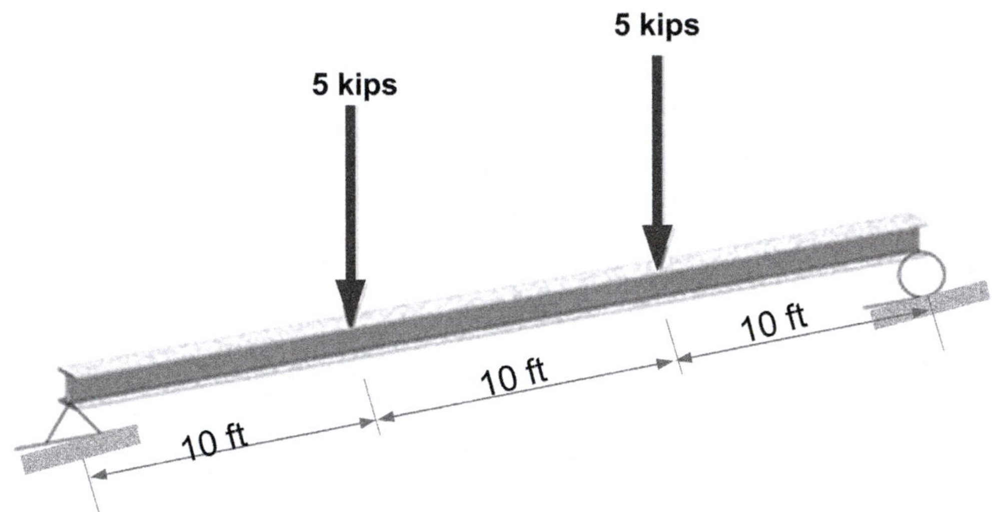

Required:

Construct the shear and moment diagrams using the equilibrium method. Indicate the magnitudes of V_{Max} and M_{Max}.

11.2 PROBLEM

Figure 11.2 depicts a part of a structural steel framing for an office building. For the given loading condition, construct the load, shear and moment diagrams for the beam *C* and the girder *ABCD* using the semigraphical approach and find V_{Max} and M_{Max}.

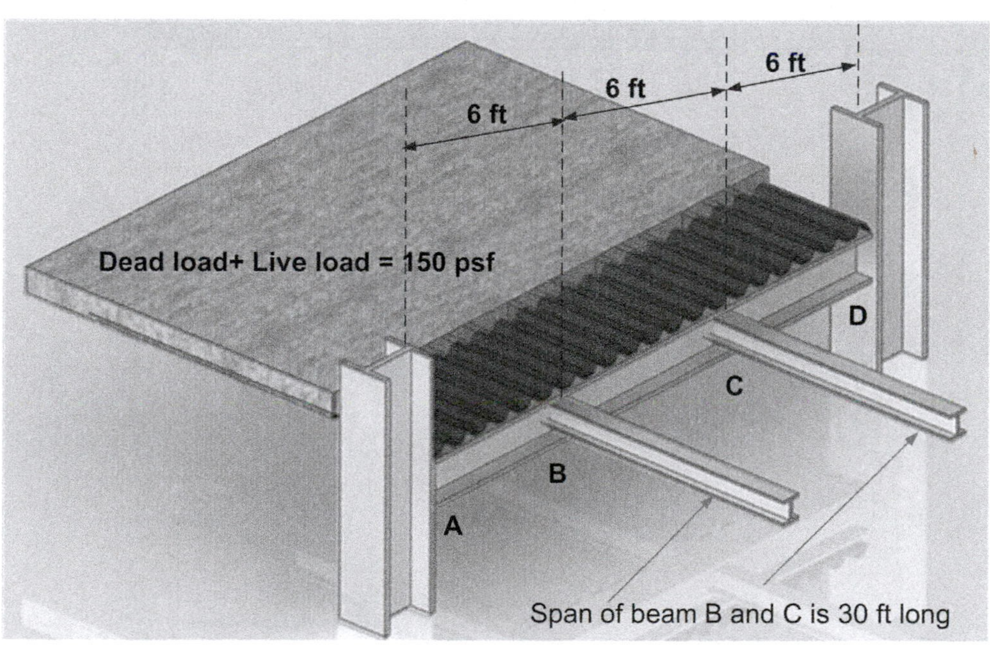

Figure 11.2

PROBLEM 11.3

Determine the degree of indeterminacy of the beams depicted in figure 11.3 below.

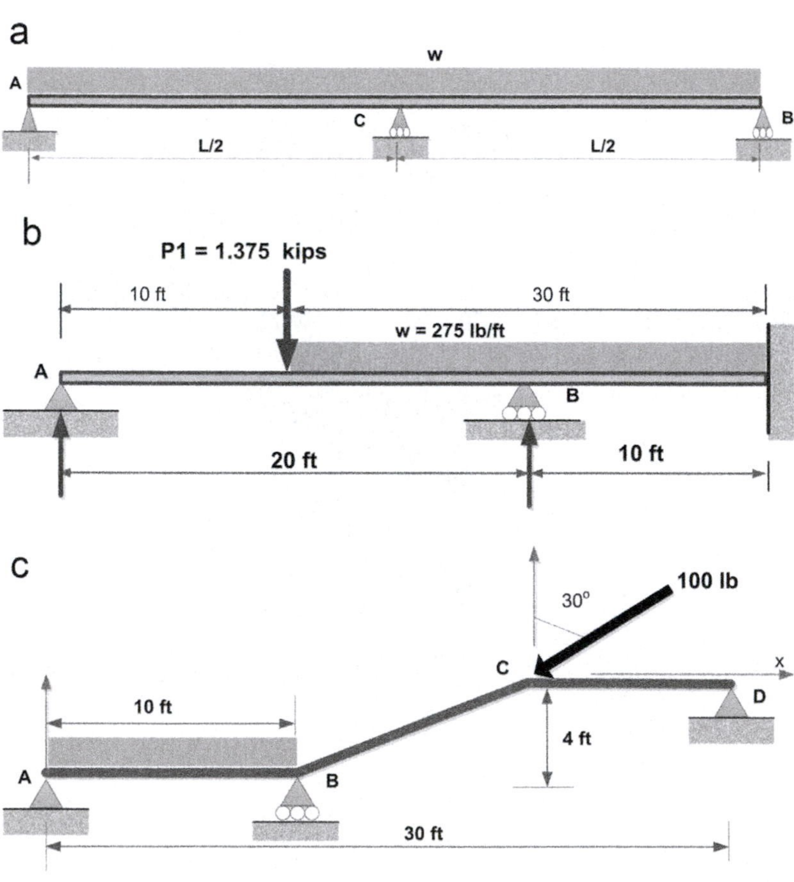

Figure 11.3

11.4 PROBLEM

For the steel beam shown in figure 11.4 below, construct the shear and moment diagrams for the given loading condition using the semigraphical approach.

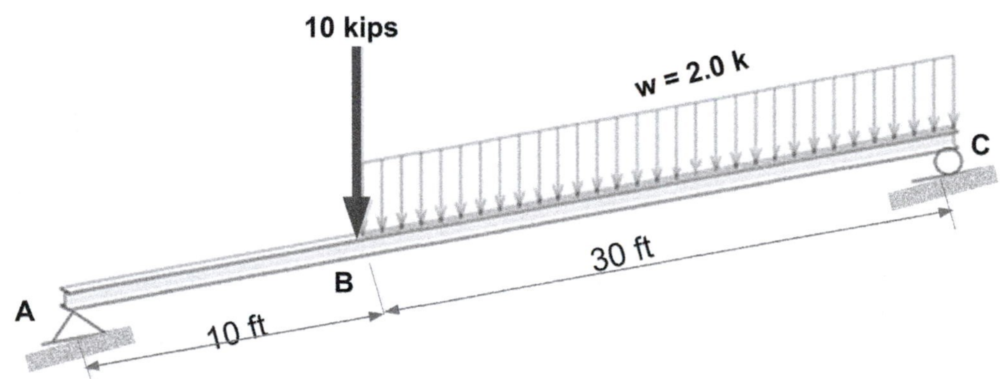

Figure 11.4

PROBLEM 11.5

The steel beam depicted in figure 11.5 is a part of a floor framing system. Construct the shear and moment diagrams for the given loading condition using the semigraphical approach and indicate the critical values.

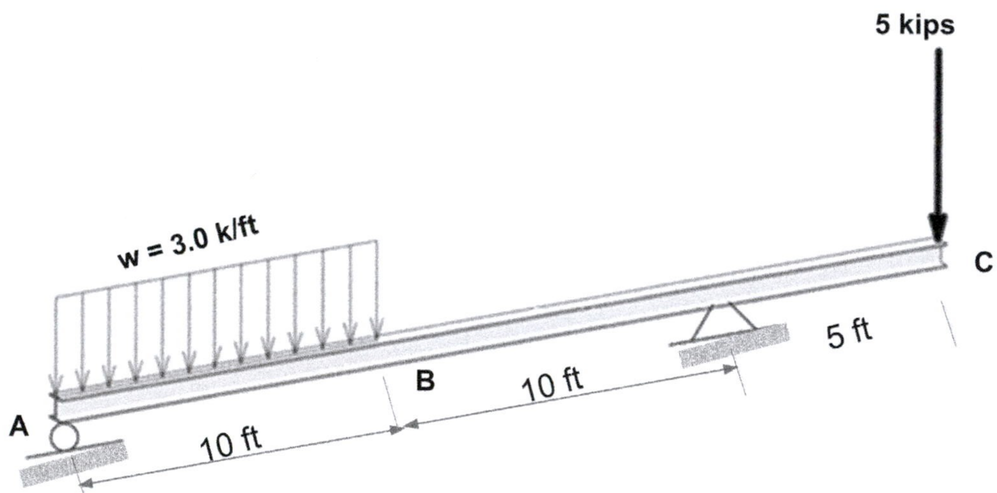

Figure 11.5

11.6 PROBLEM

A lintel steel beam over a doorway opening 6 ft wide supports a triangular load as shown. Determine the maximum shear force and bending moment acting on the lintel beam.

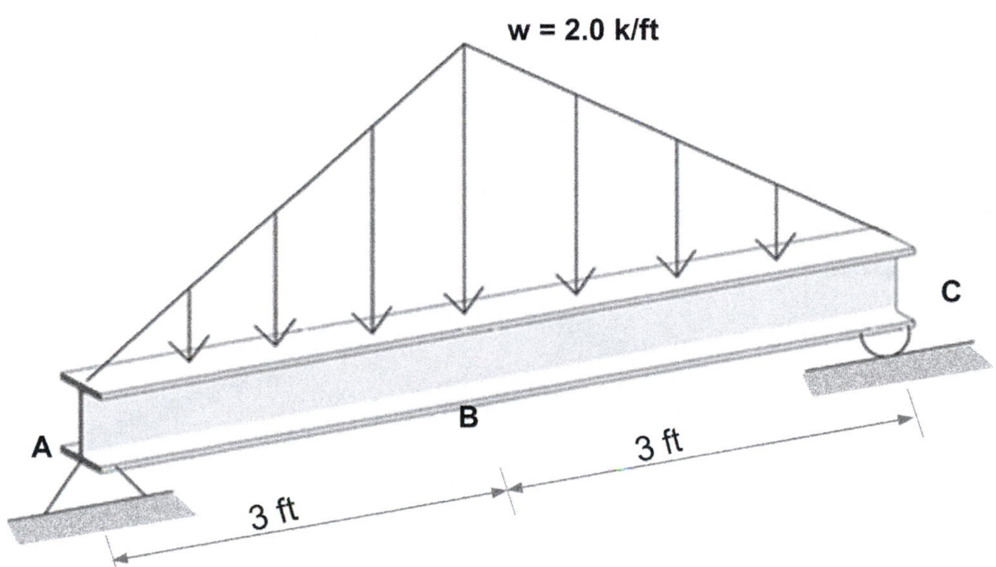

PROBLEM 11.7

Two beams crossed at midspan are subjected to a point load of 9 kips as shown in figure 11.7. The two beams have the same material and cross-section. Beam *AB*, however, is half as long as beam *CD*. How much of the 10 kips is carried by each beam?

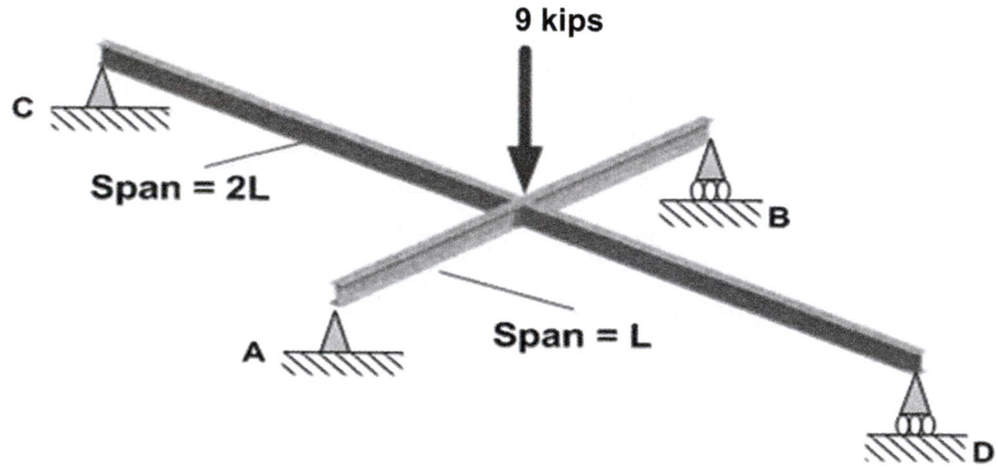

Figure 11.7

11.8 PROBLEM

In a beam grid system, two cantilever steel beams are crossed at 90° in a plan as illustrated in figure 11.8 below. The two beams have the same cross-section and beam *AB* is twice as long as beam *BC*. Determine how much of the load is taken by each beam.

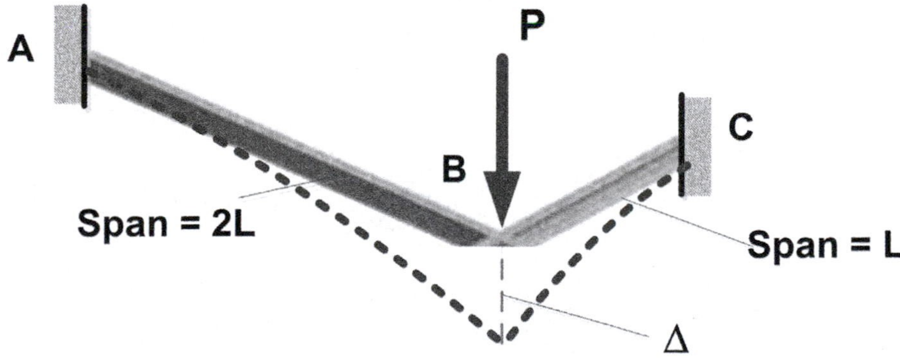

PROBLEM 11.9

A two-way waffle roof structure (figure 11.9) covers a free space of 40 ft x 40 ft for outdoor theater application and is simply supported along its four edges. The structure must support a live load of 20 psf, and a dead load of 30 psf. Assume a square grid spacing of 4 ft for the two-way square beam grids. Select a suitable wood beam section for this grid structure if the allowable bending strength of the wood is given as F_b = 1,500 psi and modulus of elasticity = E_v = 1600,000 psi.

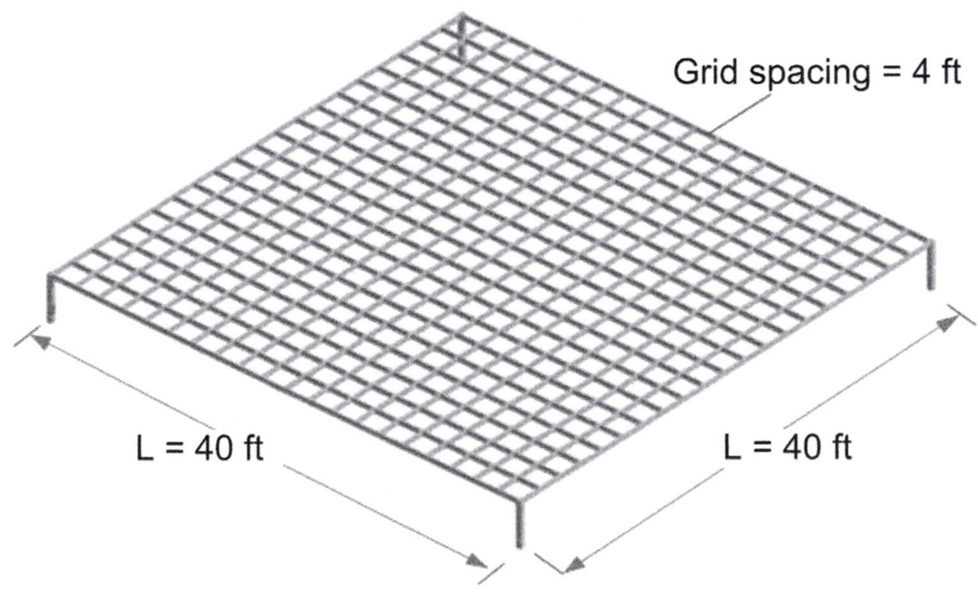

11.10 PROBLEM

The overhanging beam shown in figure 11.10a is Douglas Fir-Larch No. 1 wood, having a size of a 4 x 12 S4S member (figure 11.10b). Check the adequacy of the section in bending. (F_b = 1,300 psi)

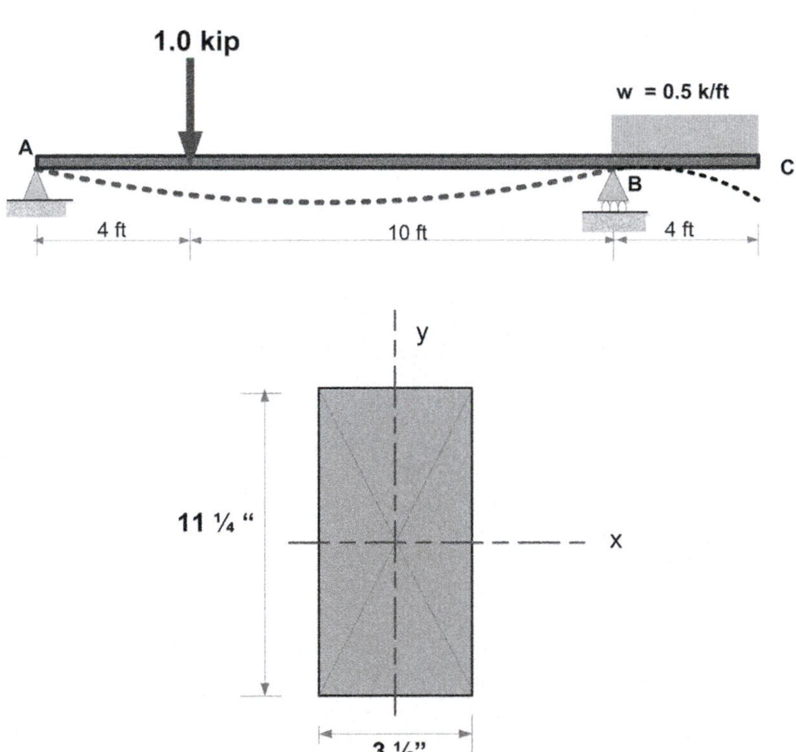

Figure 11.10

PROBLEM 11.11

For the wood framing shown below, determine the maximum bending moment and deflection for a typical interior joist and the edge joist to the opening (see figure 11.11). Assume Dead Load = 12 psf, Live Load = 68 psf. Ignore self-weight of members. What size wood joist could be used for each if F_b = 1,500 psi?

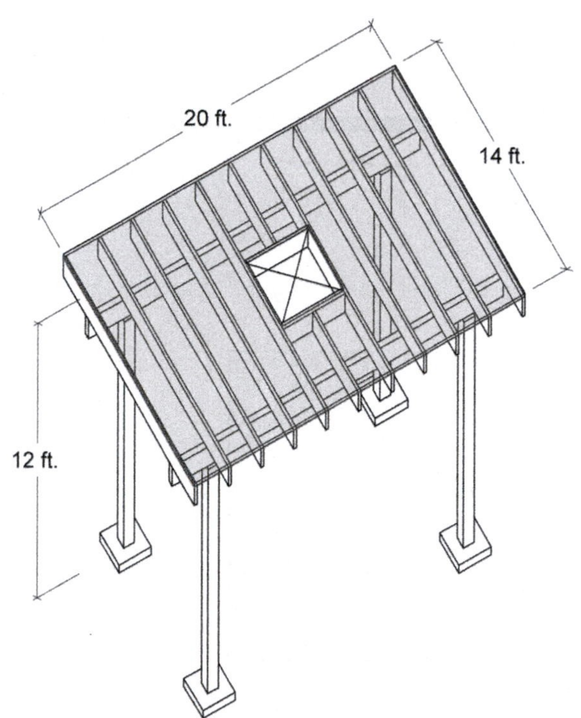

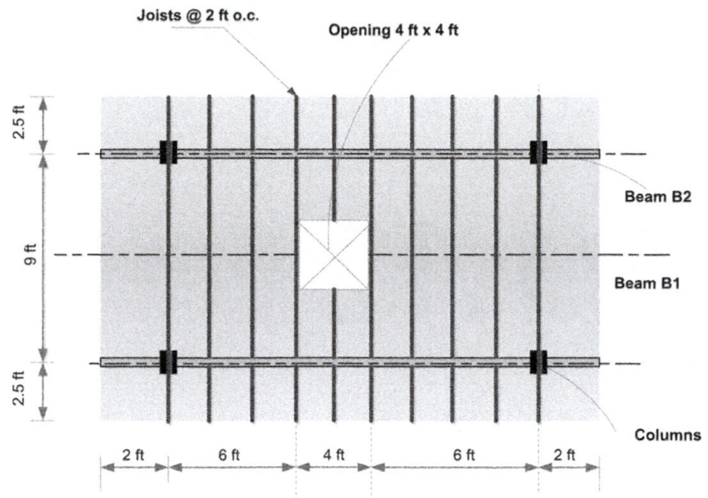
Joists @ 2 ft o.c.
Opening 4 ft x 4 ft
2.5 ft
9 ft
2.5 ft
Beam B2
Beam B1
Columns
2 ft
6 ft
4 ft
6 ft
2 ft

TYPICAL
INTERIOR
JOIST
J-1

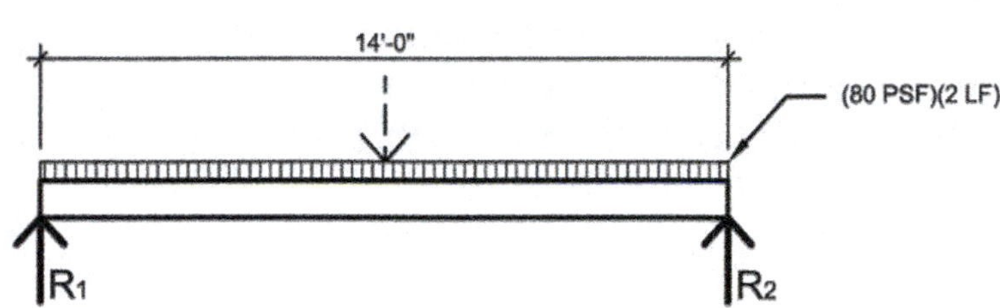
14'-0"
(80 PSF)(2 LF)
R1
R2

PROBLEM 11.12

For the lintel steel beam shown in Problem 11.6 (figure 11.6a), determine the maximum bending stress developed assuming the lintel beam to be a *W*10 x 19 (A36 steel). What size timber beam, 6" nominal width, could be used if F_b = 1,600 psi?

11.13 PROBLEM

A structural steel framing plan for a library is shown in figure 11.13 below. Determine the maximum bending moment and maximum deflection for beam *B*1. Using the rule of thumb charts, select a preliminary depth for the *W*-flange section and then check its adequacy against a bending and deflection limit of *L*/240. Use A992 steel and assume a dead load of 50 psf and a live load of 100 psf.

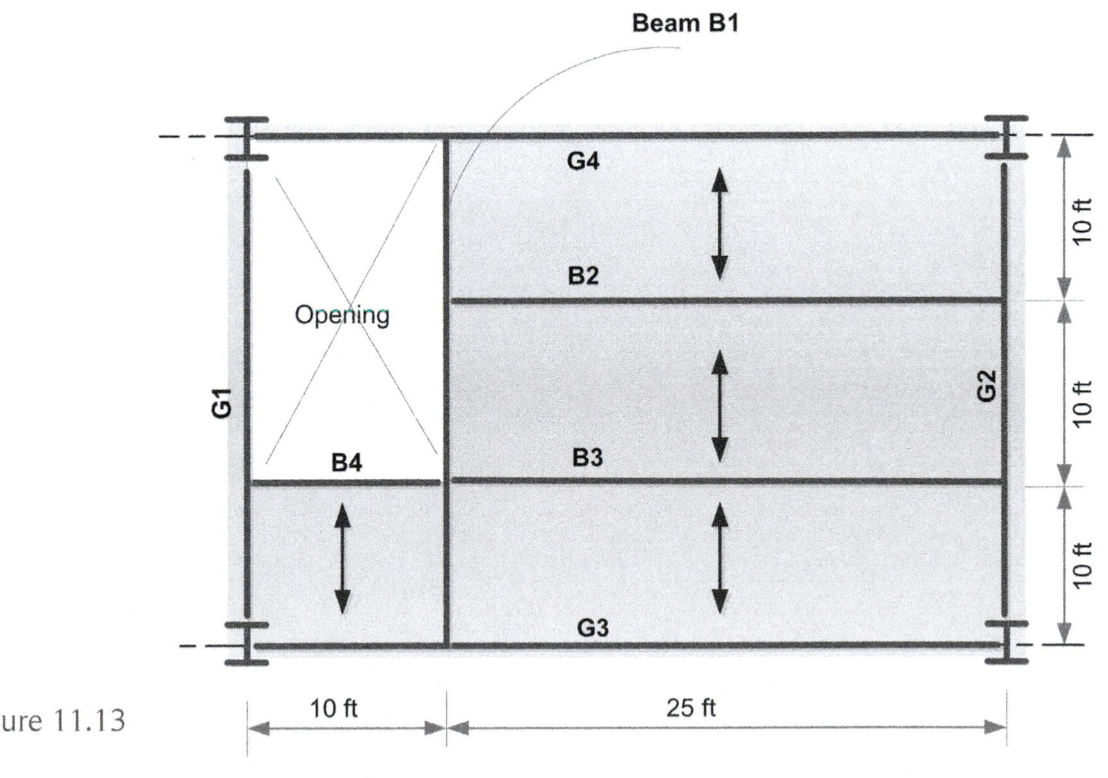

Figure 11.13

12.1 PROBLEM

i. Distinguish between short and long column behavior. Use diagrams to illustrate your answer.

ii. In the diagram shown in figure 12.1 below, specify the missing information.

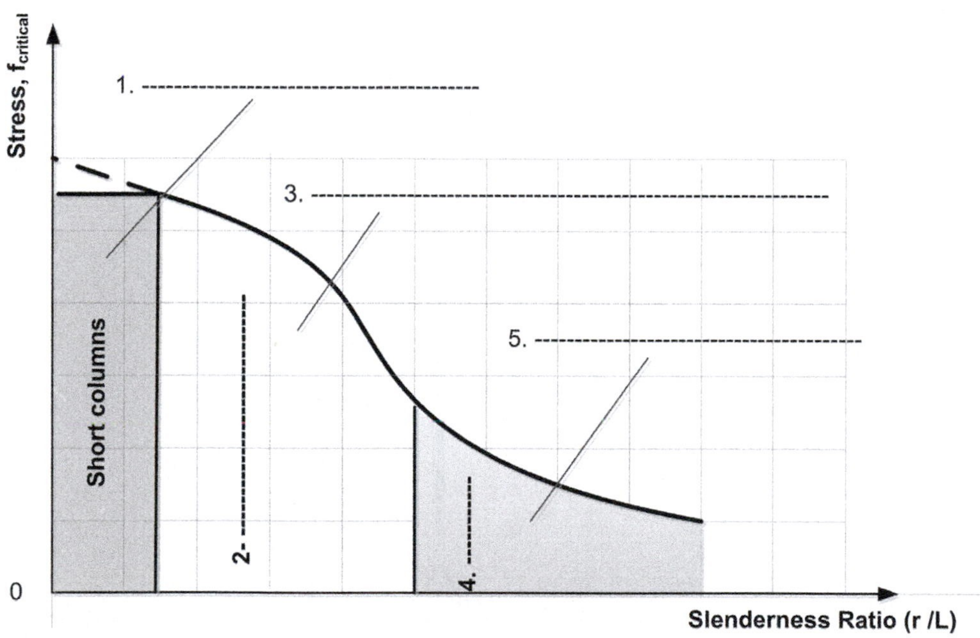

Figure 12.1

PROBLEM 12.2

A *W* 10 x 49 steel column 20 ft long is pin supported at both ends. Determine the critical buckling load and stress developed in the column. $E = 29 \times 10^3$ ksi.

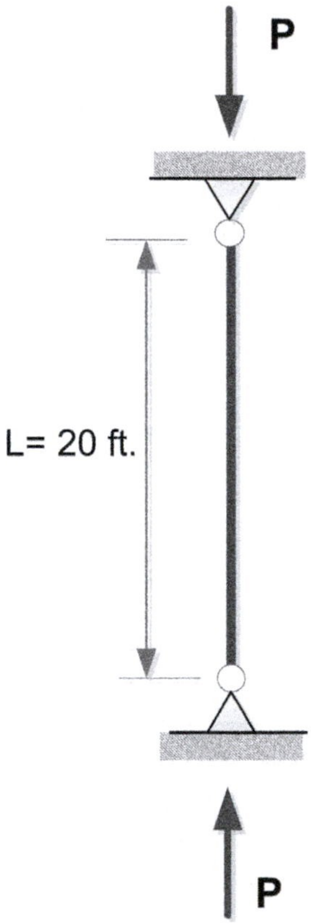

12.3 PROBLEM

Determine the maximum critical length of a *W* 8 x 31 column supporting an axial load of 250 kips. $E = 29 \times 10^3$ ksi.

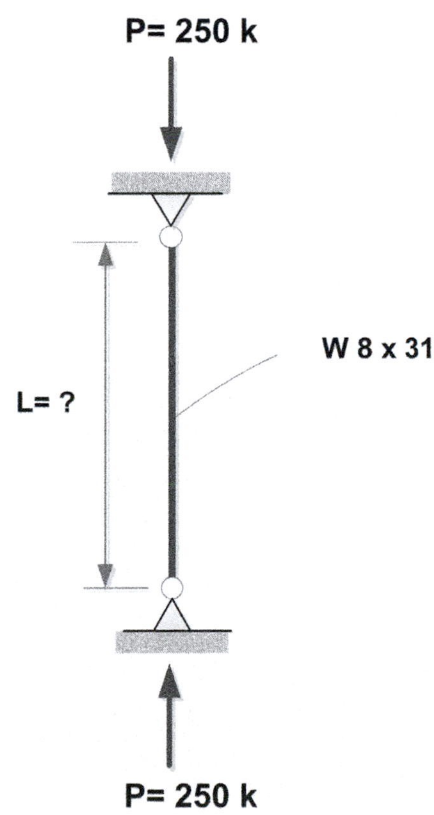

PROBLEM 12.4

A wood 4 x 6 section is used as a column 20 ft long. It has pinned ends and is braced against weak axis-buckling at mid-height (figure 12.4). Determine the critical buckling stress and load. Assume that E = 1,160 ksi.

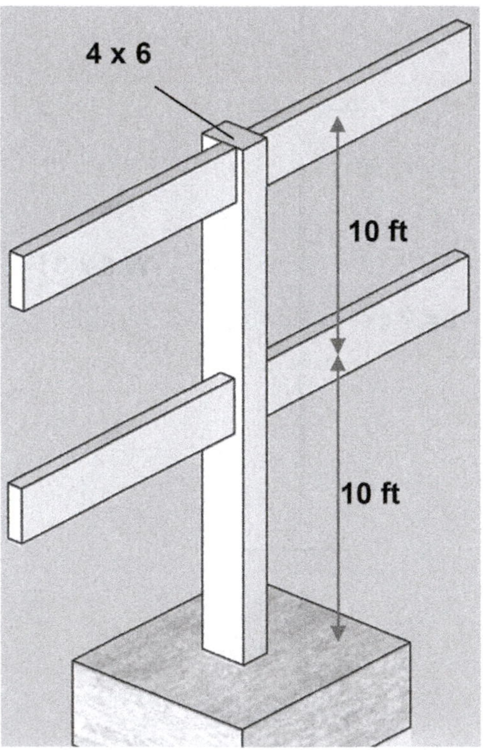

Figure 12.4

12.5 PROBLEM

Determine the critical buckling load and stress for *W* 8 x 24 column shown in figure 12.5.
Take modulus of elasticity as $E = 29 \times 10^6$ psi.

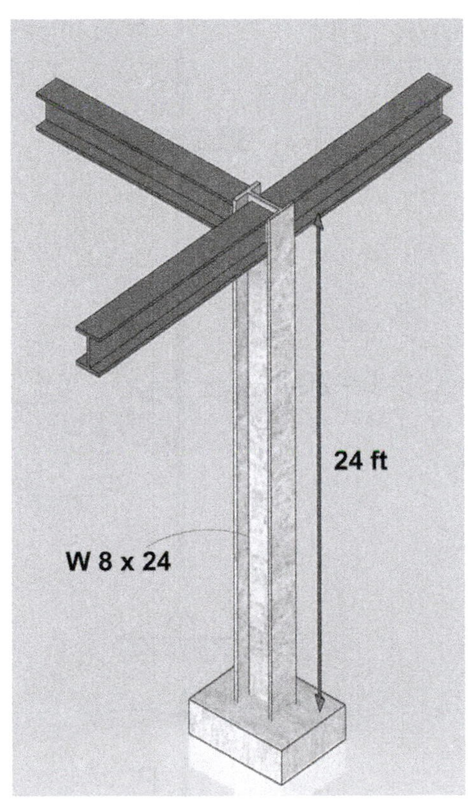

Figure 12.5

PROBLEM 12.6

Select the most economical *W*8 column (F_y = 50 ksi.) to support a load of 30 k and a length of L = 20 ft. Assume a factor of safety equal 2.0 against buckling.

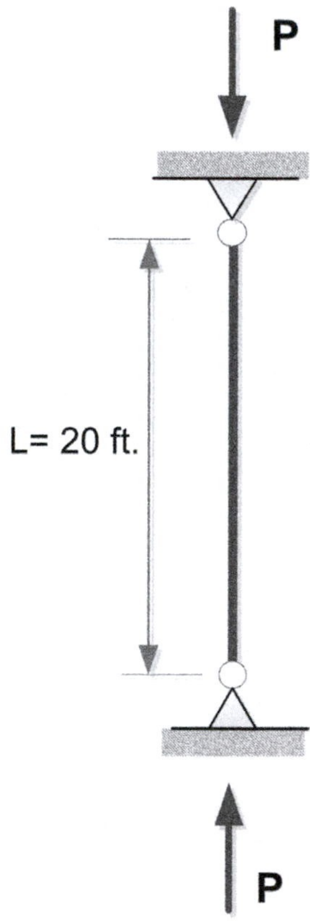

12.7 PROBLEM

Determine the critical buckling load capacity for an A992 steel column ($F_y = 50$ ksi), *W* 10 x49, shown in figure 12.7 below.

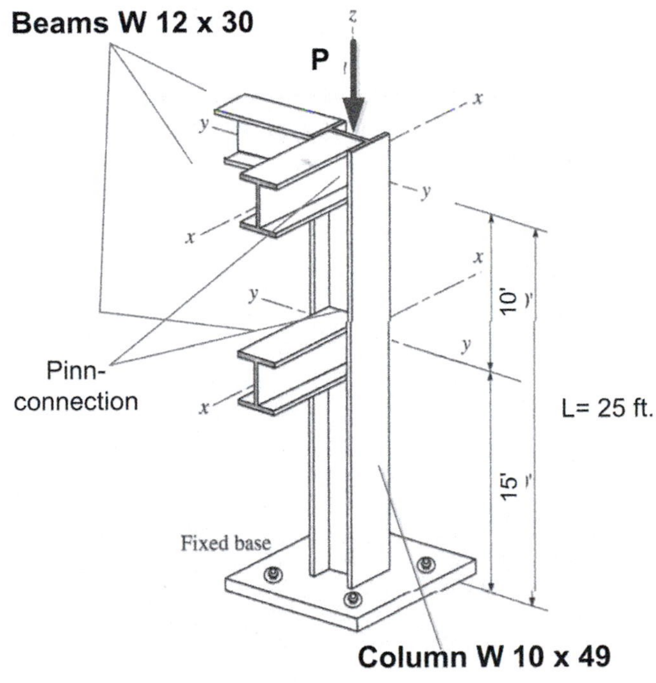

Figure 12.7

PROBLEM 12.8

The structural steel framing system for a two-story building is shown in figure 12.14 below. The governing building code specifies that the frame must be designed to withstand the dead weight of the structure, plus a roof snow load of 40 psf and a live load on each floor of 125 psf. The dead weight of the roof is estimated to be 50 psf, and each floor is 100 psf. Check the adequacy of column *AB* (*W* 8 x 31), assuming a factor of safety equal to 2.0. Consider fixed supports at the foundation levels and pinned otherwise.

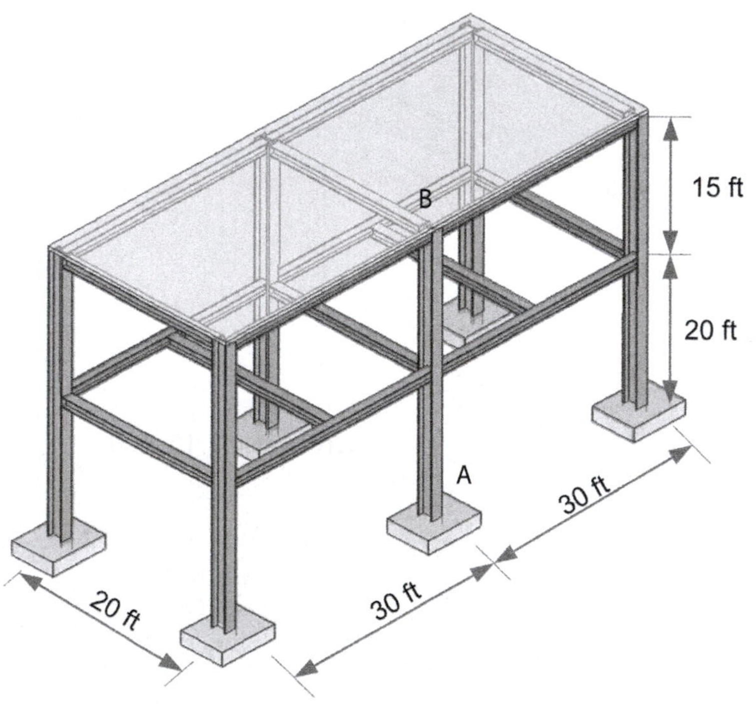

Section properties of column AB are:
$A = 9.13\ \text{in}^2$; $I_x = 110\ \text{in}^4$; $I_y = 37.1\ \text{in}^4$;
$E = 29{,}000$ ksi ; $r_y = 2.02$ in

PROBLEM 12.9

A four-story office building has a structural steel framing system that is depicted in elevation in figure 12.9. The columns are spaced 20 ft on centers in one direction and 25 ft on centers in the perpendicular direction. A typical interior column supports a tributary floor area of 500 sq. ft. The governing building code specifies that the frame must be designed to withstand the roof live load of 20 psf, dead weight of the structure, and a live load on each floor of 150 psf. The dead weight of the roof is estimated to be 80 psf, and each floor is 100 psf. The unsupported length of the ground-floor column is 20 ft, and the columns at the other floor levels are 15 ft. Design a typical interior third-floor column and the first-floor column using the *W*10 most efficient section at each level. Assume a safety factor of 2.0 for the critical buckling load. Use A992 steel.

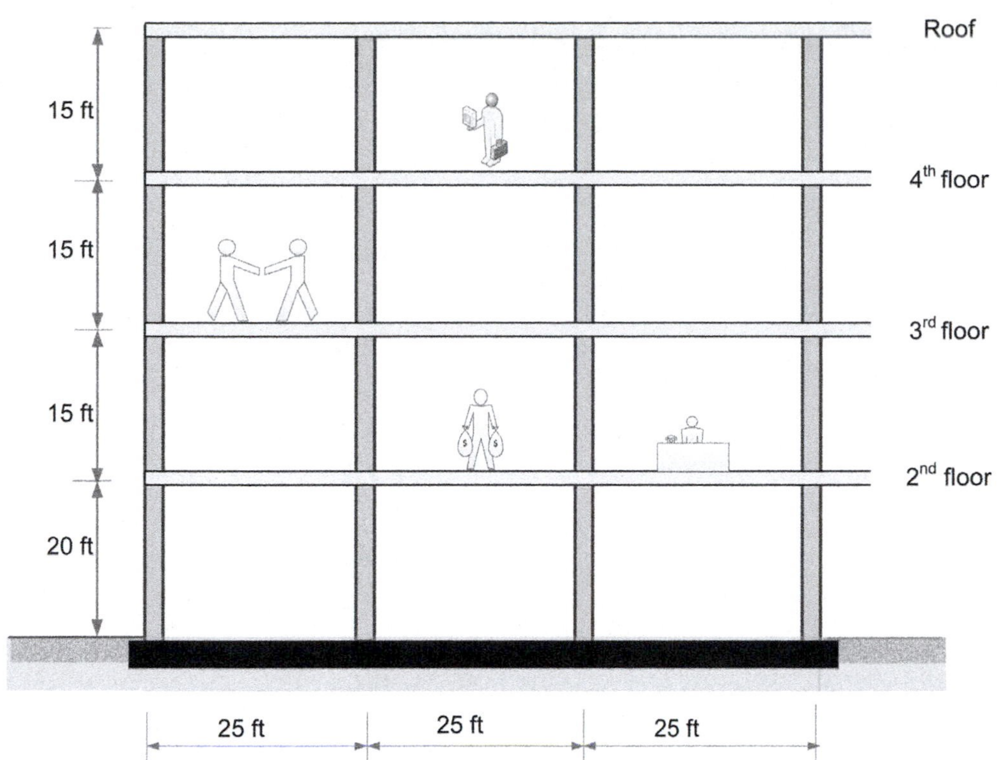
Roof
4th floor
3rd floor
2nd floor
15 ft
15 ft
15 ft
20 ft
25 ft
25 ft
25 ft

Figure 12.9

APPENDIX

PARTIAL SOLUTIONS TO PROBLEMS

CHAPTER 1

Problem 1.4

Refer to pages 19–29 in your textbook *Building Structures: Fundamentals of Crossover Design* by Nawari & Kuenstle.

Problem 1.5

Refer to pages 43–46 in your textbook *Building Structures: Fundamentals of Crossover Design* by Nawari & Kuenstle.

Problem 1.6

Refer to pages 49–54 in your textbook *Building Structures: Fundamentals of Crossover Design* by Nawari & Kuenstle.

CHAPTER 2

Problem 2.2

Refer to pages 69–70 in your textbook *Building Structures: Fundamentals of Crossover Design* by Nawari & Kuenstle.

Problem 2.3

Utilize the tip-to-tail method to find the resultant vector:

1. Draw Forces *A* and *B* to scale with their respective directions.

2. Attach the tail of Force *B* to the tip of Force *A*.

   **Note: Forces can be arranged in any tip-to-tail order to yield the resultant.*

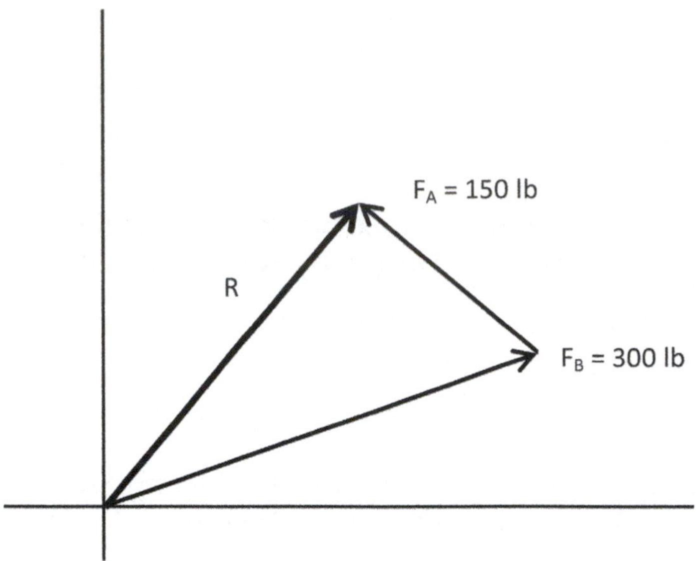

3. Draw the resultant vector from the tail of Force *A* to the tip of Force *B*.

4. Measure the length of the resultant vector and use the scale to determine the resultant fts magnitude.

5. Measure the angle of the resultant vector with respect to the x-axis to determine the resultant fts direction.

$R =$
$\theta =$ from x-axis
$\delta =$ from y-axis

Problem 2.4

Draw Forces 1, 2, and 3 to scale with their respective directions.

Arrange the forces in any tip-to-tail order.

Draw the resultant from the tail of the first vector to the tip of the last vector.

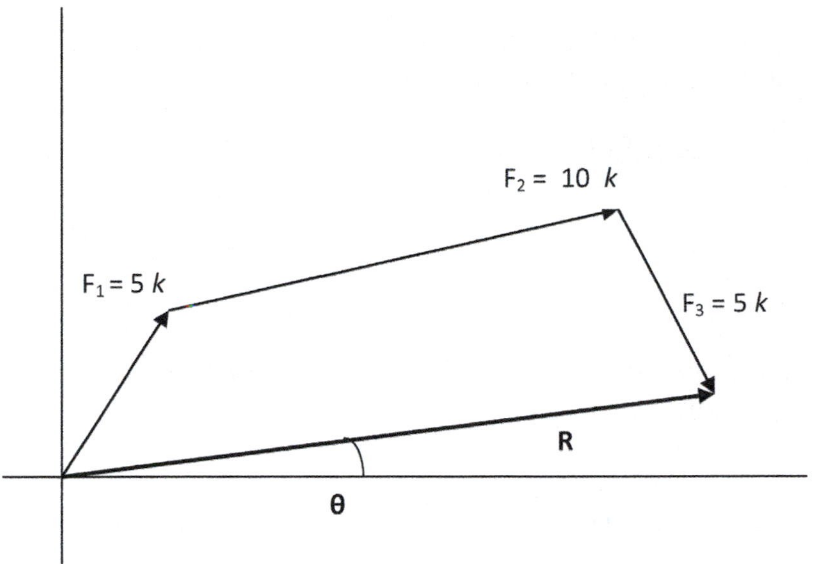

$R =$ k
$\theta =$ from x-axis

Problem 2.5

1. Redraw F_{Given} to scale and with its proper direction, using point O as the origin. According to the given scale, the length of this vector measures 2", directed 45° below the x-axis.

2. Attach the tail of force F to the tip of F_{Given}. Draw this vector until its tip meets the y-axis. The resultant force is the force of the pole, which lies on the y-axis.

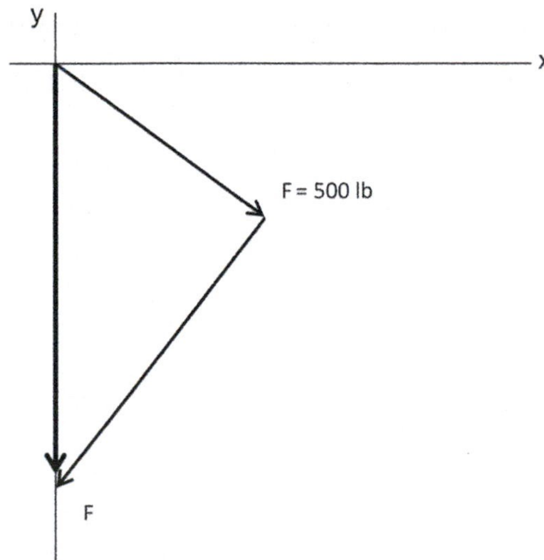

3. Using the given scale, measure the length of F to determine the force fts required magnitude.

$$F = 595.9 \text{ lb}$$

Problem 2.6

1. Resolve each of the forces into their respective x- and y-components.

$$F_x = F\,(\cos 30) \\ = (20 \text{ kips}) \cos 30° = 17.32 \text{ kips}$$

$$F_y = F\,(\sin 30) \\ =$$

2. $c = \sqrt{a^2 + b^2} = \sqrt{(1)^2 + (1)^2} = \sqrt{2}$; also we have $\frac{F}{c} = \frac{Fx}{a} = \frac{Fy}{b}$

$$\frac{30}{\sqrt{2}} = \frac{Fx}{1} = \frac{Fy}{1}$$

$F_x =$

3. Three members of a truss frame into a steel gusset plate as shown in figure 2.6c. All forces are concurrent at point C. Determine the resultant of the three forces that must be carried by the gusset plate.

F_1 = 15 k at 45° from the y-axis
F_2 = 12 k horizontally towards point C
F_3 = 20 k with at 45° from the x-axis

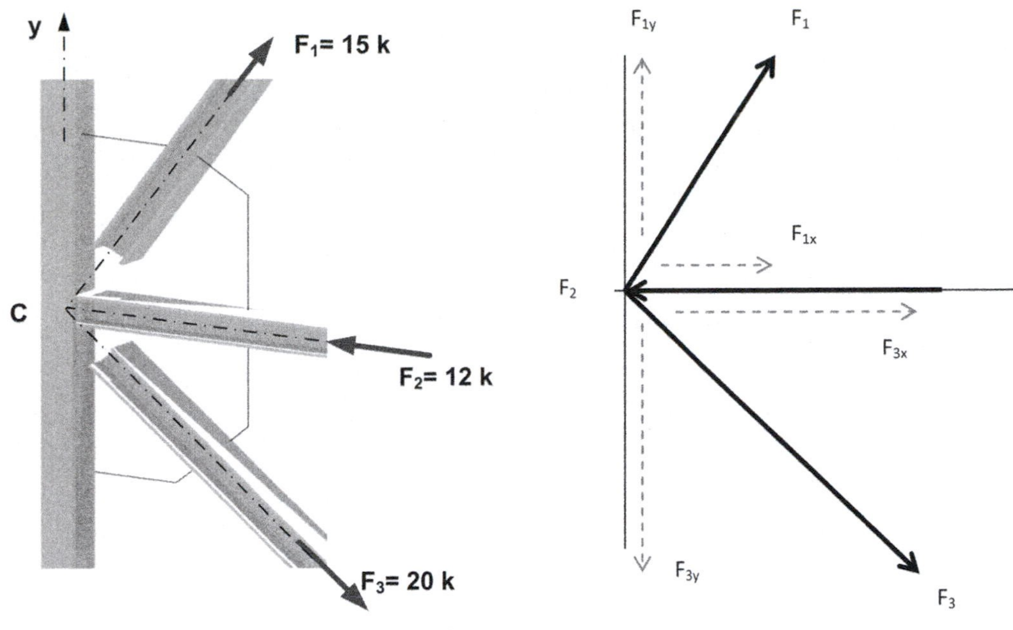

Figure 2.6c

Required:

$$F_{Resultant} = ?$$

Solution:

1. Resolve each of the forces into their respective x- and y-components.

x-components

For F_1, the complementary angle of the given angle (45°) is 45°.

Following the rule: $\cos\theta = \dfrac{Adjacent}{Hypotenuse}$

$$F_{1_x} = F_1\cos\theta = (15\text{ k})(\cos 45°) =$$
$$F_{2_x} = F_2\cos\theta = (-12\text{ k})(\cos 0°) = (-12\text{ k})(1) = -12\text{ k}$$
$$F_{3_x} = F_3\cos\theta = (20\text{ k})\left(\frac{1}{\sqrt{2}}\right) =$$

y-components

Following the rule: $\sin\theta = \dfrac{Opposite}{Hypotenuse}$

$$F_{1_y} =$$
$$F_{2_y} =$$
$$F_{3_y} =$$

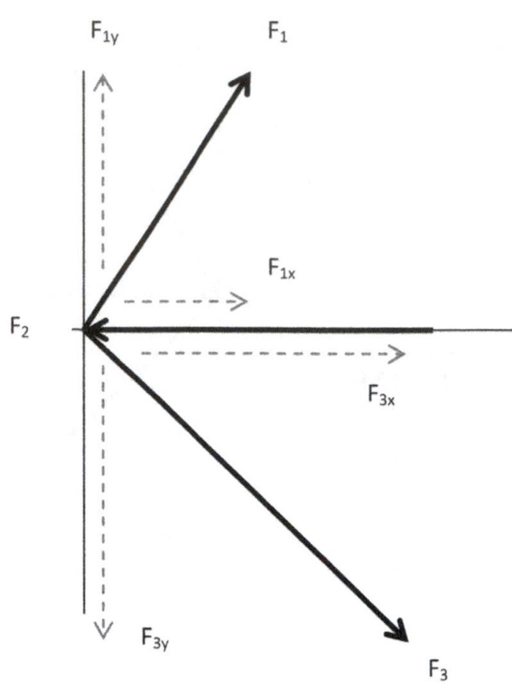

2. Add the x-components of the forces to obtain the x-component of the resultant:

$$R_x = \Sigma F_x =$$

3. Add the y-components of the forces to obtain the y-component of the resultant:

$$R_y = \Sigma F_y =$$

4. Now that the x- and y-components of the resultant force have been determined, use the Pythagorean Theorem to determine the magnitude of the resultant.

$$R_{Magnitude} = \sqrt{(R_x)^2 + (R_y)^2} =$$

$$R = \qquad \text{k}$$

Problem 2.7

1. Because the resultant must only be vertical, the summation of all horizontal forces, or the resultant horizontal force, R_x, must equal zero.

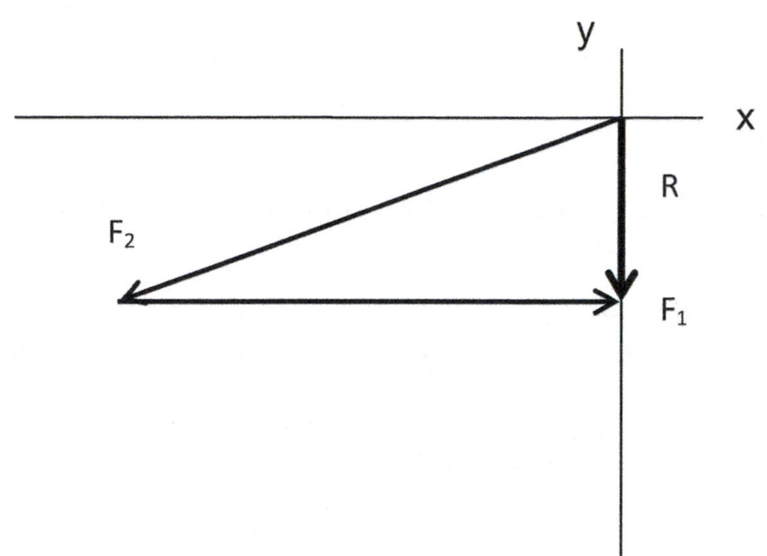

$$R_x = \Sigma F_x = 0$$
$$F_1 + (-F_{2x}) = 0$$

This equation yields:

$$F_1 = F_{2x}$$

So, $F_{2x} = F_2 \cos\theta$

$$F_1 = F_2 \cos\theta$$
$$F_1 = F_2 \cos 30°$$

2. From this equation, it can be seen that F_1 is only a fraction of F_2, that is, it is smaller than F_2.

   Because the maximum capacity of either member is 10 k, F_2 must equal 10 k:
   $$F_2 = 10 \text{ k}$$

   (If F_1 were 10 k, then F_2 would exceed the maximum capacity of 10 k).

3. Solve for $F_{1:}$

$$F_1 =$$
$$F_1 =$$
$$F_1 =$$
$$F_2 =$$

CHAPTER 3

Problem 3.1

1. Find the moment about point A created by the box fts weight using the formula:

   $M = \pm Fd$
   Moment = (± Force) (Distance to reference point)

   **Note: Positive (+) values are assigned to counterclockwise rotations, while negative (-) values are assigned to clockwise rotations with respect to the reference point.*

   $M_A =$

   **Note: Distance, d, is always an absolute value.*

2. Find the moment about point A created by the applied weight, $W = 80$ k:

   $M_A =$

3. By combining these moments, it can be determined whether the box remains static (the forces cancel each other out) or whether the concrete footing will tip over (force F overwhelms the weight of the footing).

   $\Sigma M_A =$ k–ft

   $M_A =$ k–ft

Problem 3.2

1. Using the formula $M = Fd$ for each force, find the resultant moment about A by finding the summation of all the forces:

   $M_O = F_1d_1 + F_2d_2 + F_3d_3 + F_4d_4 + \ldots$

   $M_O =$

   $M_O =$ k–ft

Problem 3.3

1. Resolve the given wind force into its x- and y-components:

$F_x = F\cos\theta$ $\qquad$ $F_y = F\sin\theta$

$=$ $\qquad$ $=$

$F_x =$ $\qquad$ $F_y =$

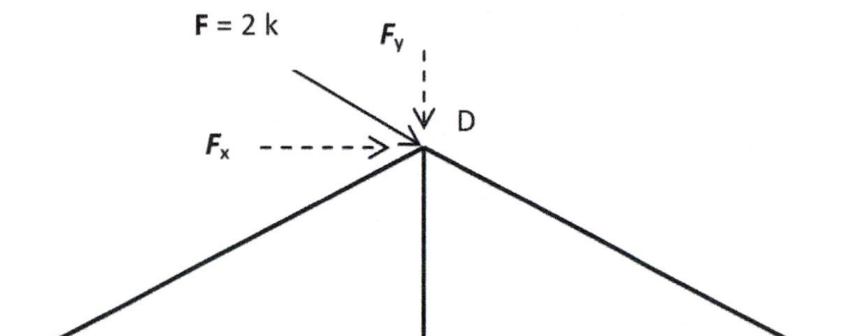

2. Find the moment created by these forces about point *B* using $M = Fd$:

$M_B = -F_x d + F_y d$

$M_B =$

$M_B =$ k–ft

3. Find the moment created by these forces about point *C*:

$M_C =$

$M_C =$ k–ft

Problem 3.4

1. Notice that the two 8 k forces are parallel and opposite to each other, creating a Couple System. The distance, *d*, between these 8 k forces can be determined using the Pythagorean Theorem:

$$\sqrt{6^2 + 6^2} = 8.485 \text{ ft}$$

2. Find the moment about point *A*:

   **Note: d is the perpendicular distance between the lines of action of F_1 and F_2. F is positive or negative depending on the direction of rotation created by these forces.*

   $M_A =$

   $M_A =$ k–ft

3. Find the moment about point *B*:

   $M_B =$

   $M_B =$ k–ft

Problem 3.5

1. By looking at the free-body diagram, it can be seen that the reaction forces, R_{Ax} and R_{Bx}, constitute a Couple System, attempting to rotate the ladder counterclockwise:

   $M_A =$

2. It can also be seen that R_{Ay} and the 200 lb man at *C* constitute a Couple System as well, attempting to rotate in a clockwise direction:

   $M_A =$

3. Find the resultant moment about A:

$$M_A =$$

4. Because the moment of a Couple System is independent of the reference point, it is a constant. Therefore:

$$M_A = \qquad \text{lb–ft}$$

Problem 3.6

1. Apply a force, $F_2 = 10$ k, downward at the column centerline while keeping the given force $F_1 = 10$ k.
2. Apply a force of $F_3 = 10$ k upward at the column centerline to counteract F_2.
3. Forces F_1 and F_3 now constitute a Couple System. These forces are now 2 ft away from each other:

$$M_{Couple} =$$

$$M_{Couple} = \qquad \text{k–ft}$$

Problem 3.7

1. To constitute a Couple System, two forces must be of equal magnitude and opposite sense with parallel lines of action.

   Resolve $F = 100$ lb into its x- and y-components:

$$F_x =$$
$$F_x =$$
$$F_y =$$
$$F_y =$$

2. Find the moment about A created by the resolved forces:

   **Note: The x-component rotates the plate counterclockwise while the y-component rotates the plate clockwise about A.*

   $M_A =$
   $M_A =$

   $M_A =$ lb–ft

3. Find the moment about B:

   $M_B =$
   $M_B =$

   $M_B =$ lb–ft

Problem 3.8

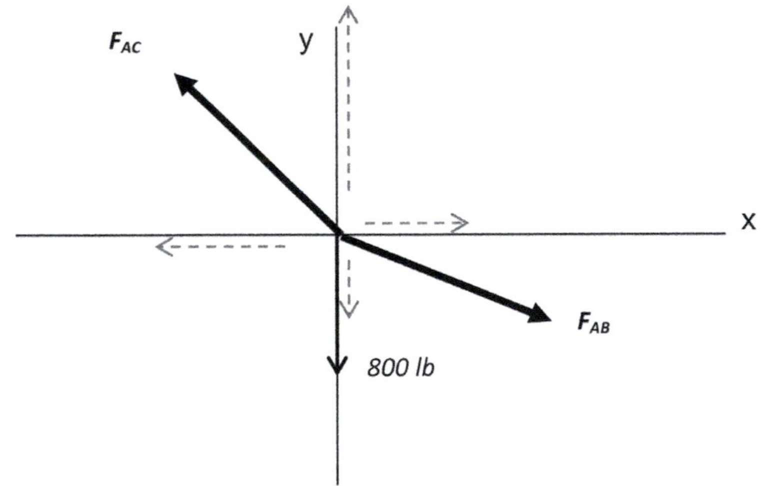

1. Because the system is in a state of equilibrium, all horizontal forces and all vertical forces must equal zero. Resolve the forces of each member into their x- and y-components:

   **Note: Because point A is the concurrent point, all forces acting on the system originate from point A. When drawing the free-body diagram, notice how column AC acts as* *a compressive force, in accordance with the Principle of Transmissibility.*

x-components:

AB: $AB_x = -\text{AB} \cos \theta$

$\text{Cos } \theta = \dfrac{12}{13}$

$AB_x =$

**Note: Given the slope, Force AB forms a 5-12-13 triangle.*

AC: $AC_x = \text{AC} \cos \theta$

$AC_x =$

$\text{AC}_x =$

y-components:

AB: $AB_y = -\text{AB} \sin \theta$

$\sin\theta =$

$AB_y =$

AC: $AC_y =$

$AC_y =$

BC: $BC_y =$

2. Add the x-components of the forces:

$R_x = [\Sigma F_x = 0] =$

3. Solve for AC:

$AC =$

4. Add the y-components of the forces:

$R_y = [\Sigma F_y = 0] =$

5. Substitute 1.066AB for AC:

6. Solve for AB:

$$AB = \quad \text{lb}$$

7. Plug AB back into previous equation to find AC:

$AC =$

$DB =$

$DB = 5{,}762.16$ lb

Problem 3.9

1. Treat points B and C as separate concurrent nodes.
2. Because the system is in a state of equilibrium, the sum of forces acting both horizontally and vertically must equal zero.
3. Resolve the forces concurrent at point B into their x- and y-components:

Force	F_x	F_y
$T_{BA} = 2,000$ lb	$(2{,}000 \text{ lb})\frac{12}{13} = 1{,}846.2$ lb	$(2{,}000 \text{ lb})\left(-\frac{5}{13}\right) =$ -769.2 lb
F_{BE}	0	$+F_{BE}$
T_{BC}		$T_{BC} \sin\theta = T_{BC}\left(-\frac{3}{5}\right)$

4. Solve for BC: add the horizontal forces and set the equation equal to zero (the state of equilibrium):

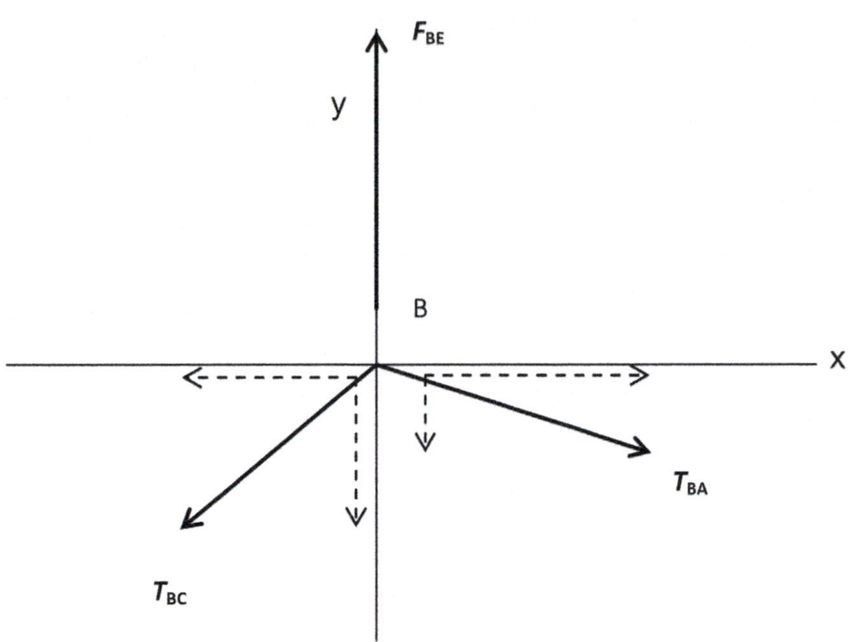

$$[\Sigma F_x = 0]\ 1{,}846.2\ \text{lb} + 0 - \frac{4}{5} T_{BC} = 0$$

$$T_{BC} = \qquad \text{lb}$$

5. Solve for F_{BE}: add the vertical forces and set the equation equal to zero:

$$[\Sigma F_y = 0]$$

$$F_{BE} = \qquad \text{lb}$$

6. Resolve the forces concurrent at point C into their x- and y-components:

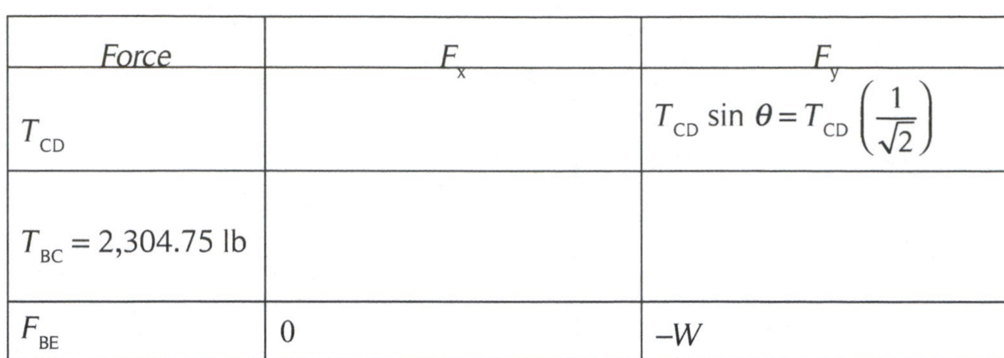

Force	F_x	F_y
T_{CD}		$T_{CD} \sin\theta = T_{CD}\left(\frac{1}{\sqrt{2}}\right)$
$T_{BC} = 2{,}304.75$ lb		
F_{BE}	0	$-W$

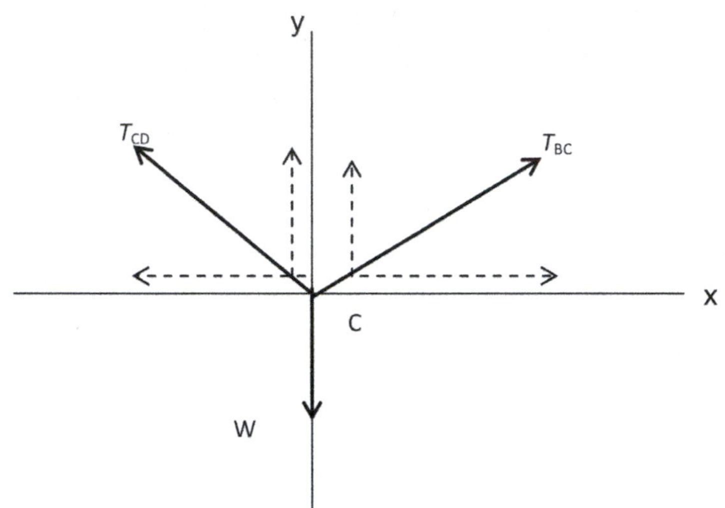

7. Solve for T_{CD}: add the horizontal forces and set the equation equal to zero (the state of equilibrium):

$$[\Sigma F_x = 0] \; -\frac{1}{\sqrt{2}} T_{CD} + 1{,}843.8 \text{ lb} + 0 = 0$$

$$T_{CD} =$$

8. Solve for W: add the vertical forces and set the equation equal to zero:

$$[\Sigma F_y = 0]$$

$W =$ lb

Problem 3.10

For the connections shown below determine the idealized (analytical) connection type for the analytical model.

Problem 3.11

1. Resolve AB and BC into their x- and y-components to determine the required reaction forces at R_A and R_C:

<u>*AB*:</u>

$$AB_x = AB\cos 60° = \left(\frac{1}{2}\right)AB$$

$$AB_y = AB\sin 60° = \left(\frac{\sqrt{3}}{2}\right)AB$$

<u>*BC*:</u>

$$BC_x = BC\cos 45° = \left(\frac{\sqrt{2}}{2}\right)BC$$

$$BC_y = BC\sin 45° = \left(\frac{\sqrt{2}}{2}\right)BC$$

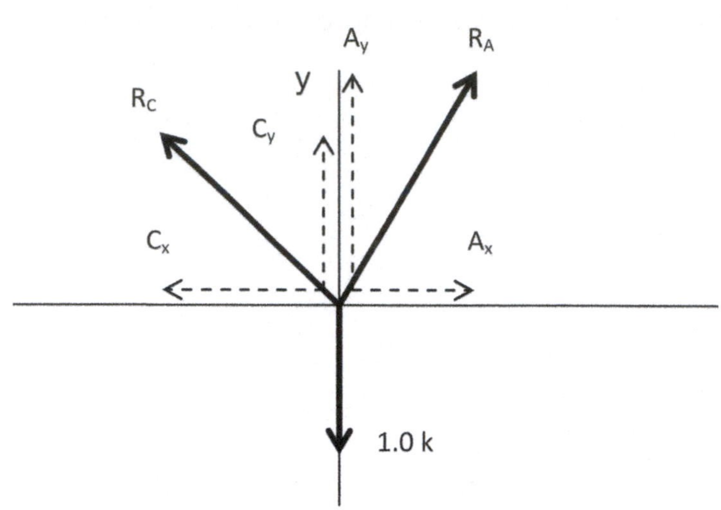

2. All horizontal and vertical forces must equal zero to be in a state of equilibrium. Add the x-components of the forces, with respect to their directions, and solve for *BC*:

$$[\Sigma F_x = 0]:$$

3. Add the y-components of the forces:

$$[\Sigma F_y = 0]:$$

4. Substitute *BC* from above:

5. Solve for *AB*:

$$AB\left(\frac{\sqrt{3}}{2}+\frac{1}{2}\right) = 1{,}000 \text{ lb}$$

$$AB(1.366) = 1{,}000 \text{ lb}$$

$$AB = 732 \text{ lb}$$

$$R_A = 732 \text{ lb}$$

6. Solve for *BC*:

$$R_C = 518 \text{ lb}$$

Problem 3.12

1. Calculate the resultant of the uniform load:

   $W = (10 \text{ ft})(500 \text{ lb/ft}) = 5{,}000 \text{ lb}$
   $\Sigma F_H = 0$ (no horizontal forces)

2. Calculate the moment about the left support point:

   $\Sigma M_{R1} = 0{:}\ -(5 \text{ ft})(6{,}000 \text{ lb}) - (15 \text{ ft})(5{,}000 \text{ lb}) + (20 \text{ ft})(R_2) = 0$
   $R_2 = 5{,}250 \text{ lb}$

3. Calculate the moment about the right support point:

   $\Sigma M_{R2} = 0{:}$

   $R_1 = \qquad \text{lb}$

4. Sum the vertical forces to verify equilibrium:

   $\Sigma F_V = 0{:}$
   $0 = 0$

Problem 3.13

1. Calculate the resultant of uniform load:

   $W = (20 \text{ ft})(250 \text{ lb/ft}) = 5{,}000 \text{ lb}$

2. $\Sigma F_H = 0$: (no horizontal forces)

3. Calculate the moment about the left support point:

$$\Sigma M_{R1} = 0: -(4\text{ ft})(10{,}000\text{ lb}) - (10\text{ ft})(5{,}000\text{ lb}) - (20\text{ ft})(5{,}000\text{ lb}) + (14\text{ ft})(R_2) = 0$$

$$R_2 = 13{,}571.43\text{ lb}$$

4. Calculate the moment about the right support point:

$$\Sigma M_{R2} = 0:$$

$$R_1 = \qquad \text{lb}$$

5. Sum the vertical forces to verify equilibrium:

$$\Sigma F_V = 0:$$

Problem 3.14

1. Calculate the resultant of uniform load:

$$W = (10\text{ ft})(400\text{ lb/ft}) = 4{,}000\text{ lb}$$

$$\Sigma F_H = 0: \text{(no horizontal forces)}$$

2. Calculate the moment about the left support point:

$$\Sigma M_{R1} = 0: -(1\text{ ft})(4{,}000\text{ lb}) - (10\text{ ft})(15{,}000\text{ lb}) + (14\text{ ft})(R_2) = 0$$

$$R_2 = 11{,}000\text{ lb}$$

3. Calculate the moment about the right support point:

$$\Sigma M_{R2} = 0:$$

$$R_1 = \qquad \text{lb}$$

4. Sum the vertical forces to verify equilibrium:

$$\Sigma F_V = 0:$$

Problem 3.16

Required:

$R1_x = ?$; $R1_y = ?$; $R2_y = ?$

Solution:

1. Calculate the moment about the left support point (*A*):

$$\Sigma M_{R1} = 0\text{: } (10\text{ ft})(5\text{ k}) + (20\text{ ft})(R2_y) = 0$$
$$R2_y = -\,2.5\text{ k}$$

2. Calculate the moment about the right support point (*B*):

$$\Sigma M_{R2} = 0\text{:}$$
$$R1_y = \qquad \text{k}$$

3. Sum the vertical forces to verify equilibrium:

$$\Sigma F_y = 0\text{:}$$

4. Calculate $R1_x$:

$$\Sigma F_x = 0\text{:}$$

$R1_x$ must be   k to achieve equilibrium.

Problem 3.17

1. Calculate the resultant of uniform load:

$$W = (20\text{ ft})(0.5\text{ k/ft}) = 10\text{ kips}$$

2. Calculate the moment about the left support point (*A*):

$$\Sigma M_{R1} = 0$$
$$R2_y =$$

3. Calculate $R1_x$:

$$\Sigma F_x = 0:$$
$$R1_x =$$

4. Now complete the calculation of moment about the right support point (B):

$$\Sigma M_{R2} = 0$$
$$R1_y =$$

5. Sum the vertical forces to verify equilibrium:

$$\Sigma F_y = 0$$

Problem 3.18

1. Calculate total resultant wind load:

$$W = (10 \text{ ft})(0.5 \text{ k/ft}) = 5 \text{ k}$$

2. Calculate the moment about the right support point (B):

$$\Sigma M_{R2} =$$
$$R_{1y} = \qquad \text{k}$$

3. Calculate R_{2H}:

$$\Sigma F_x = 0:$$
$$R_{2x} =$$

4. Calculate the moment about the left support point (A):

$$\Sigma M_{R1} = 0$$

$$R2_y = \qquad \text{k}$$

5. Sum the vertical forces to verify equilibrium:

$$\Sigma F_y = 0$$

Problem 3.19

1. Treat Joints *C* and *D* as two separate concurrent points.

   Draw the free-body diagram at Joint *D*:

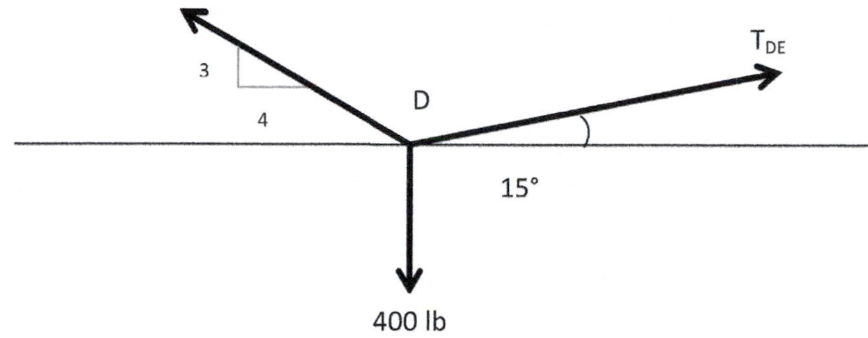

2. Resolve Forces T_{CD} and T_{DE} into their x- and y-components:

   x-component:

$$T_{CDx} = -T_{CD}\cos\theta = -\frac{4}{5}T_{CD}$$

$$T_{DEx} = T_{DE}\cos 15°$$

   y-component:

$$T_{CDy} =$$

$$T_{DEy} =$$

3. Add the x-components and set the equation equal to zero:

$$[\Sigma F_x = 0]: -\frac{4}{5}T_{CD} + T_{DE}\cos 15° = 0$$

4. Add the y-components and set the equation equal to zero:

$$[\Sigma F_y = 0]: \frac{3}{5}T_{CD} + T_{DE}\sin 15° - 400lb = 0$$

5. Substitute T_{DE} and solve for T_{CD}:

$T_{CD} =$ lb (Tension)

6. Solve for T_{DE}:

$T_{DE} =$ lb (Tension)

7. Draw the free-body diagram at Joint C:

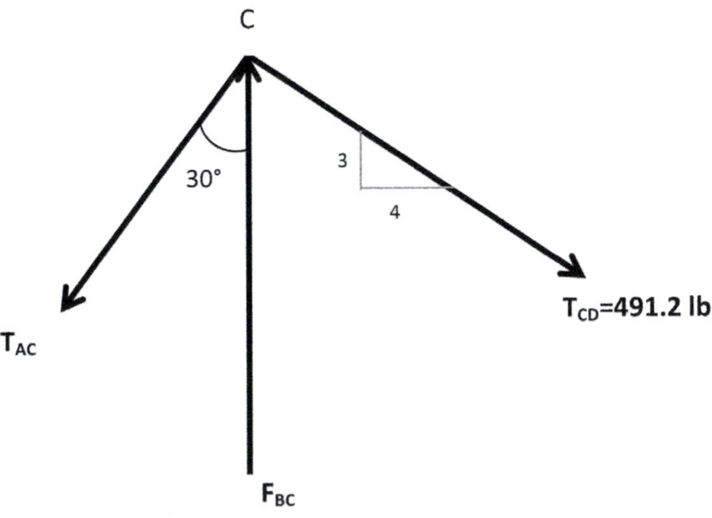

8. Resolve Forces T_{AC} and F_{BC} into their x- and y-components:

Note: Here, the reference angle of T_{AC} is given with respect to the y-axis x-component:

$$T_{ACx} =$$

$$F_{BCx} =$$

y-component:

$$T_{ACy} =$$

$$F_{BCy} =$$

9. Add the x-components and set the equation equal to zero:

$$\left[\Sigma F_x = 0\right]:$$

$$F_{AC} = \qquad \text{lb (Tension)}$$

10. Add the y-components and set the equation equal to zero:

$$\left[\Sigma F_y = 0\right]:$$

11. Substitute T_{AC} and solve for F_{BC}:

$$-(786\#)\cos 30° + F_{BC_y} = 147.4\#$$

$$F_{BC} = \qquad \text{lb (Compression)}$$

Problem 3.20

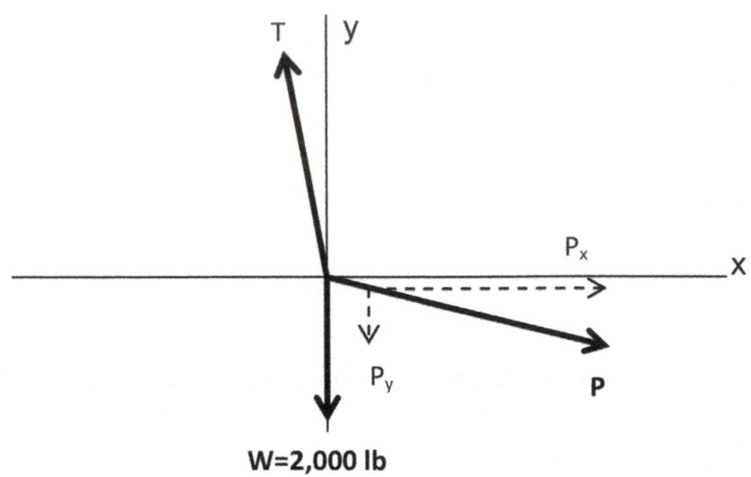

1. *AB* is a member in tension, *T*. *A* is the concurrent point.

Resolve forces *T* and *P* into their x- and y-components:

<u>*T*:</u>

$$T_x = -T\cos 80°$$
$$T_y = T\sin 80°$$

<u>*P*:</u>

$$P_x = P\cos 30°$$
$$P_y = -P\sin 30°$$

2. Horizontal and vertical forces must equal zero. Solve for *T*:

$[\Sigma F_x = 0]$: $-T\cos 80° + P\cos 30° = 0$

$T =$

3. Add the y-components and set them equal to zero:

$[\Sigma F_y = 0]$:

4. Substitute T and solve for P:

$P =$ lb

5. Substitute P and solve for T:

$T = 10.8P$
$T =$

$T =$ lb

Problem 3.21

1. Draw FBD of Girder AB

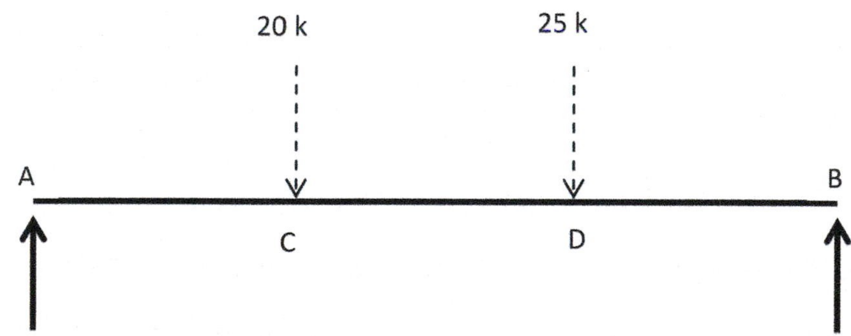

2. To constitute equilibrium, the moment about points A and B must equal zero. Find the reaction at B by taking the moment about A:

$[\Sigma M_A = 0]$:

$B_y =$ k

3. Only one unknown remains, A_y, which can be found by adding the vertical forces and setting the equation equal to zero:

$$[\Sigma F_y = 0]: \; A_y - 20k - 25k + B_y = 0$$

$$A_y = \quad\quad k$$

Note: There are no horizontal reactions necessary for this load case.

Problem 3.22

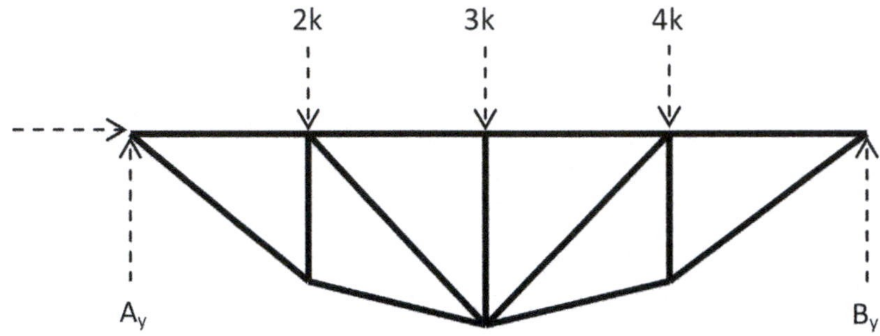

1. Because B is on a roller, there is no horizontal reaction at B_x; thus, no force exists to balance A_x. Therefore, A_x must be equal to zero:

$$[\Sigma F_x = 0]: \; A_x = 0$$

2. Find the reaction at B by taking the moment about A:

$$[\Sigma M_A = 0]: \; -2.5k(20') - 5k(40') - 7k(60') + B_y(80') = 0$$

$$-7k(60') + B_y(80') = 0$$

$$B_y = 8.375\text{k}$$

3. Find the reaction at A by 1) taking the moment about B or 2) adding the vertical forces and setting the equation equal to zero:

1) $[\Sigma M_B = 0]$:

$A_y =$

2) $[\Sigma F_y = 0]$:

$A_y =$

Problem 3.23

1. Draw FBD of the overhanging beam.

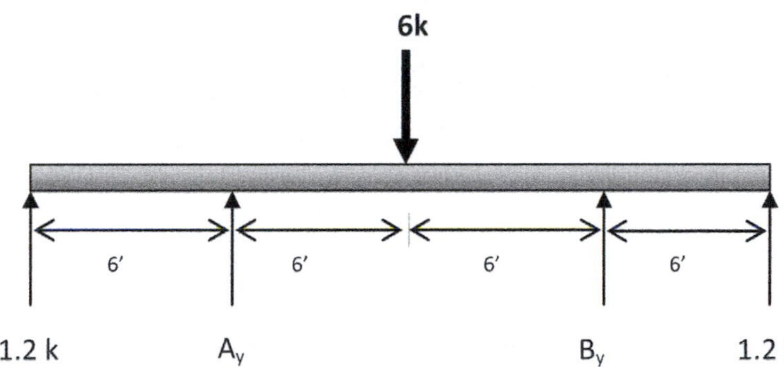

2. Take the moment about *A* to obtain *B*:
The given weight must be applied to each foot down the length of the 24 ft roof. Therefore:

$$(250\ \text{lb/ft})(24\ \text{ft}) = 6{,}000\ \text{lb}$$

This weight is then concentrated at the center of the roof.
Find the moment about A:

$[\Sigma M_A = 0]$:

$B =$

3. Solve the vertical equilibrium equation to find A:

$$[\Sigma F_y = 0]:$$

$$A =$$

Problem 3.24

1. Draw the FBD of the structure

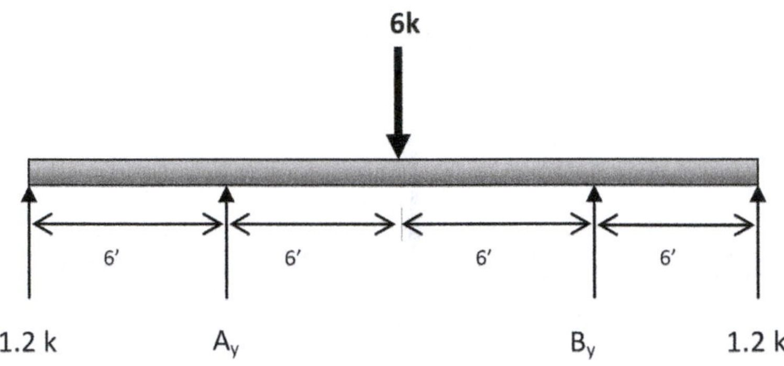

2. Because point B rests on a roller, no force exists to balance the horizontal force at A. Therefore:

$$[\Sigma F_x = 0]:$$

$$A_x = 0$$

3. Take the moment about A to find the reaction at B:

$$[\Sigma M_A = 0]:\ B(10ft) - (150lb/ft)(10ft)(9ft) = 0$$

$$B =$$

4. Solve the vertical equilibrium equation to obtain A:

**Note: The weight concentrating on the right side of the member creates a negative reaction force at A. In other words, it must pull down to maintain equilibrium.*

$[\Sigma F_y = 0]$:

$A =$

Problem 3.25

1. Because a hinge exists at B, treat AB and BC as separate members:

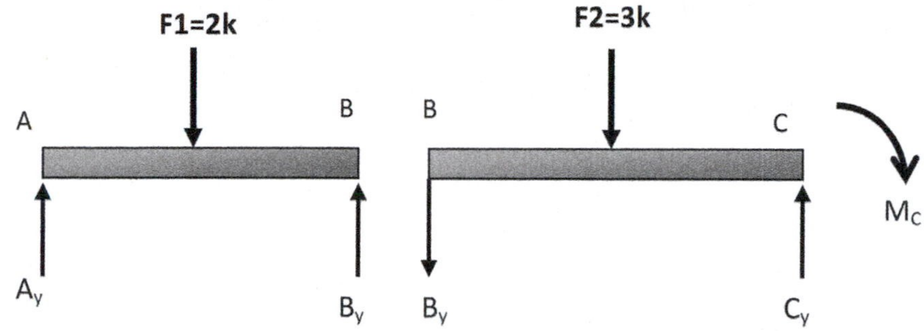

2. Because there is no horizontal reaction at A, there exists no force to balance B_x. Therefore:

   $[\Sigma F_x = 0]$:

   $B_x = 0$ k

3. Because $B_x = 0$, C_x must also equal zero:

   $C_x = 0$ k

4. Find A_y by taking the moment about B:

   $[\Sigma M_B = 0]$:

   $A_y =$ k

5. Find B_y by solving the equilibrium equation for AB:

   $[\Sigma F_y = 0]$: $A_y - 2k + B_y = 0$

   $B_y =$ k

6. Find C_y by solving the equilibrium equation of BC:

   $[\Sigma F_y = 0]$:

   $C_y =$

7. Find the resisting moment about C:

   Note: The resisting moment, M_{RC}, is opposite the moment occurring at C, M_C.

   $[\Sigma M_R = 0]$: $-M_{RC} + 3k(3ft) + 0.89k(6ft) = 0$

   $M_{RC} =$ k–ft (clockwise)

Problem 3.26

1. Resolve force $F_4 = 10$ k into its x- and y-components:

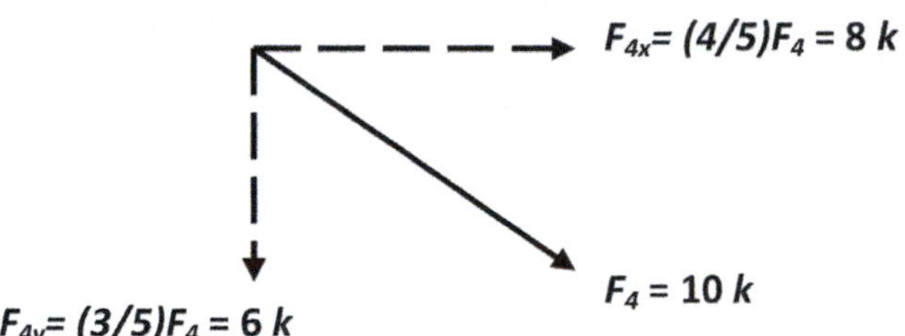

2. Force $F_4 = 10k$ has a horizontal component when resolved into its x- and y-components. Thus, there exists a reaction force, A_x. Add the horizontal forces and set the equation equal to zero:

   $[\Sigma F_x = 0]$: $-A_x + 8k = 0$

3. Find B_y by taking the moment about A:

   $[\Sigma M_A = 0]$:

   $B_y =$

4. Find A_y by resolving forces in the y-direction:

   $[\Sigma F_y = 0]$:

   $$A_y = 12\text{k}$$

Problem 3.27

1. Analyze member AB.
   Find B_y by taking the moment about point A:

   **Note: Member AB is on a ¾ slope, creating a 3-4-5 triangle. Because member AB is 10 ft in length, this creates a similar triangle with sides 6-8-10.*

   $$[\Sigma M_A = 0]: -400\ lb(5') + B_y(8') = 0$$

   $$B_y = 250 \text{ lb}$$

2. Resolve $F_2 = 200$ lb into its x- and y-components:

   $$F_{2_x} = 200\ lb(\cos\theta) = 200\ lb\left(\frac{3}{5}\right)$$

   $$F_{2_x} = -120\ lb$$

   $$F_{2_y} = 200\ lb(\sin\theta) = 200\ lb\left(\frac{4}{5}\right)$$

   $$F_{2_y} = -160\ lb$$

3. Because F_{2_x} exists, A_x must have a balancing force.

   Find A_x by solving the horizontal equilibrium equation:

   $[\Sigma F_x = 0]$:

   $$A_x =$$

4. Find A_y by solving the vertical equilibrium equation:

   $[\Sigma F_y = 0]$: $A_y - F_{2_y} + B_y = 0$

   $A_y =$

5. Resolve F_3 into its x- and y-components:

   $F_{3_x} = 100\ lb(\cos\theta) = 100\ lb\left(\frac{3}{5}\right)$

   $F_{3_x} = 60\ lb$

   $F_{3_y} = 100\ lb(\cos\theta) = 100\ lb\left(\frac{4}{5}\right)$

   $F_{3_y} = 80\ lb$

6. Now analyze the horizontal member.

   Find C_y by taking the moment about point D:

   $[\Sigma M_D = 0]$:

   $C_y =$

7. Find D_x by solving the horizontal equilibrium equation:

   **Note: Because point C is on a roller, it has no horizontal force. The same applies to point B, as it has no force acting horizontally.*

   $[\Sigma F_x = 0]$: $D_x - 60\ lb = 0$

   $D_x = 60\ lb$

8. Find D_y by solving the vertical equilibrium equation:

   $[\Sigma F_y = 0]$:

   $D_y =$

Problem 3.28

1. Analyze the dead load and its effect on each cubic foot of the system. The system can be divided into three: upper landing, stairway, and lower landing. Analyze each segment separately.

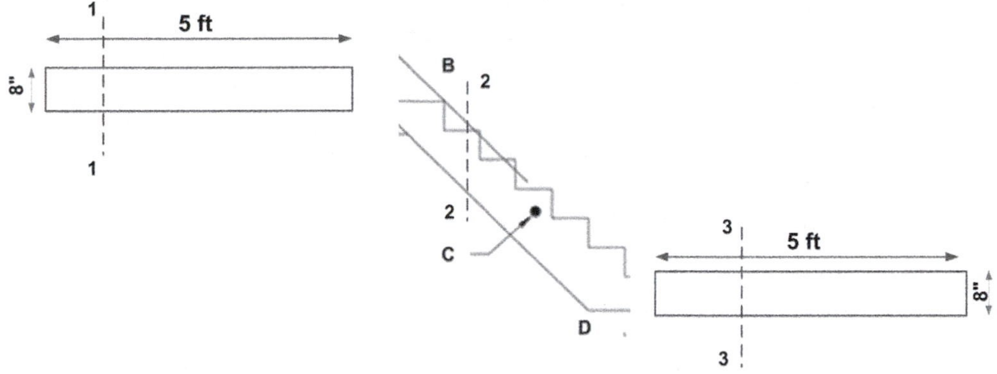

2. Draw a section [Section 1–1] of a 1-ft-wide strip of the first landing. Upon examining this, we can find the dead load (DL) amount for this strip:

$$DL_1 = (150pcf)(Thickness)(Depth)$$

$$DL_1 = (150pcf)\left(\frac{8"}{12"}\right)\left(\frac{12"}{12"}\right)$$

$$DL_1 = 100plf$$

3. Draw a section [Section 2–2] of a 1-ft-wide strip of the staircase and analyze the dead load:

$$DL_2 = (150pcf)\left(\frac{12"}{12"}\right)\left(\frac{12"}{12"}\right)$$

$$DL_2 = 150plf$$

4. Draw a section [Section 3–3] of a 1-ft-wide strip of the second landing and analyze the dead load:

$$DL_3 = (150pcf)\left(\frac{8"}{12"}\right)\left(\frac{12"}{12"}\right)$$

$$DL_3 = 100plf$$

5. Now analyze the live load placed on the system via the same method:

   **Note: Unlike dead loads, live loads do not deal with thickness.*

$$LL_1 = (100psf)(Depth)$$

$$LL_1 = (100psf)(1ft)$$

$$LL_1 = 100plf$$

$$LL_2 = (100psf)(1ft)$$

$$LL_2 = 100plf$$

$$LL_3 = (100psf)(1ft)$$

$$LL_2 = 100plf$$

6. Add the dead load and live load of each segment and multiply the sum by the length of the segment to obtain the total weight being distributed across that segment:

$$DL_1 + LL_1 =$$

$$DL_1 + LL_1 =$$

   **Note: DL_2 and LL_2 are distributed along the length of the staircase. Its length can be found by using the Pythagorean Theorem:*

$$\sqrt{(4')^2 + (5')^2} = 6.4'$$

$$DL_2 + LL_2 = 150plf + 100plf = 250plf$$

$$250lb(6.403') = 1{,}600lb$$

$$DL_2 + LL_2 = 1{,}600lb$$

$$DL_3 + LL_3 =$$

$$DL_3 + LL_3 =$$

7. Now we can find the reaction at E by finding the moment at A created by the loads:

   $[\Sigma M_A = 0]$:

   $$E = 1,800 lb$$

8. Find the reaction at A by solving the vertical equilibrium equation:

   $[\Sigma F_y = 0]$:

   $$A =$$

CHAPTER 4

Problem 4.1

Refer to page 128 in your textbook *Building Structures: Fundamentals of Crossover Design* by Nawari & Kuenstle.

Problem 4.2

1. Distributed load, w = area load x tributary width = 55 psf x 5 ft = 275 lb/ft

2. Draw FBD of beam $B1$, $B2$, and $B3$ showing loads and reactions.

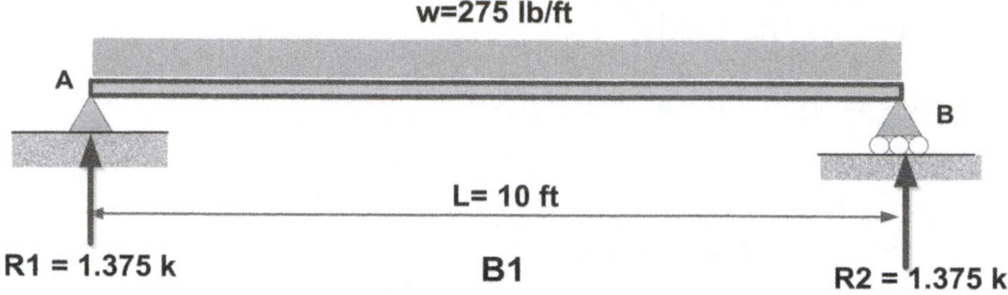

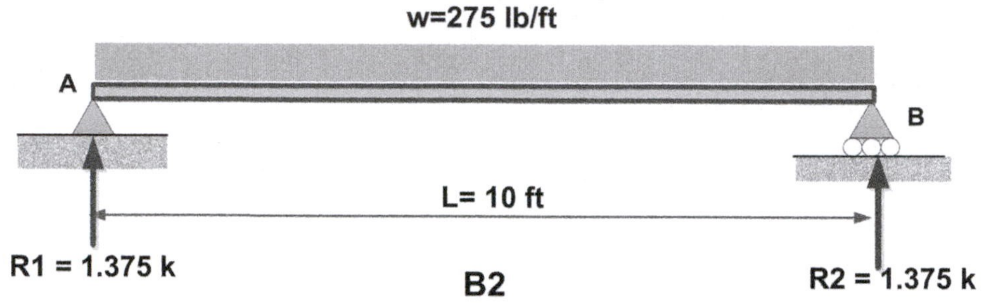

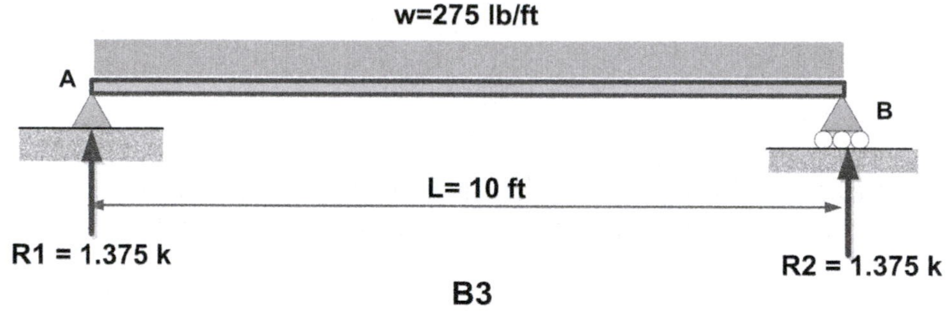

3. Draw FBD of girder $G1$:

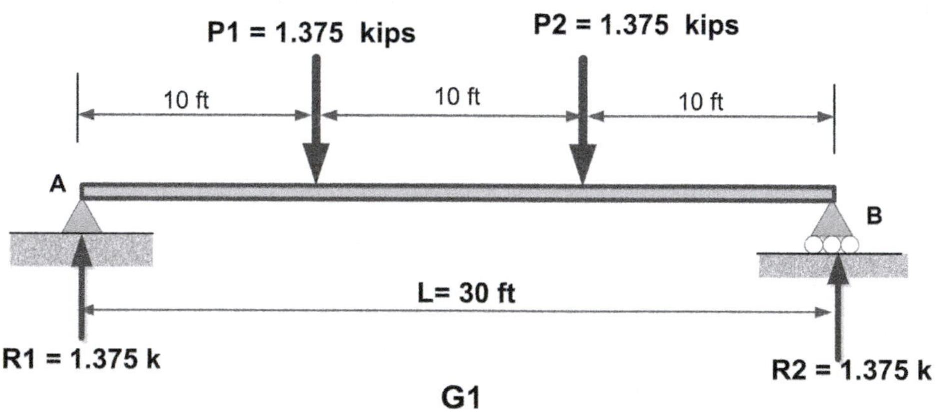

4. Draw FBD of girder *G*2

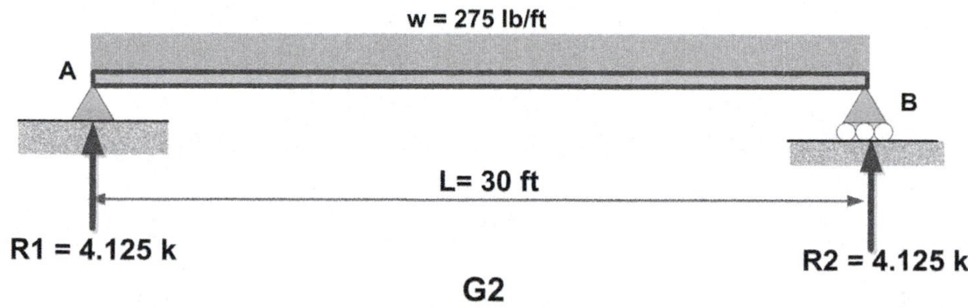

5. Draw FBD of *G*3

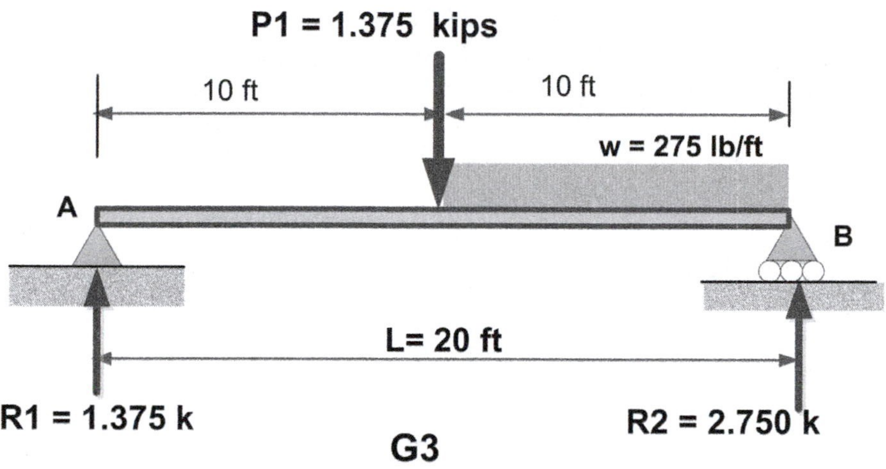

6. Total loads to the foundation:

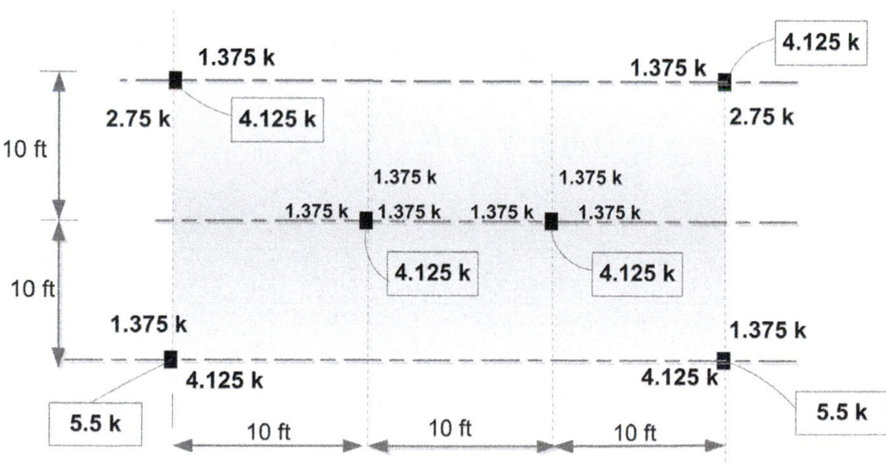

Problem 4.4

<u>Joists</u>

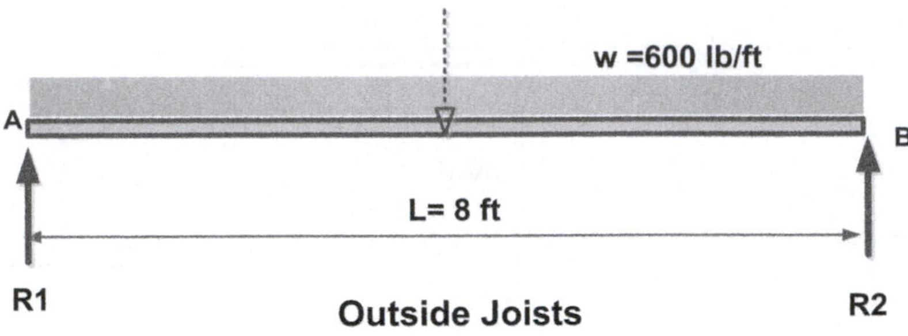

Figure 4.4b

1. Calculate total load (see figure 4.4b):

   $W = (30 \text{ psf})(2.5 \text{ ft})(8 \text{ ft}) = 600 \text{ lb}$
   Load diagram is symmetrical, therefore
   $R_1 = R_2 = W / 2 = 300 \text{ lb}$

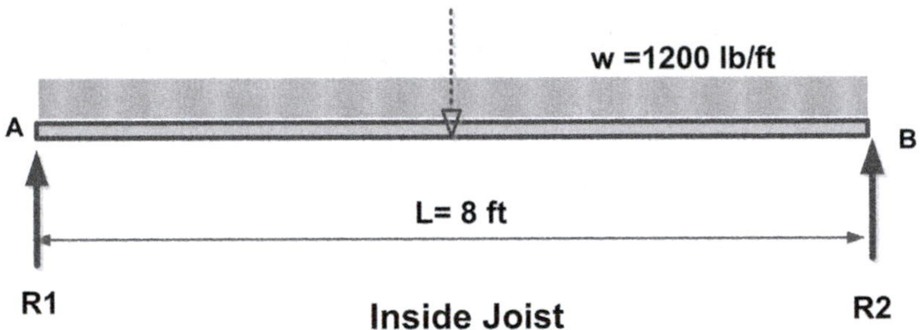

Figure 4.4c

2. Calculate total load (figure 4.4c):

   $W =$

Load diagram is symmetrical, therefore $R_1 = R_2 = W / 2 =$

Frame

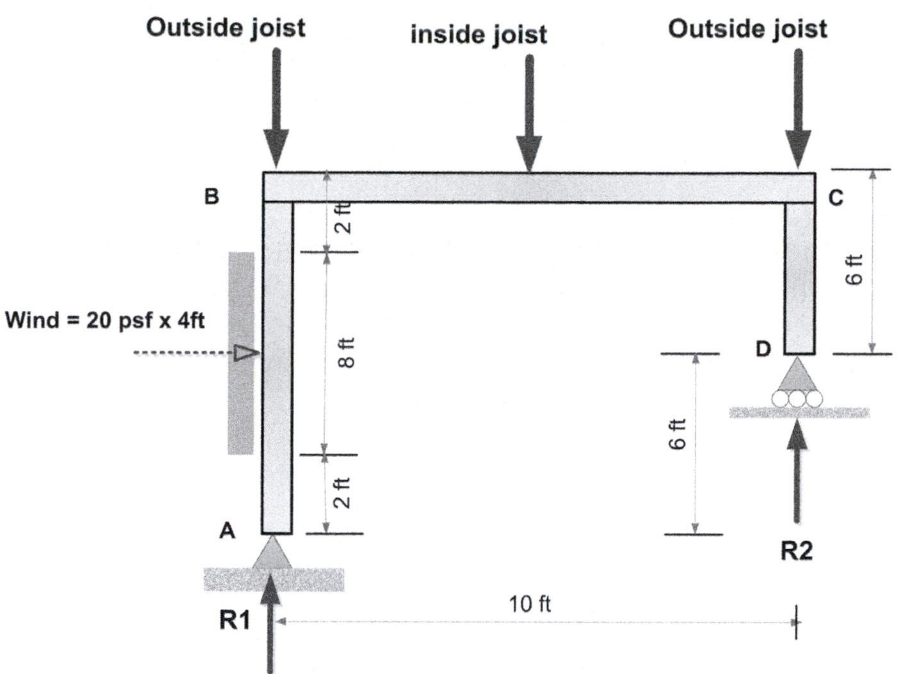

3. Calculate uniform horizontal load:

$W =$

Calculate the moment about the left support point (A):

$\Sigma M_{R1} = 0$:

$R_2 =$ lb

4. To achieve equilibrium, R_{1x}:

$640 \text{ lb} - R_{1x} = 0$

$R_{1x} = 640 \text{ lb}$

5. Calculate the moment about the right support point (D):

$\Sigma M_{R2} = 0$:

$R_{1y} =$ lb

6. Sum the vertical forces to verify the vertical equilibrium:

$\Sigma F_V = 0$:

Problem 4.5

For the wood framing shown below, calculate and show the reactions in a load diagram for each of the joists, beams, and columns necessary for determining the loads transferred to the footings. Assume Dead Load = 12 psf, Live Load = 68 psf. Ignore self-weight of members.

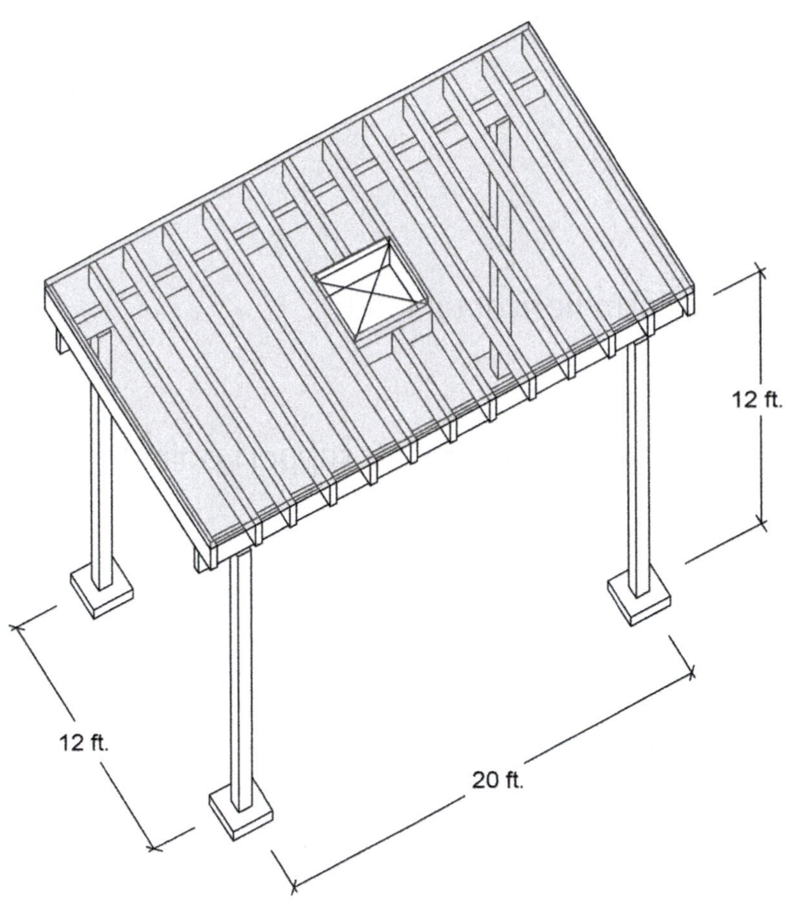

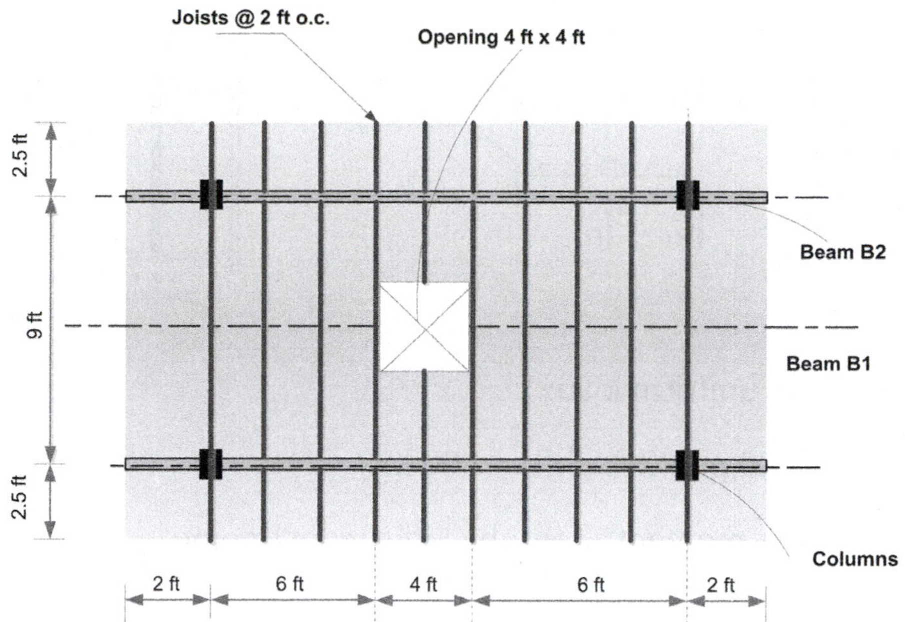

Joists

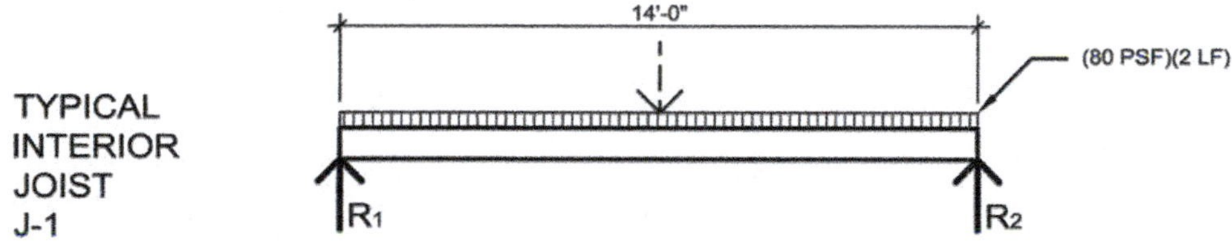

1. Calculate resultant uniform load:

   W = (80 psf)(2 ft)(14 ft) = 2,240 lb
   Load diagram is symmetrical, therefore
   $R_1 = R_2$ = 2,240 lb / 2 = 1,120 lb

TYPICAL
END
JOIST
J-2

14'-0"

(80 PSF)(1 LF)

R1 R2

2. Calculate resultant uniform load:

   W = (80 psf)(1 ft)(14 ft) = 1,120 lb
   Load diagram is symmetrical, therefore
   $R_1 = R_2$ = 1,120 lb / 2 = 560 lb

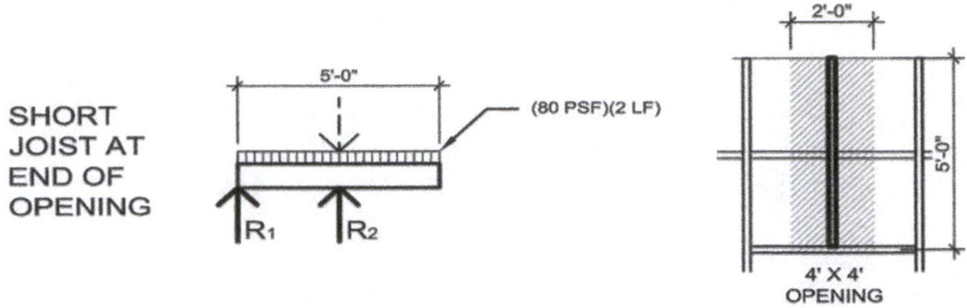

3. Calculate uniform load:

$$W = (80 \text{ psf})(2 \text{ ft})(5 \text{ ft}) = 800 \text{ lb}$$

Calculate the moment about the left support point:

$$\Sigma M_{R1} = 0:$$

$$R_2 = \qquad \text{lb}$$
$$R_1 = 0$$

SHORT
JOIST AT
EDGE OF
OPENING

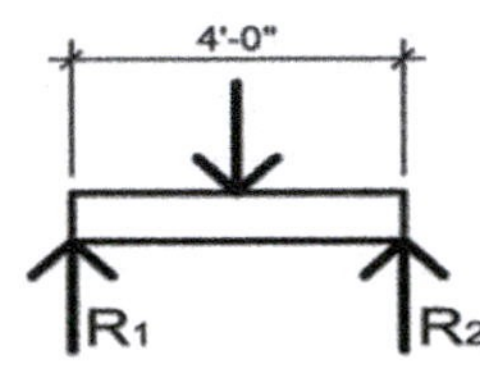

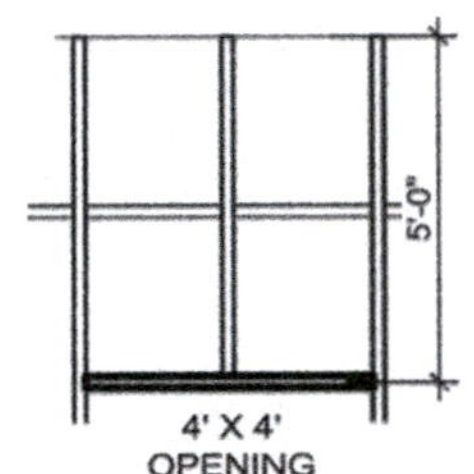

4. No reactions—point load is 0

TYPICAL
JOIST AT
EDGE OF
OPENING
J-3

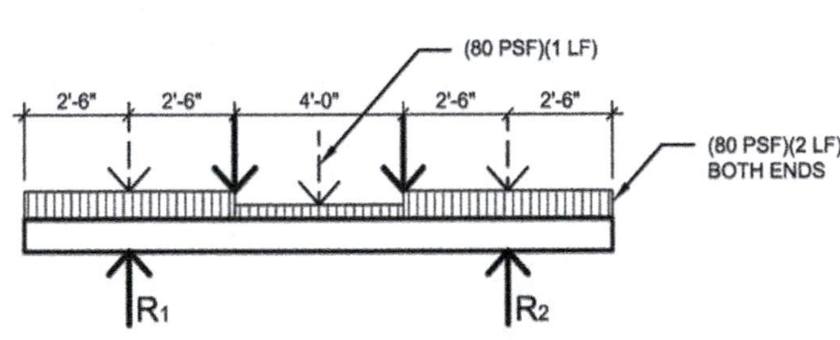

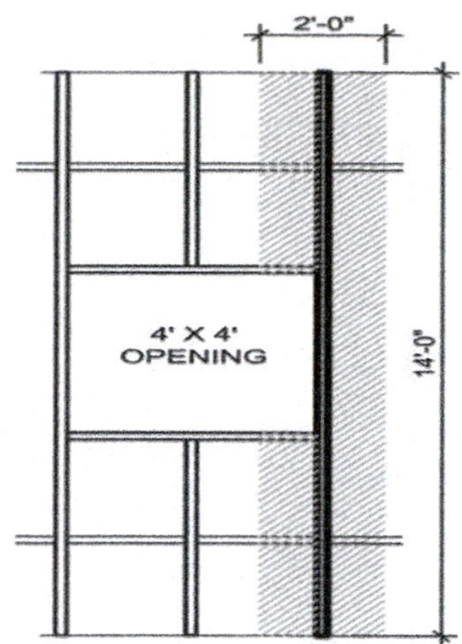

5. Total load = 800 lb + 320 lb + 800 lb = 1,920 lb

   Load diagram is symmetrical, therefore
   $R_1 = R_2 = 1{,}920$ lb / 2 = 960 lb

Beams

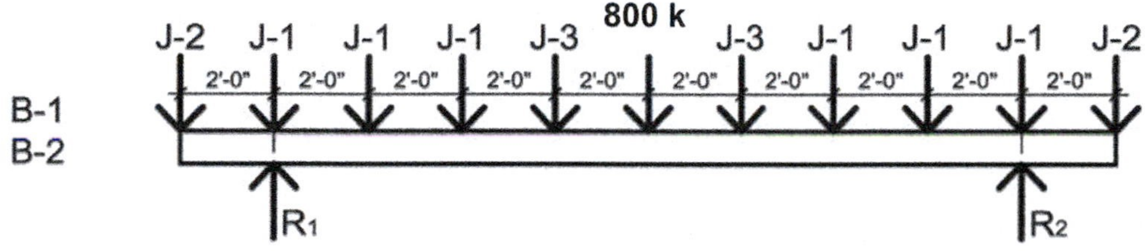

1. Total load = (2)(560 lb) + (6)(1,120 lb) + (2)(960 lb) + 800 = 10,560 lb

Columns

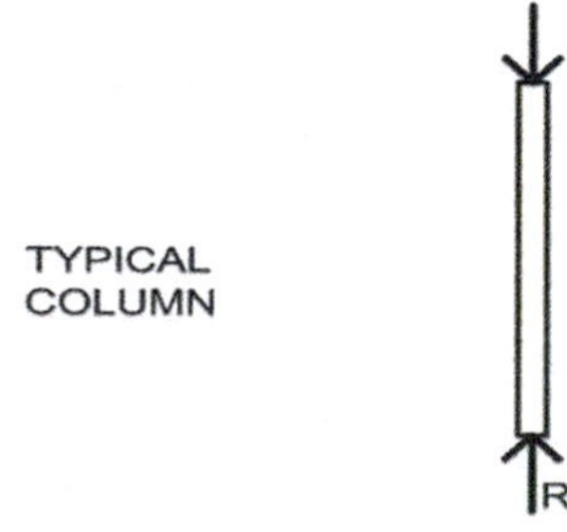

$R =$ lb

Footings

$R =$ lb

Problem 4.6

Joists

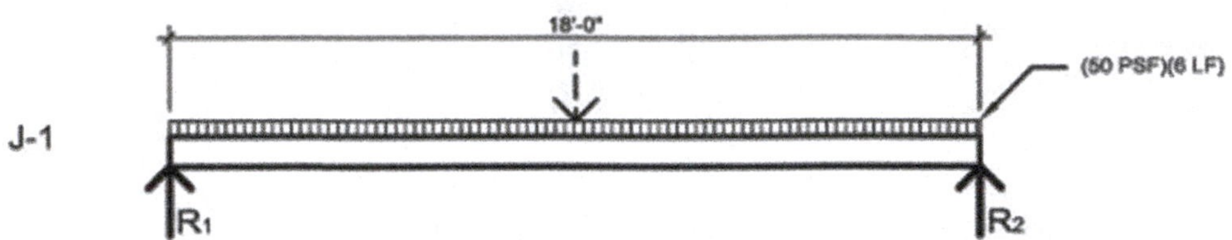

Calculate total of the uniform load:

W = area load x tributary area = (50 psf)(6 ft)(18 ft) = 5,400 lb
Load diagram is symmetrical, therefore $R_1 = R_2 =$

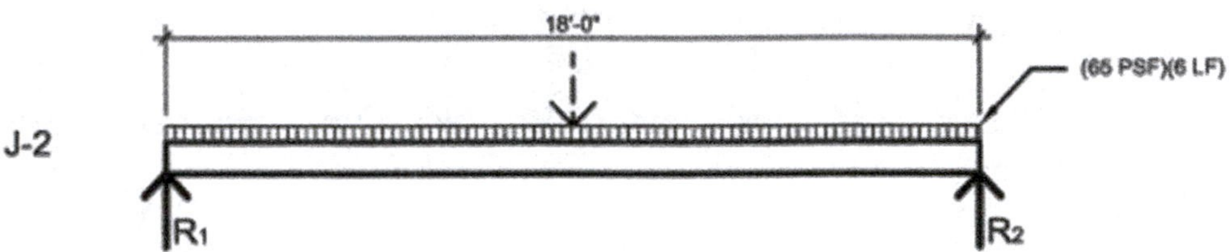

Calculate uniform load total:

W = area load x tributary area = (65 psf)(6 ft)(18 ft) = 7,020 lb
Load diagram is symmetrical, therefore $R_1 = R_2 =$

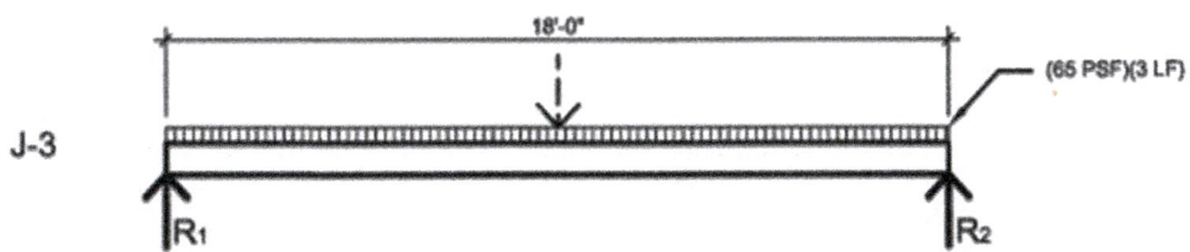

Calculate uniform load:

W = area load x tributary area =
Load diagram is symmetrical, therefore $R_1 = R_2 =$

Beams

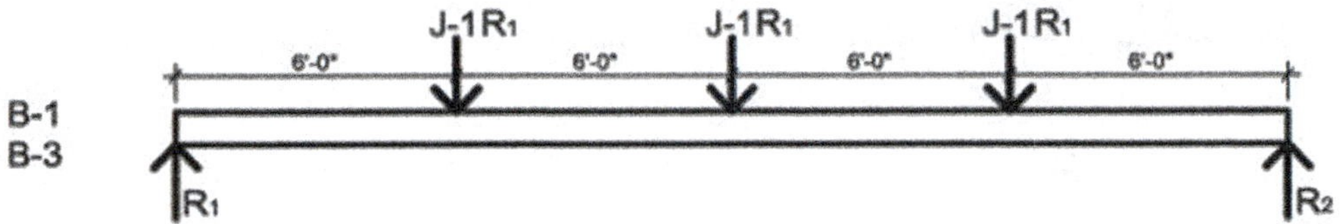

Calculate total load:

$W =$
Load diagram is symmetrical, therefore $R_1 = R_2 =$

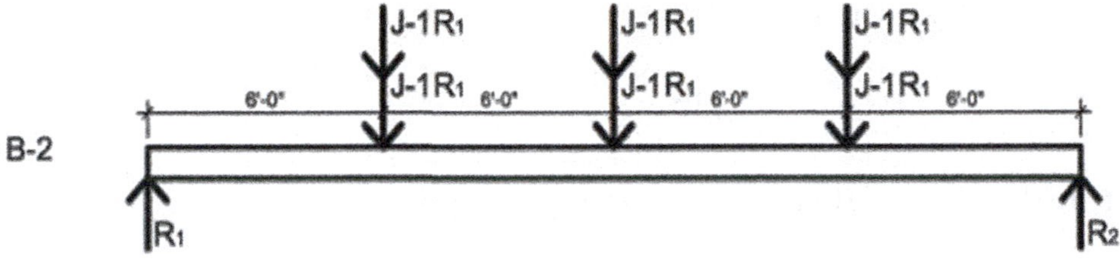

Calculate total load:

$W = (6)(2{,}700 \text{ lb}) = 16{,}200 \text{ lb}$
Load diagram is symmetrical, therefore $R_1 = R_2 = 16{,}200 \text{ lb} / 2 = 8{,}100 \text{ lb}$

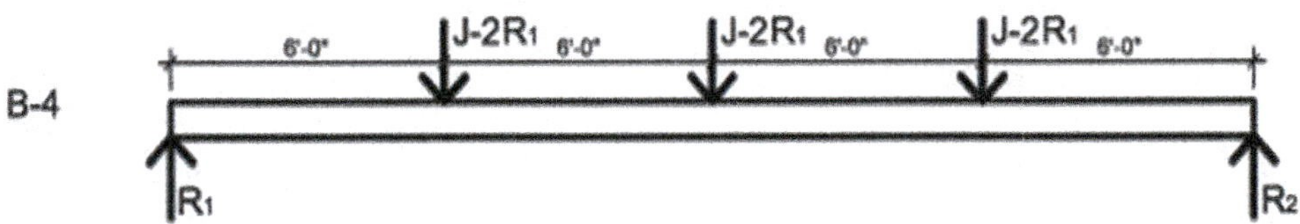

Calculate total load:

$W =$
Load diagram is symmetrical, therefore $R_1 = R_2 =$

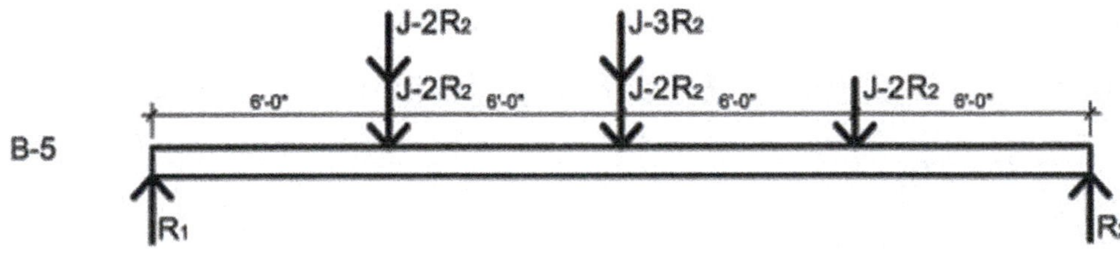

Calculate the moment about the left support point:

$\Sigma M_{R1} = 0$:

$R_2 =$ lb

Calculate the moment about the right support point:

$\Sigma M_{R2} = 0$:

$(6\text{ ft})(3{,}510\text{ lb}) + (12\text{ ft})(3{,}510\text{ lb}) + (12\text{ ft})(1{,}755\text{ lb}) + (18\text{ ft})$

$(3{,}510\text{ lb})(2) - (24\text{ ft})(R_1) = 0$

$R_1 = 8{,}775\text{ lb}$

Sum the vertical forces to verify equilibrium:

$\Sigma F_V = 0$:

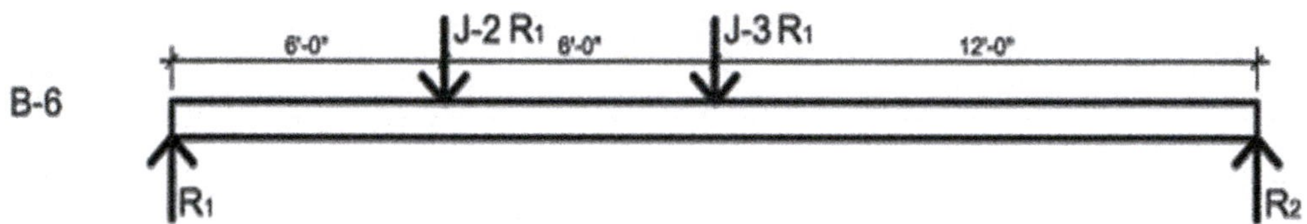

Calculate the moment about the left support point:

$\Sigma M_{R1} = 0$: $-(6\text{ ft})(3{,}510\text{ lb}) - (12\text{ ft})(1{,}755\text{ lb}) + (24\text{ ft})(R_2) = 0$

$R_2 = 1{,}755\text{ lb}$

Calculate the moment about the right support point:

$\Sigma M_{R2} = 0$:

$R_1 =$ lb

Sum the vertical forces to verify equilibrium:

$\Sigma F_V = 0$:

Girders

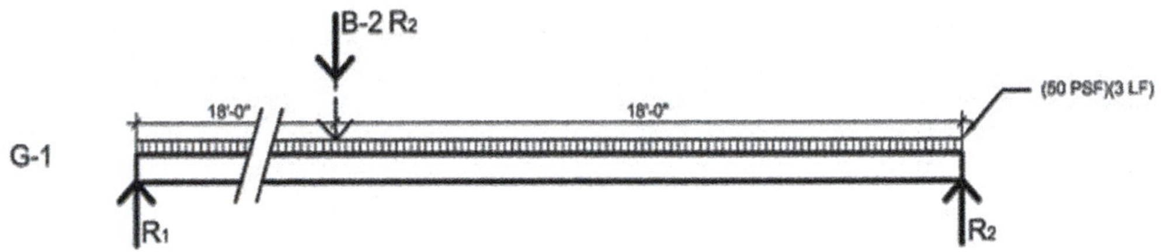

Calculate uniform load:

W = area load x tributary area = (50 psf)(3 ft)(36 ft) = 5,400 lb

Calculate total load:

5,400 lb + 8,100 lb = 13,500 lb

Load diagram is symmetrical, therefore $R_1 = R_2$ = 13,500 lb / 2 = 6,750 lb

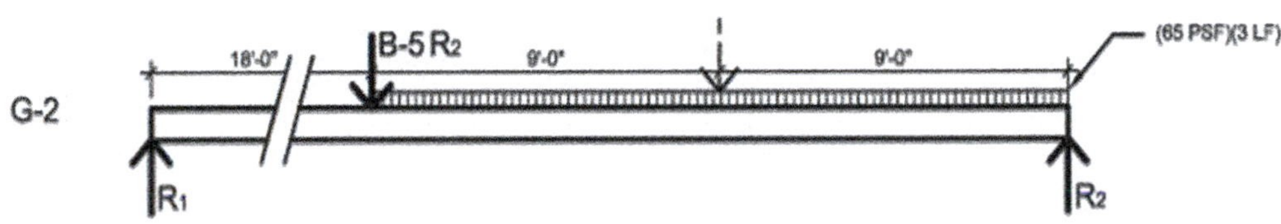

Calculate uniform load:

W = area load x tributary area = (65 psf)(3 ft)(18 ft) = 3,510 lb

Calculate the moment about the left support point:

$\Sigma M_{R1} = 0$: –(18 ft)(7,020 lb) – (27 ft)(3,510 lb) + (36 ft)(R_2) = 0
R_2 = lb

Calculate the moment about the right support point:

$\Sigma M_{R2} = 0$:
R_1 = lb

Sum the vertical forces to verify equilibrium:

$\Sigma F_V = 0$:

Columns

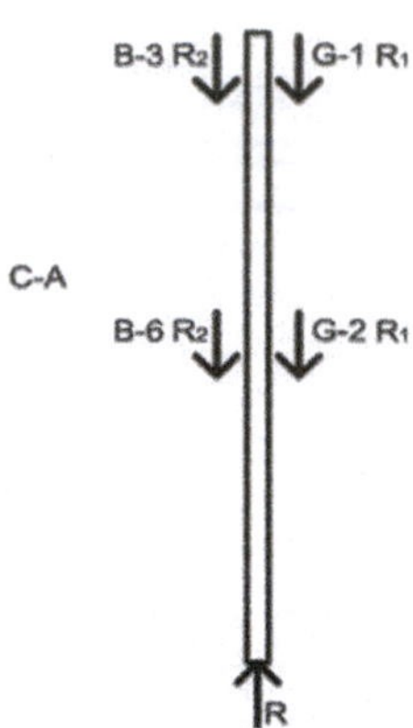

Calculate total load:

4,050 lb + 6,750 lb + 1,755 lb + 4,387.5 lb =16,942.5 lb = R

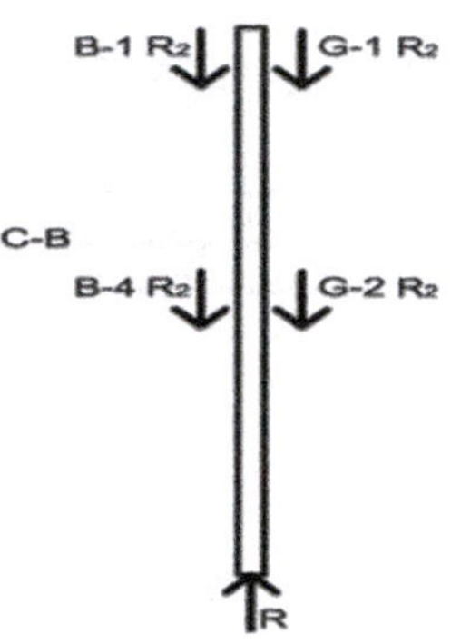

Calculate total load:

4,050 lb + 6,750 lb + 5,264 lb + 6,142.5 lb = 22,207.5 lb = R

Problem 4.7

Joists

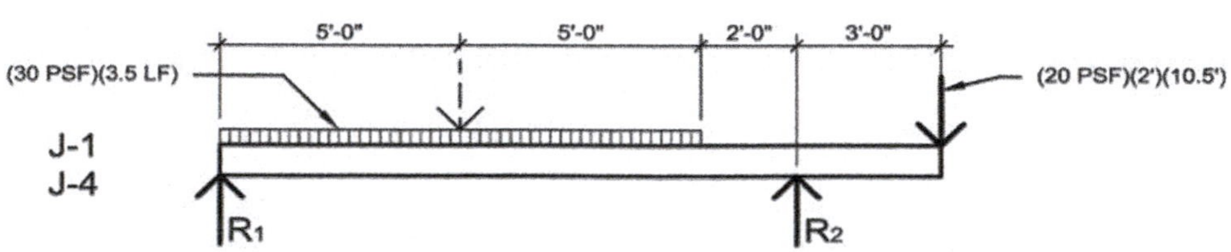

Calculate uniform load:

W = area load x tributary area = (30 psf)(3.5 ft)(10 ft) = 1,050 lb
Calculate point load:
W = (20 psf)(2 ft)(10.5 ft) = 420 lb

Calculate the moment about the left support point:

$\Sigma M_{R1} = 0:$
$R_2 =$ lb

Calculate the moment about the right support point:

$\Sigma M_{R2} = 0:$
$R_1 =$ lb

Sum the vertical forces to verify equilibrium:

$\Sigma F_V = 0:$

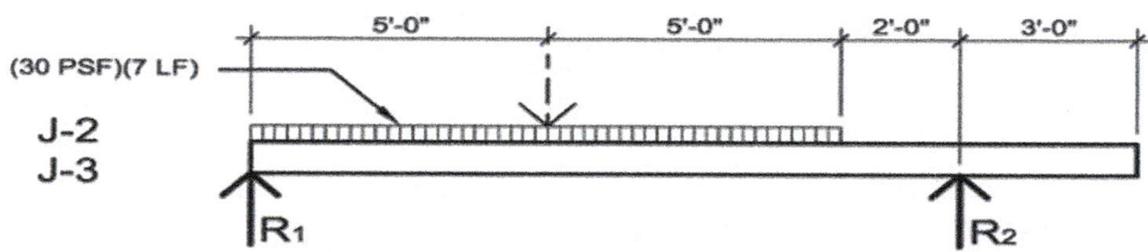

Calculate uniform load total:

W = area load x tributary area = (30 psf)(7 ft)(10 ft) = 2,100 lb

Calculate the moment about the left support point:

$\Sigma M_{R1} = 0: -(5\text{ ft})(2{,}100\text{ lb}) + (12\text{ ft})(R_2) = 0$
$R_2 = 875$ lb

Calculate the moment about the right support point:

$\Sigma M_{R2} = 0:$
$R_1 =$ lb

Sum the vertical forces to verify the vertical equilibrium:

$\Sigma F_V = 0:$

Beams

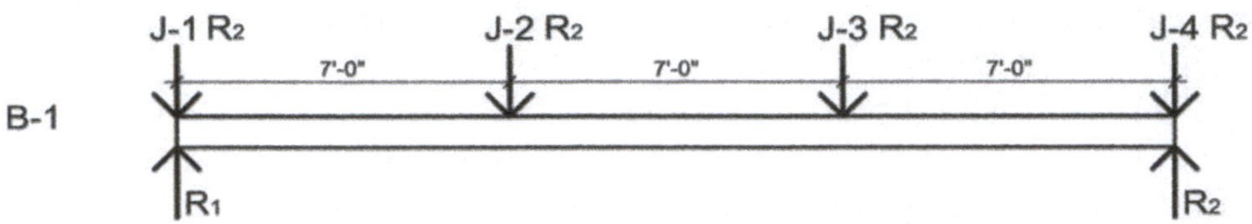

Calculate total load:

962.5 lb + 875 lb + 875 lb + 962.5 lb = 3,675 lb
Load diagram is symmetrical, therefore $R_1 = R_2$ = 3,675 lb / 2 = 1,837.5 lb

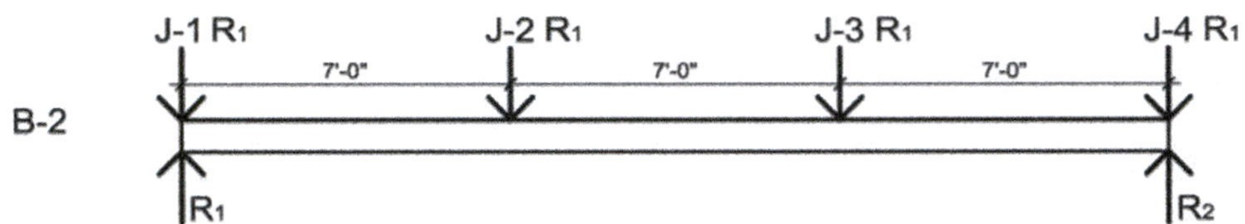

Calculate total load:

Load diagram is symmetrical, therefore $R_1 = R_2$ = 3,465 lb / 2 =

Columns

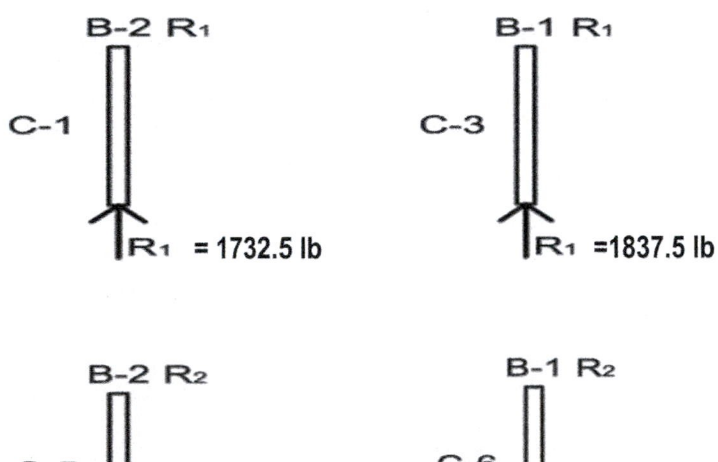

Girders

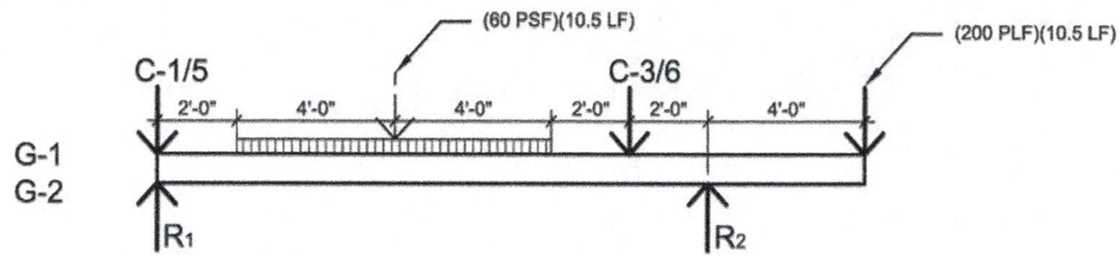

Calculate uniform load total:

W = area load x tributary area = (60 psf)(10.5 ft)(8 ft) = 5,040 lb

Calculate point load:

W = (200 lb/ft)(10.5 ft) = 2100 lb

Calculate the moment about the left support point:

$\Sigma M_{R1} = 0$: –(6 ft)(5,040 lb) – (12 ft)(1,837.5 lb) – (18 ft)(2,100 lb)

+ (14 ft)(R_2) = 0

R_2 = 6,435 lb

Calculate the moment about the right support point:

$\Sigma M_{R2} = 0$:

R_1 = lb

Sum the vertical forces to verify equilibrium:

$\Sigma F_V = 0$:

Columns

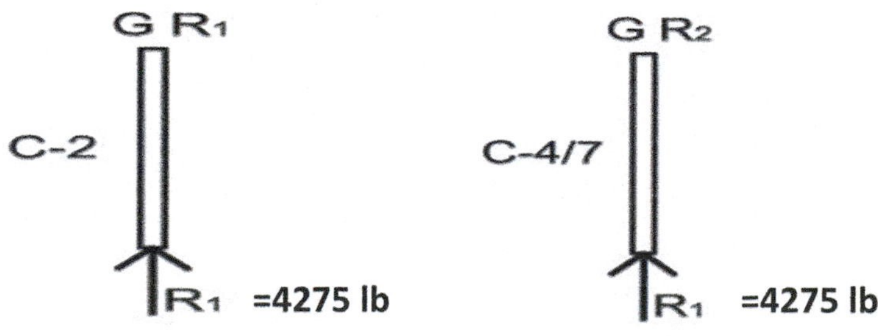

Footings

F–1 (C–2)

Area = 2 ft x 2 ft = 4 sf
4,275 lb / 4 sf = 1,068.75 psf

F–2 (C–4)

Area = 2 ft x 2 ft = 4 sf

CHAPTER 5

Problem 5.1

Answer:

Problem 5.2

Answer:

Problem 5.3

Refer to page 153–154 in your textbook *Building Structures: Fundamentals of Crossover Design* by Nawari & Kuenstle.

Problem 5.4

Answer:

Problem 5.5

1. Moment = Force x distance

2. Find the moment caused by the 12 kip lateral force:

$$M = (20\ kips)\ (\frac{150ft}{2}) = 1500\ kip - ft$$

3. Now find the shear on the north and south walls:

$R_{north} = R_{south}$ = rotational shear = Moment / Length of the wall (or depth of diaphragm)

$$= \frac{1500\ kip}{50\ ft} = 30\ kip$$

Problem 5.6

1. Determine the wind pressure using:

   p = 0.0021 V^2 psf (see chapter 5 in *Building Structures*, by Nawari & Kuenstle)
   = 0.0021 $(110)^2$ = 25.4 psf

2. Moment = Force x distance

3. To find the total wind pressure (Force), we multiply the design wind pressure by the surface area it is acting on, which is the surface area of the sign *BCDE* (see figure 5.6b)

   F =

4. Since the distance from the midpoint of the sign surface to the ground is 22.5 ft, then

   $M =$ k–ft

Problem 5.7

1. Determine the wind pressure using:

$p = 0.0021\ V^2$ psf (see chapter 5 in *Building Structures*, by Nawari & Kuenstle)
$= 0.0021\ (100)^2 = 21$ psf

2. Determine the resultant wind pressure, *P* (see figure 5.7b and 5.7c):

   P = wind pressure x surface area = (21 psf) (5 ft x 3ft) x 5
   = 1,575 lb = 1.575 kips

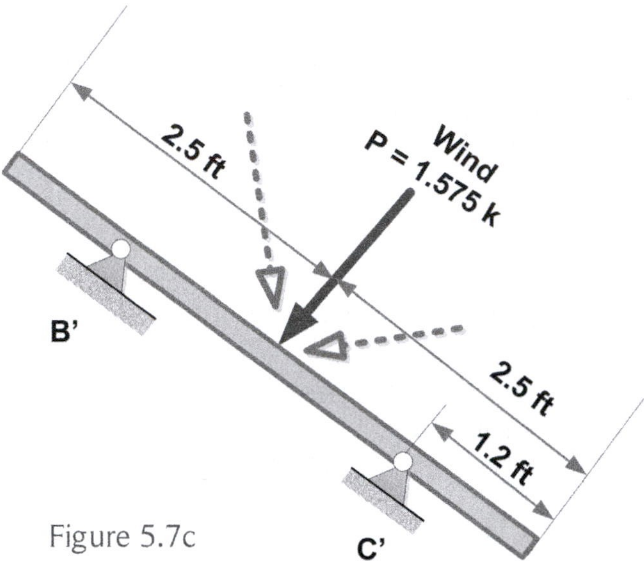

Figure 5.7c

3. Moment = Force x distance

4. Since the distance from the midpoint of the PV panel to point *C'* is 2.5 – 1.2 = 1.3 ft, then

   $M =$ k–ft

Problem 5.8

Refer to page 163 in your textbook *Building Structures: Fundamentals of Crossover Design* by Nawari & Kuenstle.

Problem 5.9

Step 1: Compute wind pressure using the approximate method

$p = 0.0021\ V^2$ psf
$= 0.0021\ (100)^2 = 21$ psf

The resultant wind force at the roof level is
$F = (21\text{ psf})\ (7.5\text{ ft} + 2\text{ ft})\ (120\text{ ft}) = 23{,}940\text{ lb} = 23.94\text{ kips}$

Step 2: Compute the fundamental period

$T = C_t h_n^x$; for this type of structure, we have

$T = 0.02150.75 = 0.15$ s

Step 3: Determine the total dead load of the building

$W =$ weight of the roof + weight of the upper half of the wall

$=$

Step 4: Compute the base shear force V

Using the equations given in chapter 5 in *Building Structures*, by Nawari & Kuenstle, we have (note the importance factor $I = 1.0$ for office buildings)

$$V = \frac{S_{D1}W}{T\ (R/I)} = \qquad \text{kips, but this value should not exceed}$$

$$V = \frac{S_{DS}W}{\left(\frac{R}{I}\right)} =$$

and not less than
$V = 0.044\ S_{DS} I\ W =$

Therefore, use $V =$ kips

Problem 5.10

The correct answer is A:

A solid shear wall of concrete provides the most resistance to deflection under lateral loading. This is used in conjunction with a steel frame, which carries the vertical loads. Shear wall systems are often used to form a central core in the building for elevators and mechanical ducts.

Bracing is an economical method of providing rigidity to a steel frame and is commonly seen as X-bracing and K-bracing. They are usually placed in the central set of bays and act as vertical trusses cantilevered from the ground.

Moment-resisting connections are used between columns and beams and may consist of simple welded joints or may include small brackets when larger loads are involved. These connections are the least capable of the three at resisting deflection.

Problem 5.11

Refer to pages 181–182 in your textbook *Building Structures: Fundamentals of Crossover Design* by Nawari & Kuenstle.

Problem 5.12

1. The principal purpose of these joints is to control relative movements of building components or entire building sections to minimize cracks and stresses. These movements can be attributed to different causes such as changes in material volume and plan configuration, soil and foundation settlement, seismic actions, and direct force actions. Whatever the source of the displacement of the members, if they are held back from free movement, additional forces will be induced into the component itself as well as the adjacent members, preventing the free deformation.

2.

Problem 5.13

Answer:

Problem 5.14

Step 1: Determine the resultant wind force assuming wind is against the long building façade.

P = (20 psf) (100 ft x 24 ft) = 48,000 lb = 48 kips

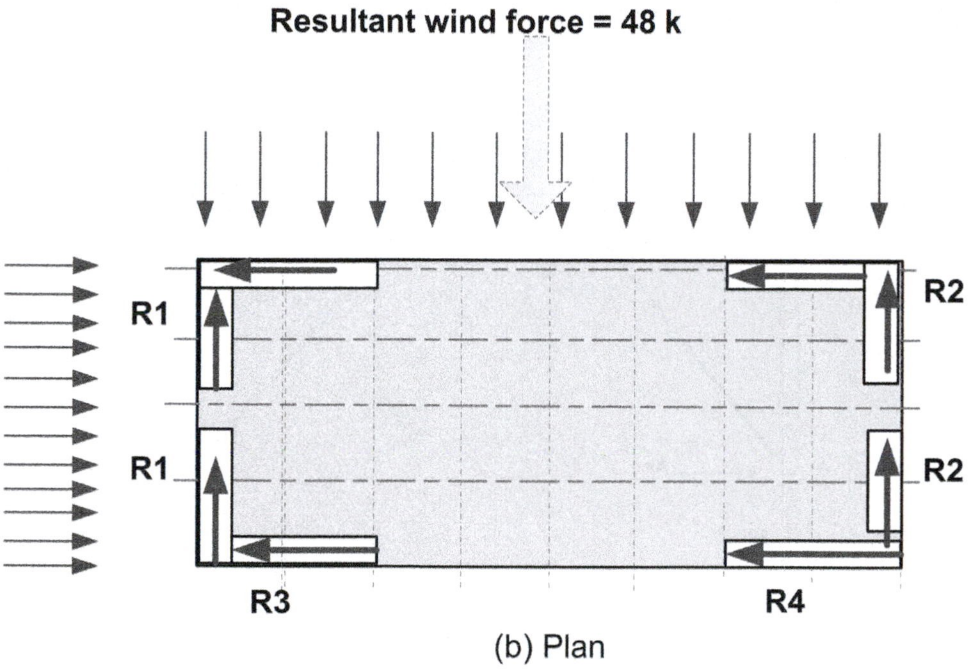

Figure 5.14b

Step 2: Find shear wall reactions.

From the symmetrical condition shown in figure 5.14b, we have $R1 = R2$, then $2\ R1 + 2\ R2 = 48$ k or $4R1 = 48$ k, which gives,

$R1 = R2 = 12$ k

Step 3: Determine the resultant wind force assuming wind is against the short building façade.

P = kips

Step 4: Find shear wall reactions.

Again, from the symmetrical condition we have $R3 = R4$, then:

Problem 5.15

Answer:

Problem 5.16

An industrial building with a plan dimension of 25' x 45' and a height of 15' is subjected to a wind load of 5 kips as shown in figure 5.16. Two braced exterior walls parallel to the wind direction are used to resist the horizontal diaphragm force in the roof. Assuming horizontal reactions at *A* and *B* are equal, determine the magnitude of force developed in each brace member.

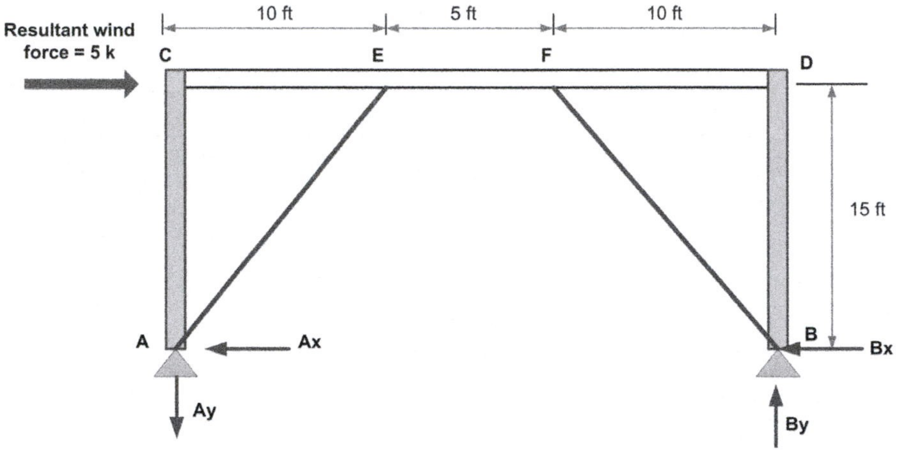

Figure 5.16

1. Determine the vertical reaction B_y:

$[\Sigma M_A = 0]:$

$B_y =$

2. Determine the vertical reaction A_y:

$[\Sigma F_y = 0]: \quad -A_y + B_y = 0$

$-A_y + 3\ k = 0$

$A_y =$

3. Assuming $A_x = B_x$:

$$[\Sigma F_x = 0]: \quad 5k - A_X - B_X = 0$$

$$A_X = B_X =$$

4. Take a section through members *AE* and *CE* (figure 5.16c):

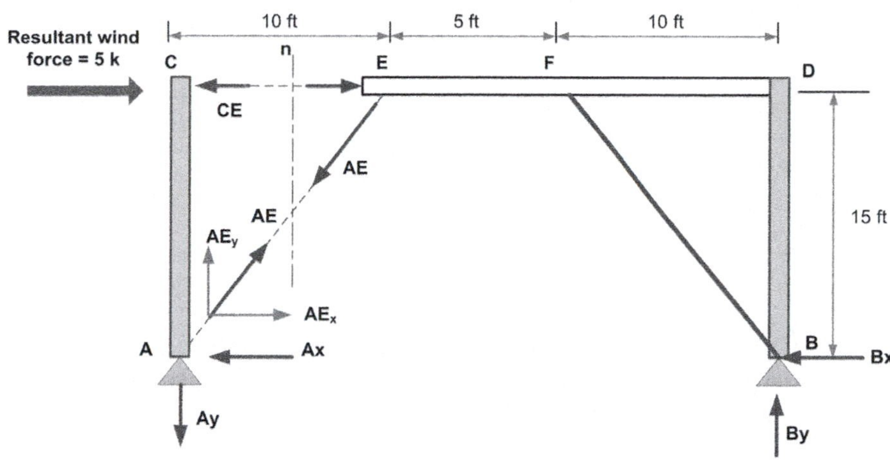

Figure 5.16c

5. Determine the reaction forces of member *AE* by resolving the member into its x- and y-components, AC_x and AE_y, and taking the moment about *C*:

Note: Member AE is acting in tension, while CE is acting in compression.

$$[\Sigma M_C = 0]:$$

$$AE_x =$$

$$AE_x = AE\cos\theta = AE(2/\sqrt{13})$$

Therefore,

$$AE =$$

6. Take a section through members *BF* and *DF* (figure 5.16d):

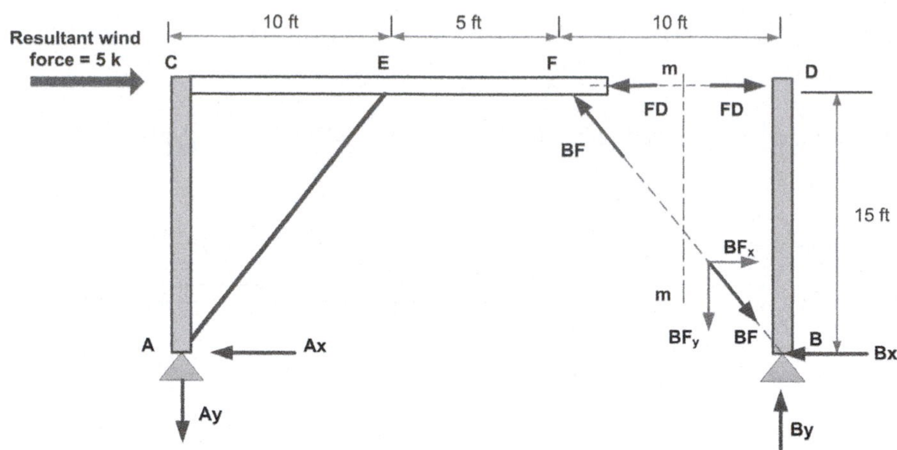

Figure 5.16d

7. Determine the reaction forces of member *BF* by resolving the member into its x- and y-components, BF_x and BF_y, and taking the moment about *D*:

$$[\Sigma M_D = 0]: \quad BF_x(15') - B_x(15') = 0$$

$$BF_x(15') - 2.5k(15') = 0$$

$$BF_x =$$

$$BF_x = BF\cos\theta = BF(2/\sqrt{13})$$

Therefore,

$$BF =$$

CHAPTER 6

Problem 6.1

Refer to page 198–199 in your textbook *Building Structures: Fundamentals of Crossover Design* by Nawari & Kuenstle.

Problem 6.2

1. It can be seen that the reaction force at point E must be equal and opposite to the force applied by member DE. By analyzing DE, we can see that it forms a triangle with a rise of 1 and a run of 2. From this, we can deduce that the value of its hypotenuse is $\sqrt{5}$.

2. Therefore, we can resolve reaction E into its x- and y-components:

$$E_x = E\left(\frac{2}{\sqrt{5}}\right)$$

$$E_y = E\left(\frac{1}{\sqrt{5}}\right)$$

3. Find E by taking the moment about A:

$$[\Sigma M_A = 0]: E_y(40') - 250\#(30') - 250\#(20') - 250\#(10') = 0$$

$$E =$$

4. Plug the value of E back into the x and y equations to obtain E_x and E_y:

$$E_x = E\left(\frac{2}{\sqrt{5}}\right)$$

$$E_y = E\left(\frac{1}{\sqrt{5}}\right)$$

$$E_x = \qquad E_y =$$

5. Find C by analyzing the forces that are concurrent at point C. Determine CB_x and CB_y by solving the equilibrium equations:

**Note: The horizontal component of the tension force is the same at any point of the cable, because* $[\Sigma F_x = 0]$.

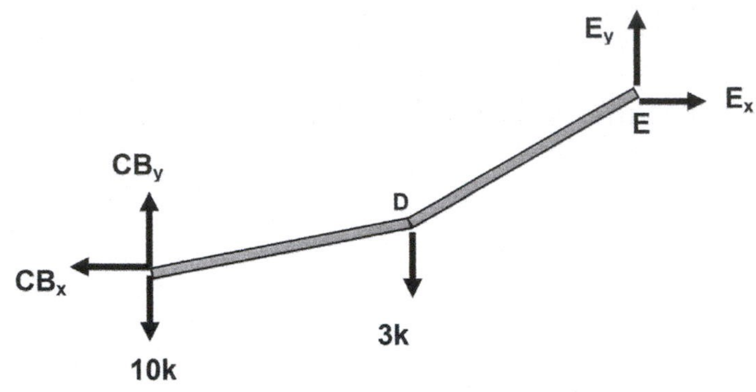

$$[\Sigma F_x = 0] \qquad CB_x = E_x$$

$$CB_x = 750 lb$$

$$[\Sigma F_y = 0] \qquad CB_y - 250 lb - 250 lb + E_y = 0$$

$$CB_y =$$

6. To find h_c, solve the triangle formed by CB, CB_x, and CB_y:

It is given that CB_x has a length of 10 ft, while CB_y has an unknown length.
Therefore, we can use the method of proportions to find the length of CB_y:

$$\frac{y}{CB_y} = \frac{10'}{CB_x}$$

$$y(CB_x) = 10'(CB_y)$$

$$y =$$

7. Find h_c by adding y and the given $h_b = 5$ ft:

$$h_c = y + h_b$$

$$h_c =$$

Problem 6.3

For the cable structure shown in figure 6.3, determine the cable tension between each force, and determine the required length of the cable for the system shown. Assume the sag at C as $h_c =$ 10 ft.

1. First, solve for the support forces at A and E.

   Find E_y by taking the moment about A:

   $[\Sigma M_A = 0]$: $\quad -6k(12') - 10k(32') - 3k(42') + E_y(60') = 0$

   $$E_y = 8.633k$$

2. Find A_y by solving the vertical equilibrium equation:

   $[\Sigma F_y = 0]$: $\quad A_y - 6k - 10k - 3k + E_y = 0$

   $$A_y =$$

3. Solve the forces in CDE. Don't forget that force ED is equal and opposite to the force E. This means that we only have one unknown to solve for, E_x.

   **Note: In regard to CB_y, we know that CB_x must equal E_x. Therefore, we can later find CB_y by solving the vertical equilibrium equation.*

Draw the right side FBD using point C as the concurrent point:

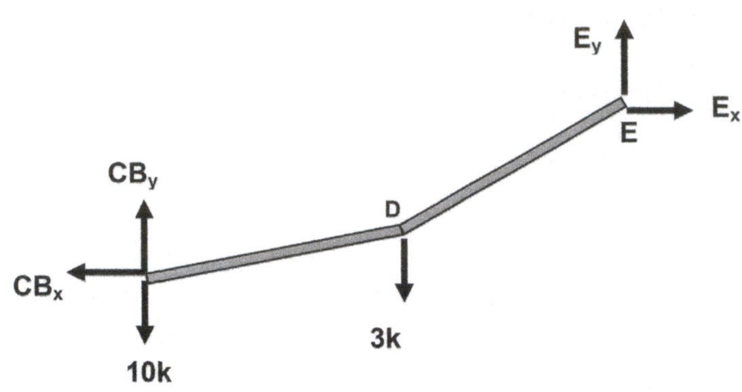

Find E_x by taking the moment about point C:

$$[\Sigma M_c = 0]: \quad -3k(10') + E_y(28') - E_x(10') = 0$$

$$E_x =$$

4. From the Pythagorean Theorem, we can obtain E:

$$E = \sqrt{E_x^{\,2} + E_y^{\,2}}$$

$$E = ED =$$

5. Now that E_x has been found, we know that its value is the same for all horizontal components. Therefore, we can find A_x:

$$E_x = A_x$$

$$A_x =$$

6. The reaction at A can now be found using the Pythagorean Theorem:

$$A = \sqrt{A_x^{\,2} + A_y^{\,2}}$$

$$A = AB =$$

7. Already determined is force CB_x:

$$[\Sigma F_x = 0]: \quad CB_x = E_x$$

$$CB_x =$$

8. Find CB_y by solving the vertical equilibrium equation of FBD(6.3b):

$$[\Sigma F_y = 0]: \quad CB_y - 10k - 3k + E_y = 0$$

$$CB_y =$$

9. CB can now be obtained by the Pythagorean Theorem:

$$CB = \sqrt{CB_x^{\,2} + CB_y^{\,2}}$$

$$CB =$$

10. Draw the left side, FBD (6.3c), using point C as the concurrent point:

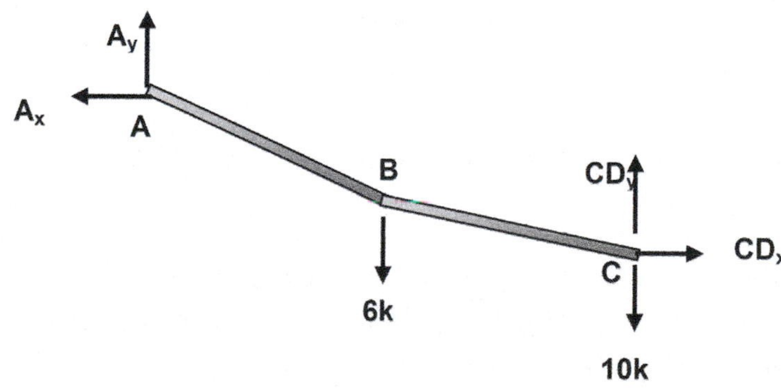

11. CD_x is a horizontal force and is thus equal to E_x:

$$E_x = CD_x$$

$$CD_x =$$

12. Using FBD (6.3c) solve the vertical equilibrium equation:

$$[\Sigma F_y = 0] \qquad A_y - 6k - 10k + CD_y = 0$$

$$CD_y =$$

13. Use the Pythagorean Theorem to find CD:

$$CD = \sqrt{(CD_x)^2 + (CD_y)^2}$$

$$CD =$$

Problem 6.4

Step 1: Draw the FBD of the cable AB

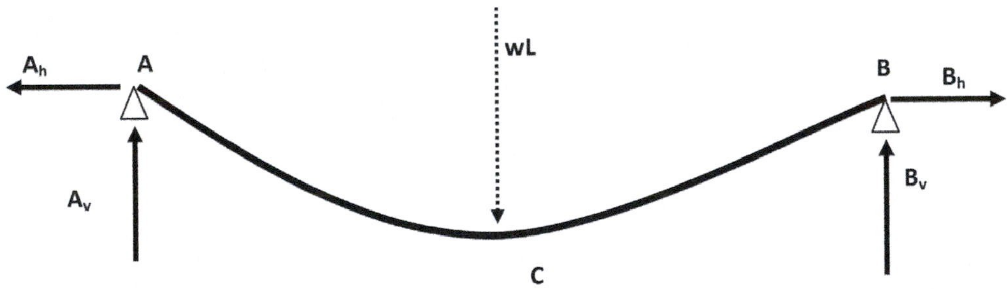

The maximum horizontal component of the cable force will occur at point C.

Step 2: To determine the horizontal component of the cable force, consider the FBD of half of the cable and sum the moments about point A

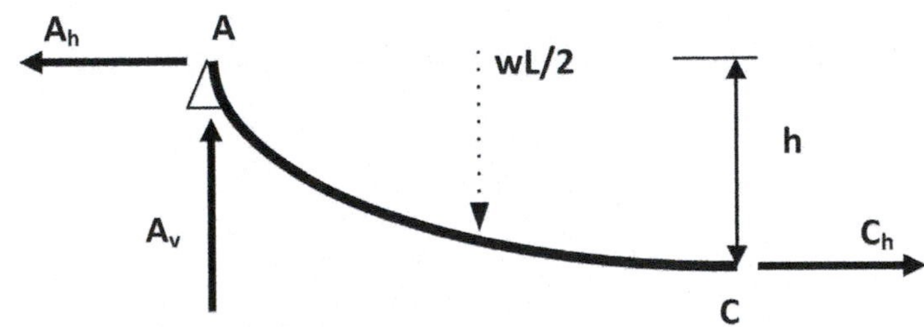

$$\sum M_A = 0 : C_h x h - wL/2 x \frac{L}{4} = 0$$

Therefore, the maximum horizontal component of the cable force is:

CHAPTER 7

Problem 7.1

Answer:

Problem 7.3

Refer to pages 221–224 in your textbook *Building Structures: Fundamentals of Crossover Design* by Nawari & Kuenstle.

Problem 7.4

1. Determine the vertical reactions A_y and B_y:

$[\Sigma M_A = 0]$: $-4k(25') - 4k(75') + B_y(100') = 0$

$B_y = 4k$

$[\Sigma F_y = 0]$:

$A_y =$

2. Determine the horizontal reaction A_x:

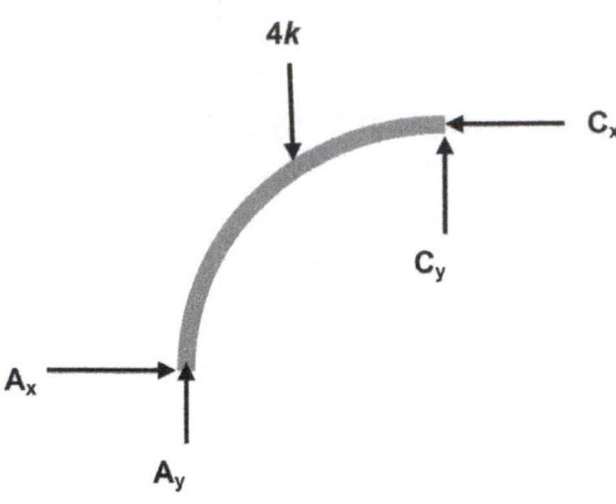

$[\Sigma M_C = 0]$:

$$A_x =$$

3. Determine the vertical reaction C_y:

$[\Sigma F_y = 0]$: $A_y - 4k - C_y = 0$

$$C_y =$$

4. Determine the horizontal reaction C_x:

$[\Sigma F_x = 0]$: $A_x - C_x = 0$

$$C_x = A_x =$$

5. Determine the horizontal reaction B_x:

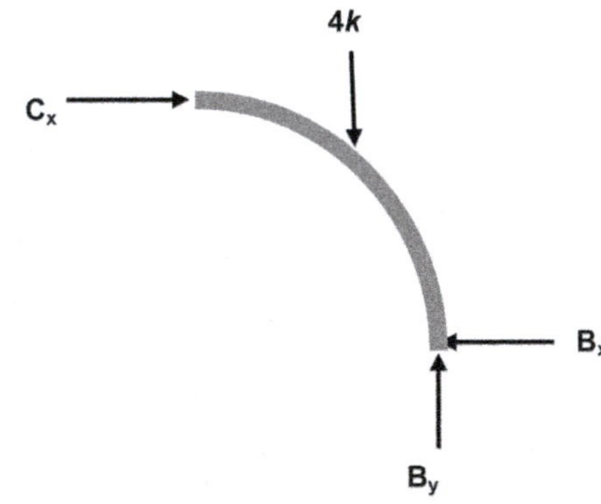

$[\Sigma F_x = 0]$: $C_x - B_x = 0$

$B_x = C_x =$

Problem 7.5

Step 1: Determine the vertical reactions at support A and B

$\Sigma F_y = 0$: $A_y + B_y - (w)(L) = 0$

Then, $A_y = B_y = wL/2$ (symmetry)

Step 2: To determine the horizontal reactions, draw FBD for the left half of arch (figure 7.5b):

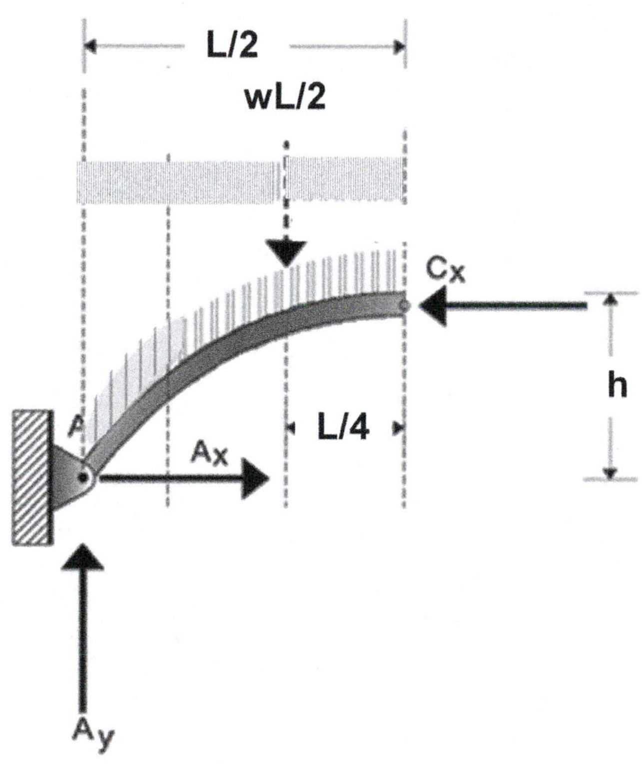

Figure 7.5b

Resultant of the loading on the left half is $(w) \times L = wL$
For half of the arch:

$\Sigma M_c = 0$:

$A_x(h) - (wL/2)(L/2) + (wL/2)(L/4) = 0$

$A_x =$

By symmetry $B_x = A_x =$

<u>Step 3</u>: The resultant of these two reactions will be equal to the compression force on the arch member (figure 7.4c):

$R_c =$

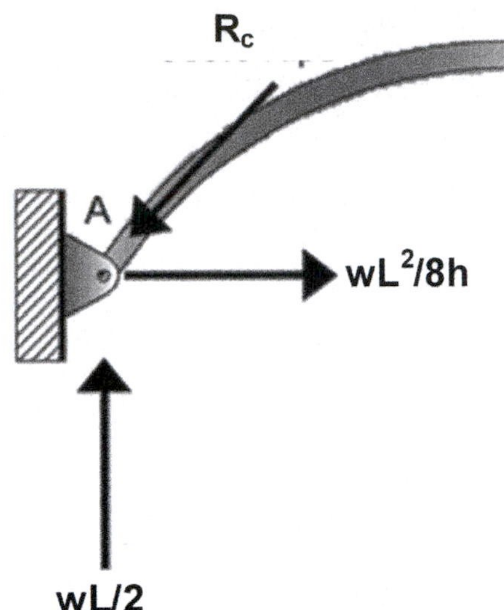

Figure 7.5c

CHAPTER 8

Problem 8.2

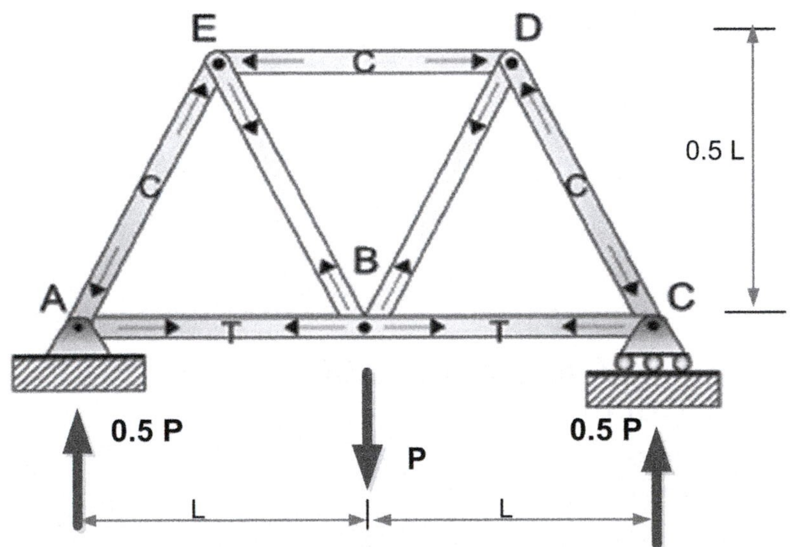

Problem 8.3

Refer to page 245–246 in your textbook *Building Structures: Fundamentals of Crossover Design* by Nawari & Kuenstle. Figure 8.3b

Problem 8.4

1. Draw the FBD of the entire truss system:

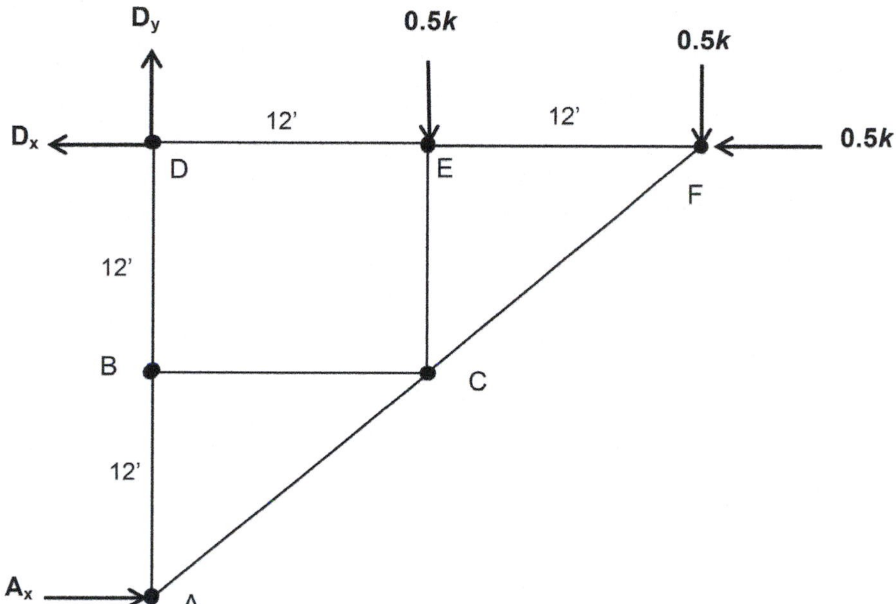

2. Solve for the external reactions of the system, D_x, D_y, and A_x.

   **Note: By finding the moment about D, we deal with only one unknown, A_x.*

Find A_x by taking the moment about D:

$[\Sigma M_D = 0]$:

$$A_x =$$

Find D_x by solving the horizontal equilibrium equation:

$[\Sigma F_x = 0]: \quad A_x - 0.5k - D_x = 0$

$$D_x =$$

Find D_y = by solving the vertical equilibrium equation:

$[\Sigma F_y = 0]$:

$$D_y =$$

3. Isolate Joint A to determine the forces in members AB and AC:

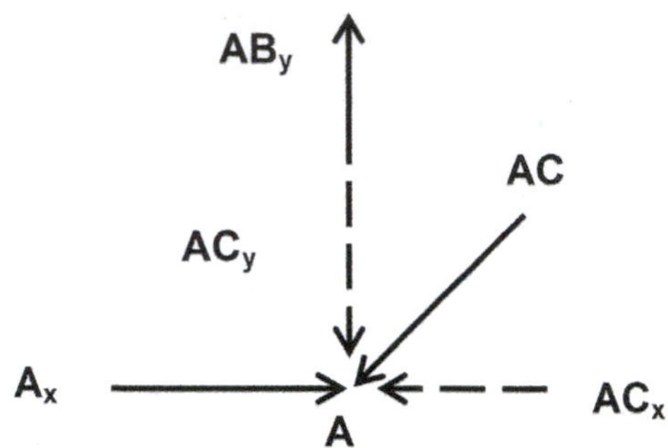

We can resolve AC into its x- and y-components in order to find AC:

$$AC_x = AC\cos 45^\circ = .707AC$$

Using the horizontal equilibrium equation, solve for AC:

$[\Sigma F_x = 0]$:

$AC =$ (Compression)

Using the vertical equilibrium equation, solve for AB:

$[\Sigma F_y = 0]$: $AB + AC_y = 0$

$AB =$ (Tension)

4. Isolate Joint B to determine the forces in members BC and BD:

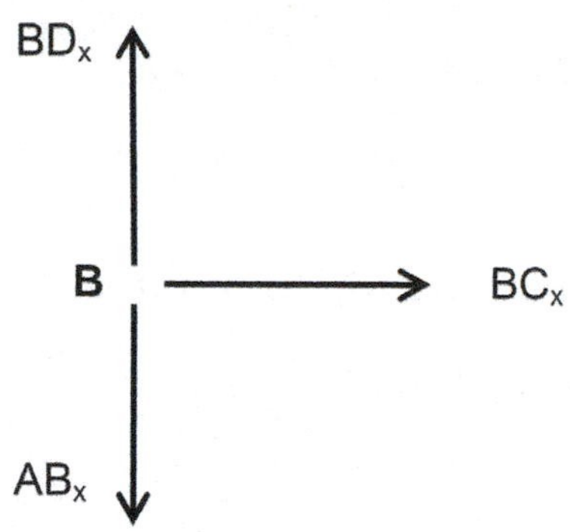

In examining member BC, we can see that no horizontal forces are acting on the member. Therefore:

$$[\Sigma F_x = 0]:$$

$$BC = 0$$

Find BD by solving the vertical equilibrium equation:

$$[\Sigma F_y = 0]: \quad BD_y - AB_y = 0$$

$$BD =$$

5. Isolate Joint D to find the forces in members DC and DE. Because DC only has one unknown, we begin with this member. Member DE cannot be solved without knowing the horizontal force DC_x.

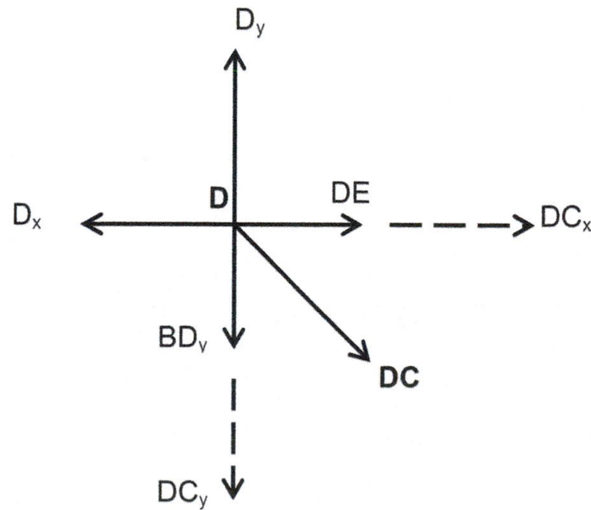

Resolve DC into its x- and y-components in order to solve for DC:

$$DC_x = DC\cos 45° = .707DC$$

$$DC_y = DC\cos 45° = .707DC$$

Find DC by solving the vertical equilibrium equation:

$$[\Sigma F_y = 0]: \quad D_y - BD - DC_y = 0$$

$DC =$ (Tension)

Find DE by solving the horizontal equilibrium equation:

$$[\Sigma F_x = 0]: \quad -D_x + DE + DC_x = 0$$

$DE =$

6. Isolate Joint E to solve for the forces in members EF and CE:

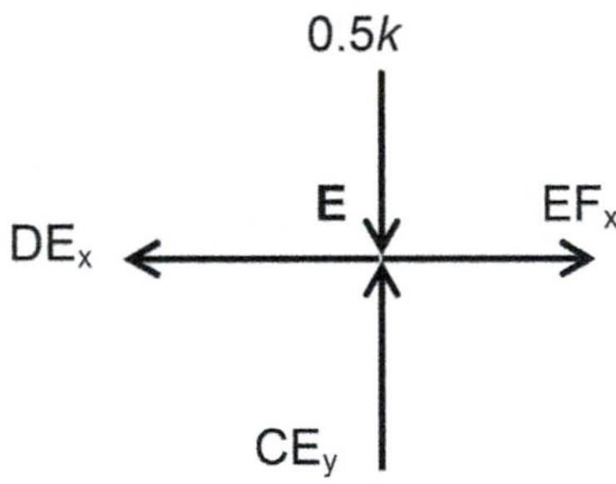

$[\Sigma F_x = 0]:$

$EF_x =$

$$[\Sigma F_y = 0]: \quad CE_y - 0.5k = 0$$

$CE =$ (Compression)

7. Isolate Joint F to solve for the forces in members CF:

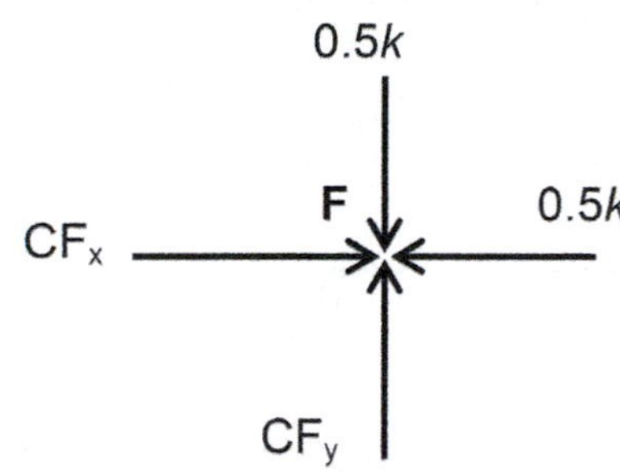

$[\Sigma F_x = 0]$:

$CF=$ (Compression)

Problem 8.5

Refer to page 256–257 in your textbook *Building Structures: Fundamentals of Crossover Design* by Nawari & Kuenstle.

Problem 8.6

Answer:

Problem 8.7

1. Draw the FBD of the entire system:

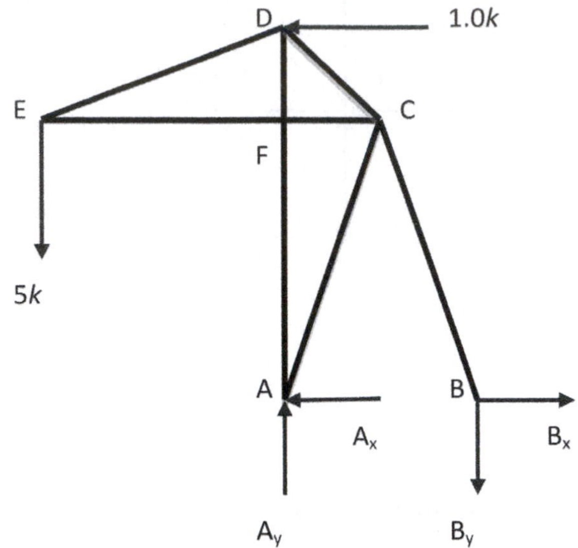

Note: Notice the absence of rollers at either A or B. Both A and B have pin connections.

2. Solve for the reactions at A and B.

Take the moment about A to find the reactions at B:
Keep in mind the following:

$$B_x = \frac{1}{\sqrt{5}} CB$$

$$B_y = \frac{2}{\sqrt{5}} CB$$

$$[\Sigma M_A = 0] \quad 5k(10') + 1k(15') + 1k(20') - B_y(10') = 0$$

$$\text{Since } B_y = \left(\frac{2}{\sqrt{5}}\right) CB,$$

$$5k(10') + 1k(15') + 1k(10') - \frac{2}{\sqrt{5}} CB(10') = 0$$

$$CB =$$

$$B_x =$$

$$B_y =$$

3. Solve the horizontal and vertical equilibrium equations to obtain the reactions at A:

$$[\Sigma F_x = 0]:$$

$$A_x =$$

$$[\Sigma F_y = 0]:$$

$$A_y =$$

4. Because Joint E has the fewest unknowns, isolate and solve for the forces of the members associated with that joint.

   Draw the FBD of the isolated joint:

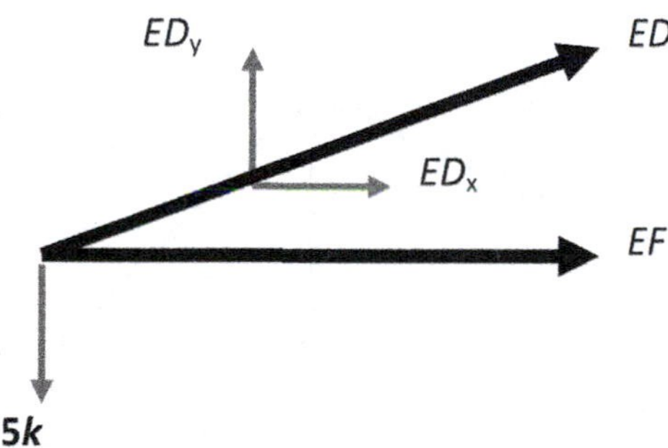

5. Resolve ED into its x- and y-components, and solve the horizontal and vertical equilibrium equations to find the force of member ED:

$$ED_x = \frac{2}{\sqrt{5}} ED$$

$$ED_y = \frac{1}{\sqrt{5}} ED$$

In this case, the vertical equation has only one unknown, *ED*, while the horizontal equation has two unknowns, *ED* and *EF*. Thus, we must first solve the vertical equation to obtain *ED* in order to solve the horizontal equation.

$$[\Sigma F_y = 0]:$$

$$ED = 11.2k \text{ (T)}$$

$$[\Sigma F_x = 0]:$$

$$EF = \qquad \text{(C)}$$

6. Next, examine Joint *D*, and find the forces of members *DC* and *DF*.

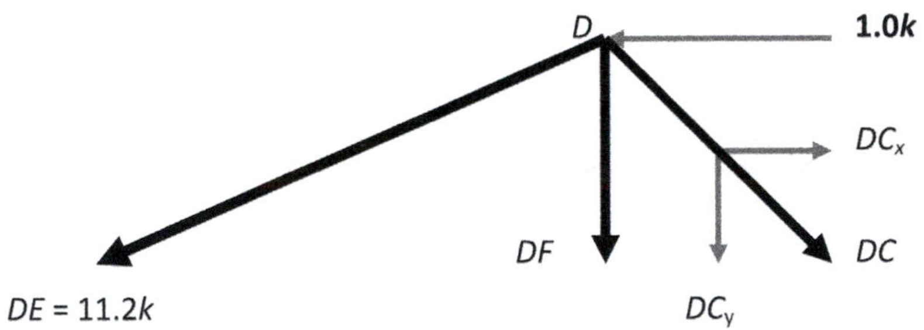

7. Resolve *DC* into its x- and y-components:

$$DC_x = \frac{\sqrt{2}}{2} DC = .707DC$$

$$DC_y = \frac{\sqrt{2}}{2} DC = .707DC$$

8. Solve the horizontal and vertical equilibrium equations. In this case, the horizontal equation has fewer unknowns, *DC*, than the vertical equation, *DC* and *DF*.

$$[\Sigma F_x = 0]: \quad -ED_x - 1k + DC_x = 0$$

$$DC = \qquad (T)$$

$$[\Sigma F_y = 0]: \quad -ED_y - DF - DC_y = 0$$

$$DF = \qquad (C)$$

9. Next, examine Joint *F*, and find the forces of members *CF* and *FA*.

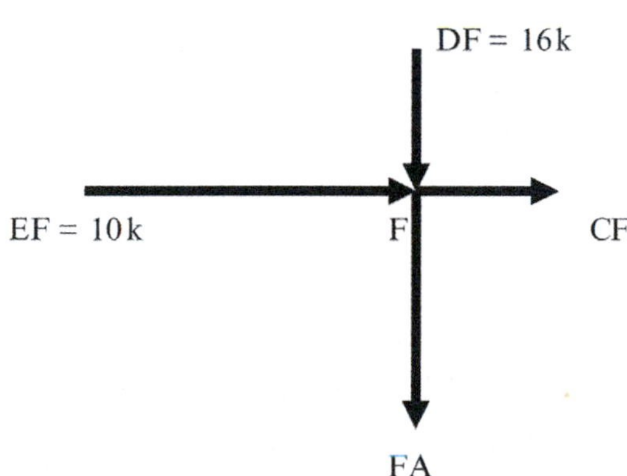

10. Solve the vertical and horizontal equilibrium equations:

$$[\Sigma F_x = 0]:$$

$$CF = \qquad (C)$$

$$[\Sigma F_y = 0]: \quad -16k - FA = 0$$

$$FA = 16k(C)$$

11. Finally, examine Joint C, and find the forces of member CA.

Note: CB_x *and* $CB_y = B_x$ *and* B_y

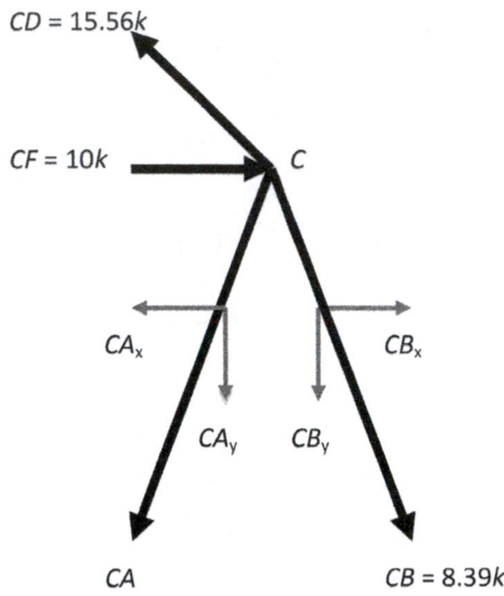

12. Solve the vertical and horizontal equilibrium equations to obtain CA. However, because we have already found CB, only one equilibrium equation needs to be solved to find CA.

$$[\Sigma F_x = 0]: \quad CF - CD_x - CA_x + CB_x = 0$$

$$CA = \qquad (T)$$

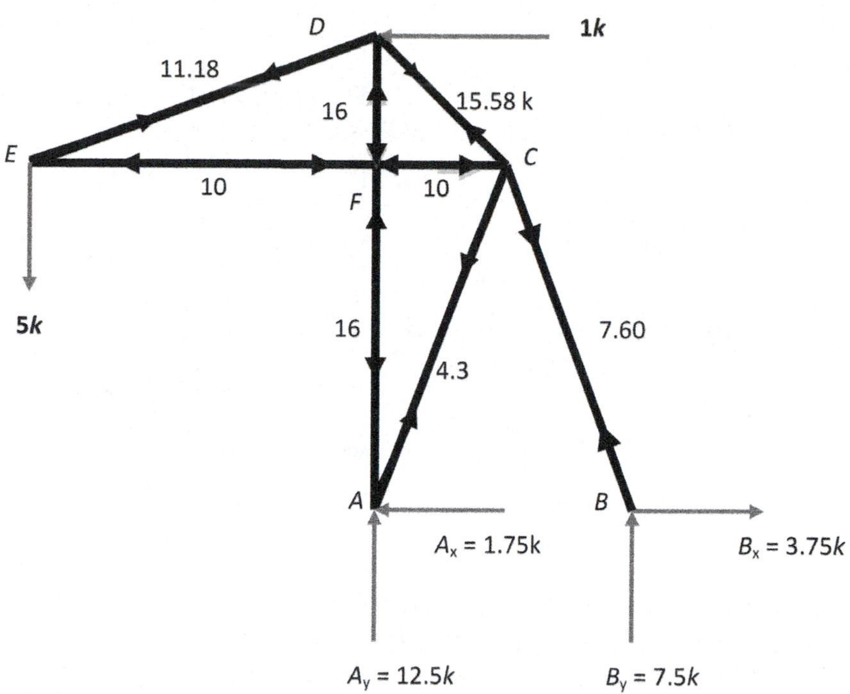

Problem 8.8

Step 1: Draw a FBD of the entire truss and determine the support reactions.

From symmetry of structure and loading, the reactions at support *A* and *G* are equal to 5*P*/2.

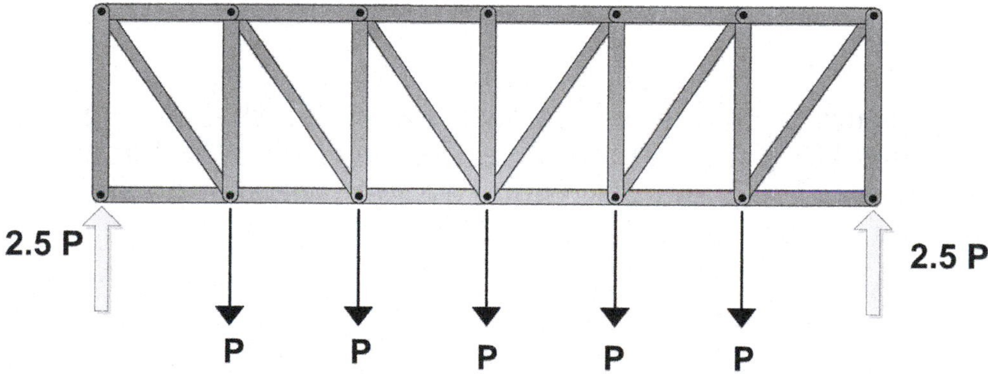

Step 2: Pass a vertical section as shown below and determine the sense of the internal forces.

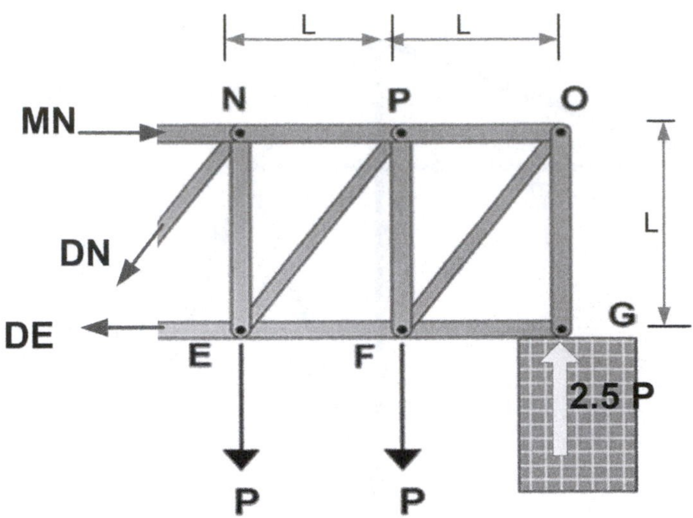

From the equilibrium equation in the y-direction, it is clear that the force in the diagonal member *DN* is tension. Also from the summation of moments about Joint *N*, the force in the member *DE* is in tension. Equilibrium of forces in the horizontal direction yields a compression force in the member *MN*.

Step 3: Repeat step 2 above to cover all the bays in the right side half of the truss. Since the truss is symmetrical, internal forces in the left half will be the same.

Step 4: Display the sense of the internal forces in the truss

Problem 8.9

The cantilever truss shown below is a part of a shading support structure. Using the method of section determine the forces in members *AC*, *BC*, and *BD*. (Hint: Pass only one section and then use the right side part of your section.)

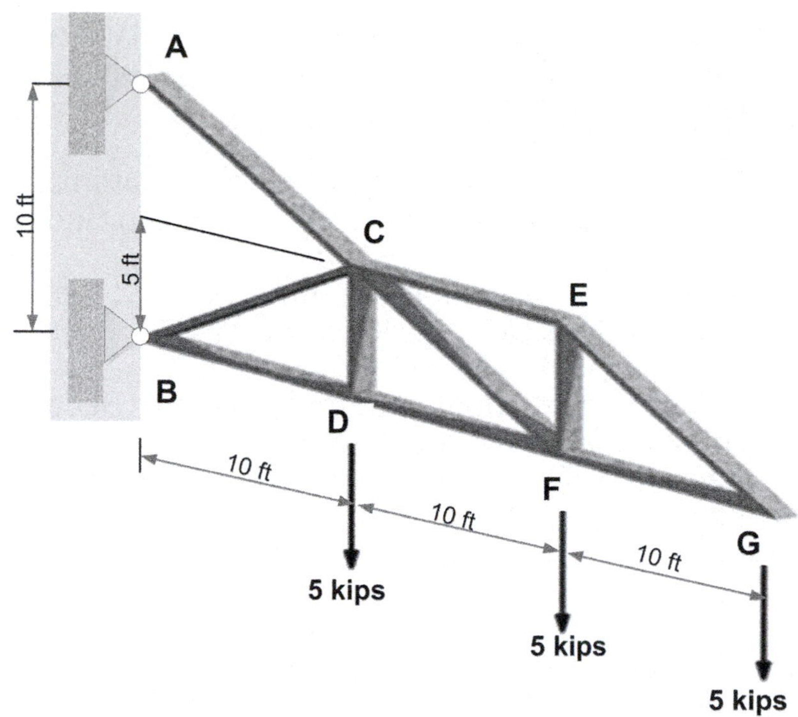

1. Draw the FBD of the sectioned system. We may make the section cut through members *AC*, *BC*, and *BD*:

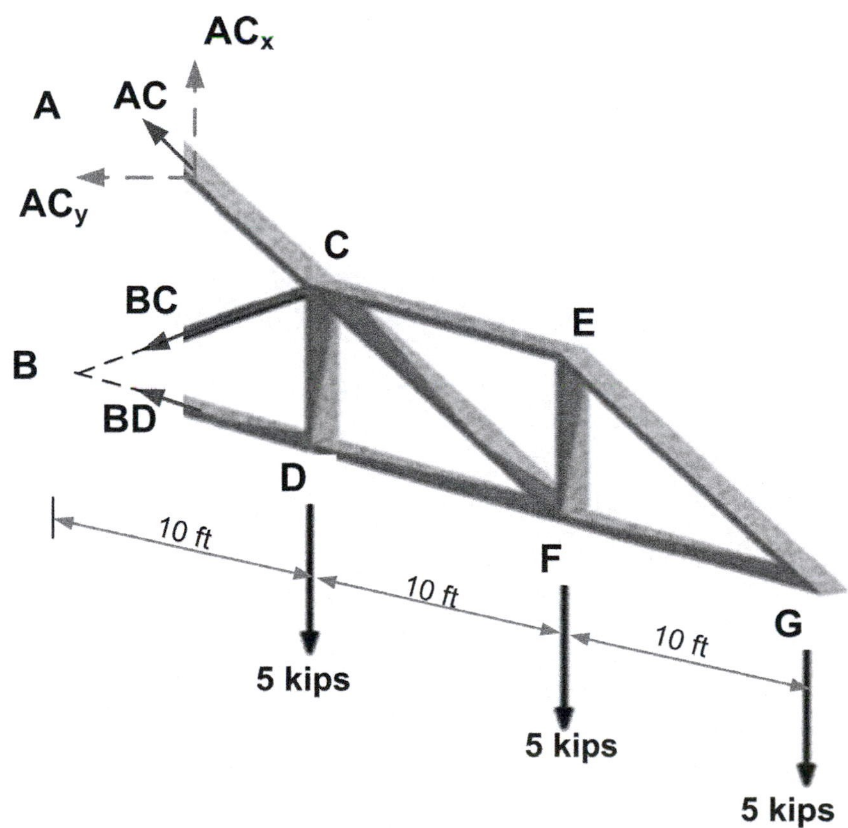

2. Take the moment about any point at which any two of the three unknown members intersect in order to solve for the third unknown.

For example, it is possible to take the moment about imaginary point *B*, the intersection of members *BC* and *BD*, to find *AC*.

It is also possible to take the moment about point *C*, the intersection of members *BC* and *AC*, to find *BD*.

We will take the moment about imaginary point *B*. Because *BC* and *BD* intersect at *B* and are, therefore, acting along the same line of action of *B*, they have absolutely no effect on the moment equilibrium of the system. They do not affect the moment about *B*. Thus, the solution of the third unknown, in this case *AC*, is completely independent of *BC* and *BD*.

3. Take the moment about point *B* to find the force of *AC*:

$$[\Sigma M_B = 0]:$$

$$AC_x(5') + AC_y(10') - 5k(10') - 5k(20') - 5k(30') = 0$$

$$AC = \qquad (T)$$

4. We are now left with two unknowns, *BC* and *BD*. Find the force of *BC* by taking the moment about *F*: $[\Sigma M_F = 0]$:

$$BC_x(5') + BC_y(10') + 5k(10') - 5k(10') = 0$$

$$BC =$$

5. Find the remaining force of member *BD* by taking the moment about *C*:

$$[\Sigma M_C = 0]:$$

$$BD = \qquad (C)$$

Problem 8.10

1. Since the total resultant force is 100 kips at bridge mid-span, each truss will support 50 kips as illustrated in figure 8.10.

2. Consider one truss and find the reactions at *A* and *E*:

$$[\Sigma M_A = 0]: \quad -50k\ (30') + E_y(60') = 0$$

$$E_y(60') = 1500$$

$$E_y = 25k$$

$$[[\Sigma F_y = 0]: \quad A_y + E_y - 50k = 0$$

$$A_y =$$

3. We may take the section cut through members *AB*, *BH*, and *HG*. Draw the FBD of the sectioned system and then use the left portion of the system.

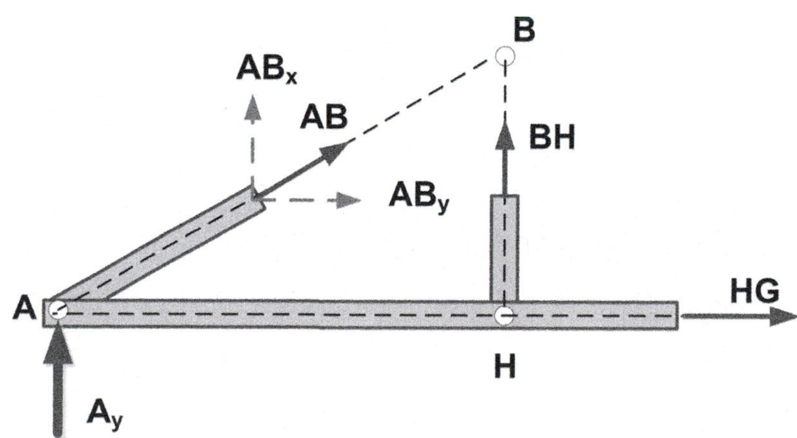

4. Resolve AB into its x- and y-components to find AB:

$$AB_x = \frac{3}{\sqrt{13}} AB$$

$$AB_y = \frac{2}{\sqrt{12}} AB$$

5. Take the moment about H to find AB:

$[\Sigma M_H = 0]$:

$AB =$ (C)

6. Take the moment about A to find BH:

$[\Sigma M_A = 0]$: $BH(15') = 0$

$BH = 0$

7. Take the moment about B to find HG:

$[\Sigma M_B = 0]$:

$HG =$ (T)

Problem 8.11

1. Find the reactions at A and J by taking the moment about either point:

$$\Sigma M_A = 0: \quad -20\text{ k }(30') - 20\text{ k }(60') - 25\text{ k }(90') - 25\text{ k }(120'\text{m}) + J_y\,(30') = 0$$

$J_y =$

2. Equilibrium of vertical forces to find A_y:

$$\Sigma F_y = 0: \quad 235\text{ k} - A_y = 0$$

$A_y =$

$\Sigma F_x = 0$:

$J_x =$

3. Cut a section through AB, AI, and JI (see figure 8.11b).

$AB = 235$ kips (Tension)

$\Sigma F_x = 0$: $\quad BJ_x - J_x = 0$

$BJ_x =$

$BJ_y = BJ_x =$

$\Sigma F_y = 0$:

$IJ =$

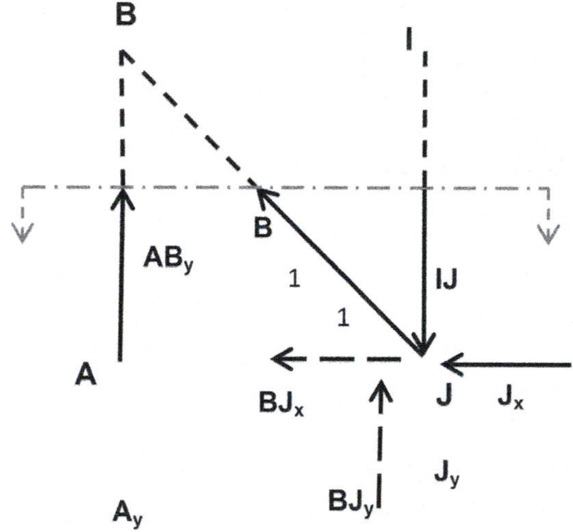

Figure 8.11b

Problem 8.12

1. Find the reactions at F and A by taking the moment about either point:

$$[\Sigma M_F = 0]:$$

$$-2k(12') - 1k(48') - 2k(36') + 2k(24') + 1k(12') - A_y(60') = 0$$

$$A_y(60') = 192$$

$$A_y = 3.2k$$

$[\Sigma F_y = 0]$:

$$F_y =$$

$[\Sigma F_x = 0]$: $A_x - 2k = 0$

$$A_x = 2k$$

2. Cut a section through members *BC*, *BJ*, *IC*, and *IJ* (figure 8.12b):

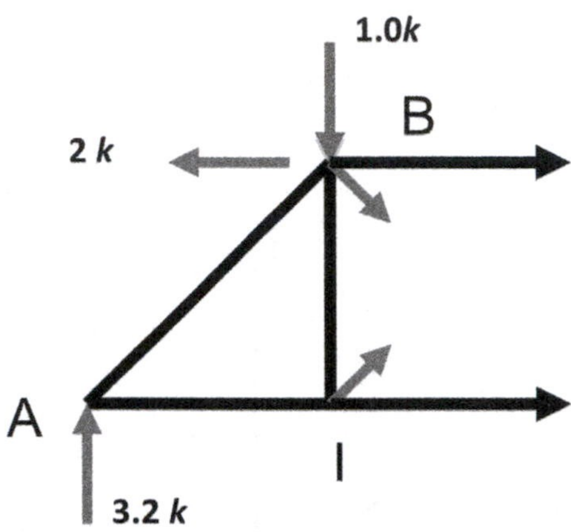

Figure 8.12b

3. Solve the vertical equation of equilibrium to determine the effective tension counter.

   Note: The unbalance between the upward force of 3.2k at A and the downward applied force of 1.0 k at B is a downward force of 2.2k. Therefore, member BJ is the effective tension counter. Counter CI, therefore, is ineffective.

   $[\Sigma F_y = 0]$: $3.2k - 1k - BJ_y = 0$

$$BJ = \frac{2}{\sqrt{2}} BJ_y$$

$$BJ = \quad \text{(T)}$$

4. Cut a second section through members *CD*, *DH*, *JD* and *JH*:

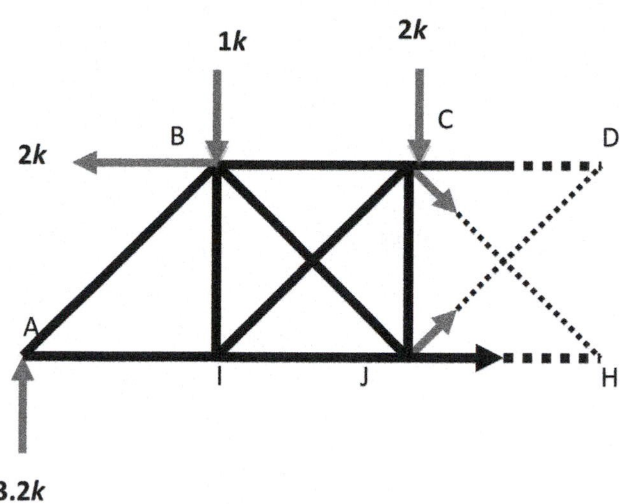

5. Solve the vertical equation of equilibrium to determine the effective tension counter:

$[\Sigma F_y = 0]$:

$HC =$ (T)

6. Cut a third section through members *CB*, *CJ*, *IB*, and *IJ*:

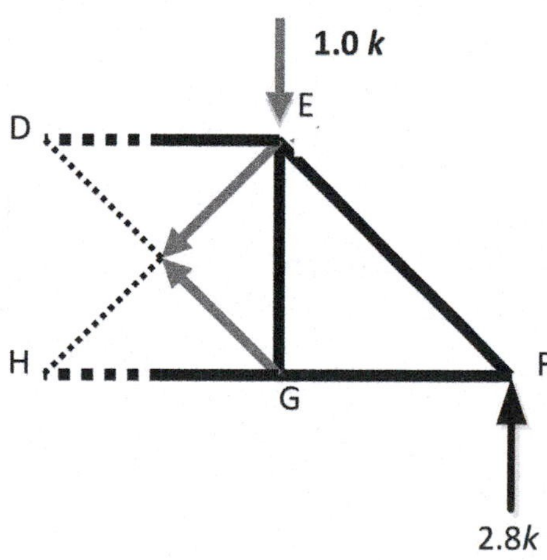

7. Solve the vertical equilibrium equation to determine the effective tension counter:

$$[\Sigma F_y = 0]:$$

$$EH = \qquad \text{(T)}$$

CHAPTER 9

Problem 9.1

Refer to page 265 in your textbook *Building Structures: Fundamentals of Crossover Design* by Nawari & Kuenstle.

Problem 9.2

For the structural members cross-sections shown below determine the moment of inertia about the x- and y-axis along with the respective values for the radii of gyration.

(a) For a rectangular section, the moment of inertia is given by:

$I_x = bh^3/12$

$$I_{xx} = \frac{(4)(12)^3}{12} = 576 in^4$$

$I_y = hb^3/12$

$$I_{xx} = \frac{(12)(4)^3}{12} = 64 in^4$$

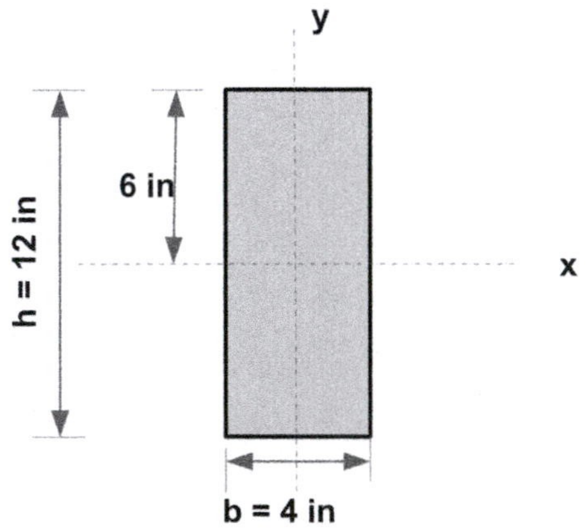

(b) $$I_{xx} = I_{xx\,rectangle} - I_{xx\,hole}$$

$$I_{xx} = \frac{bh^3}{12} - \frac{\pi r^4}{4}$$

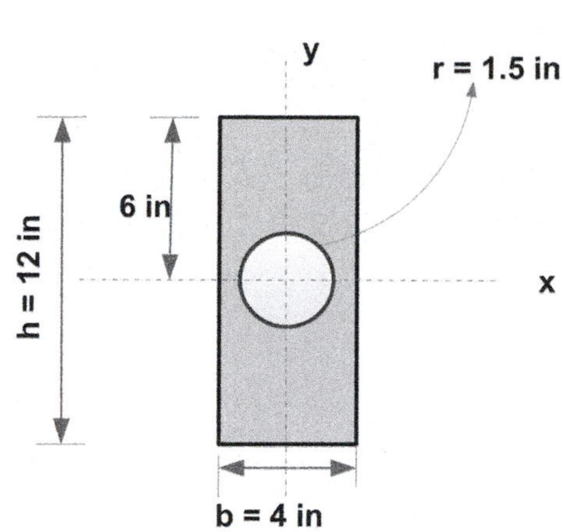

$$I_{xx} =$$

$$I_{yy} = I_{yy\,rectangle} - I_{yy\,hole}$$

$$I_{yy} = \frac{hb^3}{12} - \frac{\pi r^4}{4}$$

$$I_{yy} ==$$

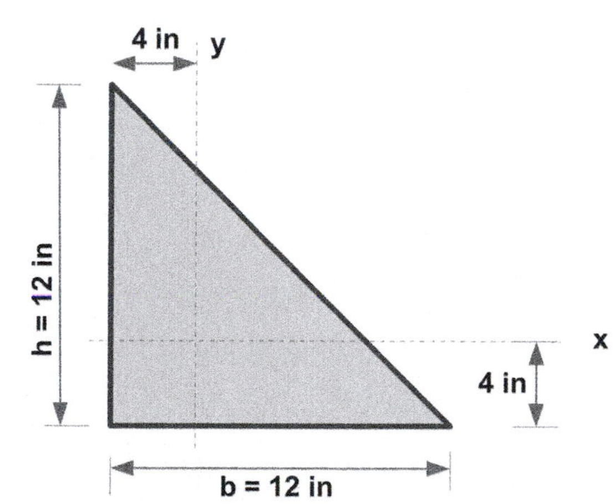

(a) $$I_{xx} = \frac{bh^3}{36}$$

$$I_{xx} = \frac{(12)(12)^3}{36} = 576in^4$$

$$I_{yy} = I_{yy} =$$

(b) $$I_{xx} = I_{xx\,triangle} - I_{xx\,hole}$$

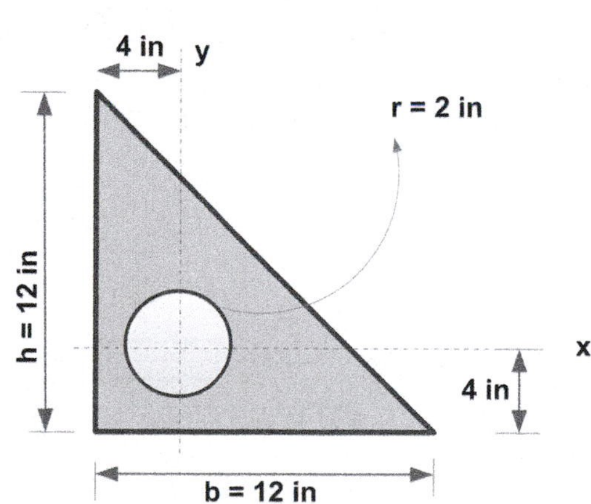

$$I_{xx} ==$$

$$I_{yy} = I_{yy\,triangle} - I_{yy\,hole}$$

$$I_{yy} ==$$

CHAPTER 10

Problem 10.1

Refer to pages 273–275 in your textbook *Building Structures: Fundamentals of Crossover Design* by Nawari & Kuenstle.

Problem 10.2

Answer:

Problem 10.3

$$f_c = \frac{P}{A}$$

$$f_c =$$

Problem 10.4

1. Consider the equilibrium of Joint *D* and determine the force in member *CD*:

$$[\Sigma F_x = 0]: \quad CD - 1\,kip = 0$$

Therefore, the force in member *CD* is compressive and equal to 1.0 kips.

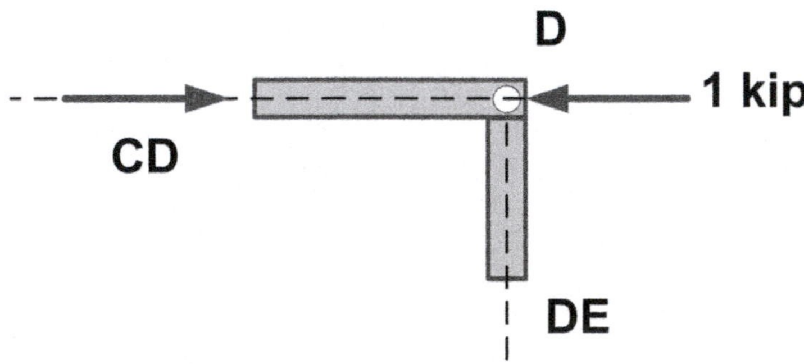

2. Determine the compressive stress of member AB:

$$f_c = \frac{P}{A}$$

$$f_c =$$

Problem 10.5

1. Find the total load of the marquee produced by the dead load and wind load:

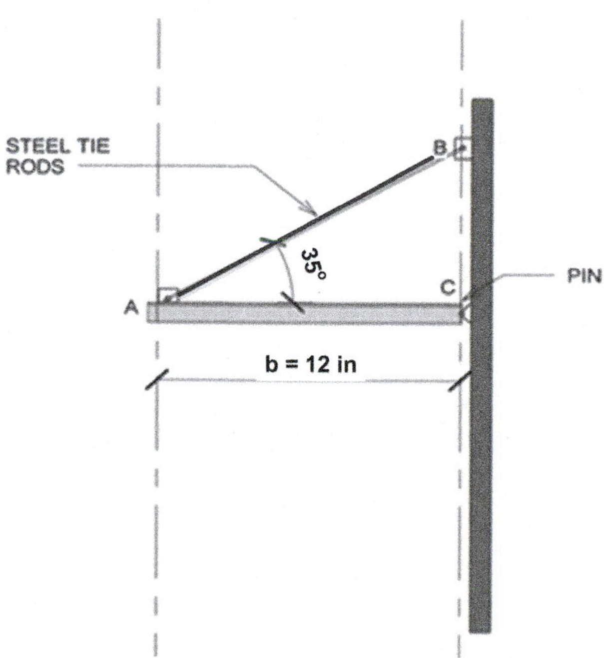

$$\text{Total load} = (150psf)(12')(24') = 43,200\ lb = 43.20\ k$$

2. Determine the load supported by each cable:

$$\frac{43.2k}{2} = 21.6k \text{ per cable}$$

3. Find the force in AB by taking the moment about C:

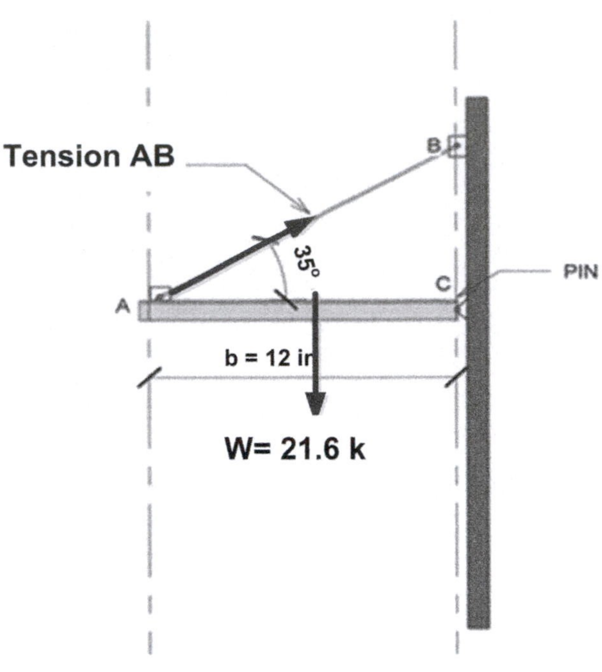

$$[\Sigma M_C = 0]: \quad 216k(6') - AB_y(12') = 0$$

$$AB =$$

4. Find the cross-sectional area of the cables required to hold up the marquee:

$$f_t = \frac{P}{A}$$

$$A =$$

5. The closest available size rod, to the nearest $\frac{1}{16}$" is:

6. Determine if the actual tensile stress in *AB* can be accommodated by the allowable stress of the A-36 steel:

$$f_{t_{Actual}} =$$

$$f_{t_{Allowable}} = 24ksi$$

7. Find the diameter of the required cable:

$$A = \frac{\pi D^2}{4}$$

Solving for *D*, we have $D =$

Problem 10.6

Using the given information, evaluate the strain by using the strain equation:

$$\varepsilon = \frac{\delta}{L}$$

$$\varepsilon =$$

Problem 10.7

1. Determine the applied load of a 12" strip of the wall.

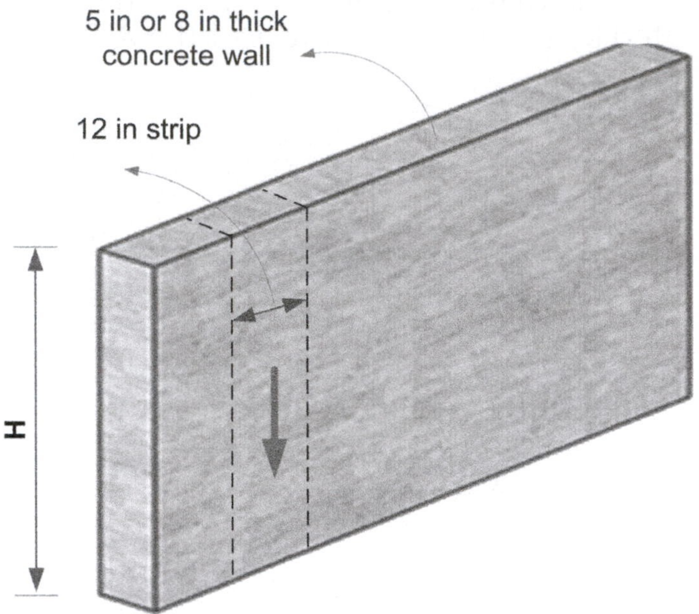

Volume of wall = length X width X height

= 12" x 5" x H
= 60H in^3

Weight of wall = Density X Volume
= 145 lb/ft^3 x 60Hin^3 x (1/1728)
= 5.035H lb

2. Determine the compressive stress at the bottom of the wall:

$f_c = P/A$
= (5.035H lb) / (12" x 5")
=

3. Given that the maximum allowable compressive stress is 0.15 ksi find the height of the wall.

0.15 ksi = 0.0839H psi
H =

4. Repeat the problem with the wall 8" wide:

Problem 10.8

1. For (a), determine the total weight of the wire:

$$0.040\, {}^{lb}\!/\!_{ft} \times 500ft = 20lb$$

2. Determine the bearing area of the wire:

$$A = \frac{\pi D^2}{4}$$

$$A =$$

3. Find the tensile stress of the wire:

$$f_t = \frac{P}{A}$$

$$f_t =$$

4. For (b), determine the allowable tensile stress given the ultimate tensile stress and the safety factor, *S.F.*:

$$F_{Allowable} = \frac{F_{Ultimate}}{S.F.}$$

$$F_{Allowable} =$$

5. Determine the allowable load, $P_{Allowable}$, that can be safely supported:

$$P_{Allowable} = F_{Allowable} \times Area$$

$$P_{Allowable} =$$

6. Subtract the weight of the wire from the allowable load to obtain the maximum weight that can be safely supported:

$$W_{Maximum} =$$

$$W_{Maximum} =$$

Problem 10.9

1. Here, the shortening of the cylinder is the total deformation of the cylinder, δ.

$$\varepsilon = \frac{\delta}{L}$$

2. Solve for δ:

$$\varepsilon = \frac{\delta}{L}$$

$$\delta = \varepsilon L$$

$$\delta =$$

Problem 10.10

1. Consider a 1 ft length of wall:

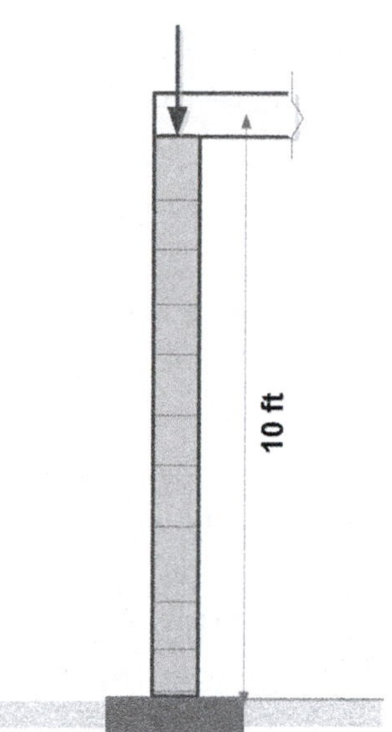

2. Find the total load at the base of each wall:

$$Roof = 1' \times 24' \times 100 psf = 2,400\ lb$$

$$Wind = 1' \times 24' \times 30 psf = 720\ lb$$

Brick =

Total Load at Base of Wall =

3. Determine the bearing area of the brick:

Bearing Area =

4. Determine the compressive stress at the base of the wall:

$$f_p = \frac{P}{A}$$

$$f_p =$$

Problem 10.11

(i). The thermal axial expansion is given by: $\Delta L = L\alpha \Delta T$

(ii). If the concrete beam is prevented from rotation at both ends, the maximum thermal bending stress is given by:

$$f_{bt} = E\Delta T/2 =$$

Problem 10.12

An office building has exposed steel framing of 100 ft high (see figure 10.12). The south side of the building is subjected to direct sun and reaches a temperature of 60 °F while the north side remains at 5 °F. Determine the overall change in length of columns under this condition. Assume the thermal expansion coefficient of steel as $\alpha = 7.3\ (10^{-6})\ °F^{-1}$

The thermal axial expansion is given by: $\Delta L = L\alpha \Delta T$
Where $\Delta T = 60 - 10 = 50\ ^0F$

$$\Delta L =$$

Problem 10.13

1. The thermal strain is expressed as: $\varepsilon = \alpha \Delta T$

Assuming the curtain wall and the supporting concrete frame are not connected and free to deform, then we have:

The total thermal strain in the curtain wall is

$$\varepsilon_{al} = \alpha \Delta T = (13.5 \text{ x}10\text{–}^{6})(75\text{–}30) = 607.5 \text{ x}10\text{–}^{6}$$

And the total thermal strain in the concrete frame is

$$\varepsilon_{conc} = \alpha \Delta T =$$

2. Since the wall is attached to the concrete frame, then, the net strain is obtained from:

$$\varepsilon_{net} = \varepsilon_{al} - \varepsilon_{conc} =$$

3. Thermal compressive stress on the curtain wall is expressed as:

$$f_T = \varepsilon_{net} E =$$

CHAPTER 11

Problem 11.1

1. Determine the reactions at A and D:

$$[\Sigma M_A = 0]: \quad -5k(10') - 5k(20') + D_y(30') = 0$$

$$D_y = 5k$$

$$[\Sigma F_y = 0]: \quad A_y - 5k - 5k + 5k = 0$$

$$A_y = 5k$$

2. Construct the shear diagram and determine V_{Max}:

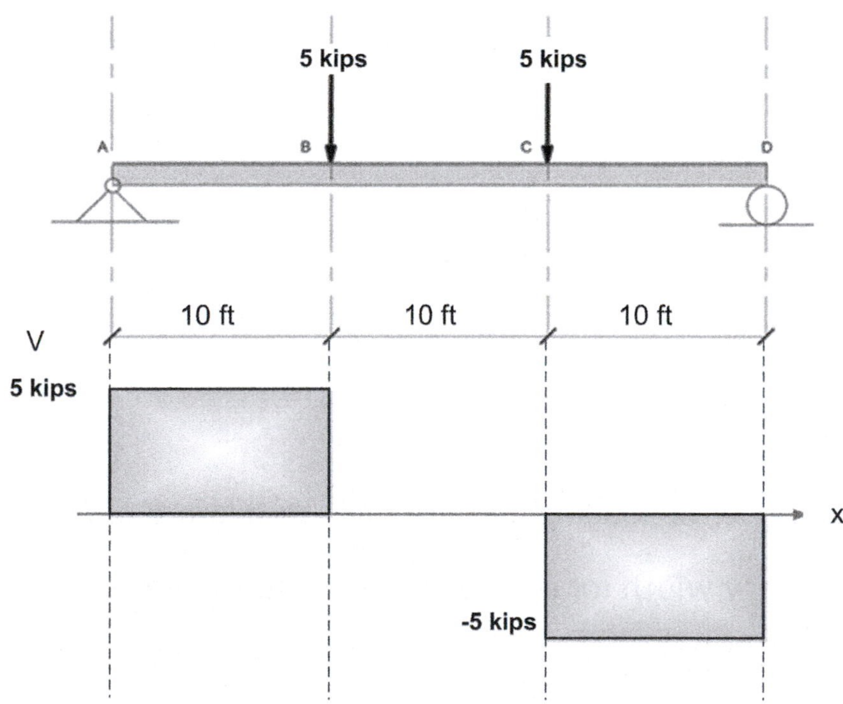

3. Construct the moment diagram and determine M_{Max}:

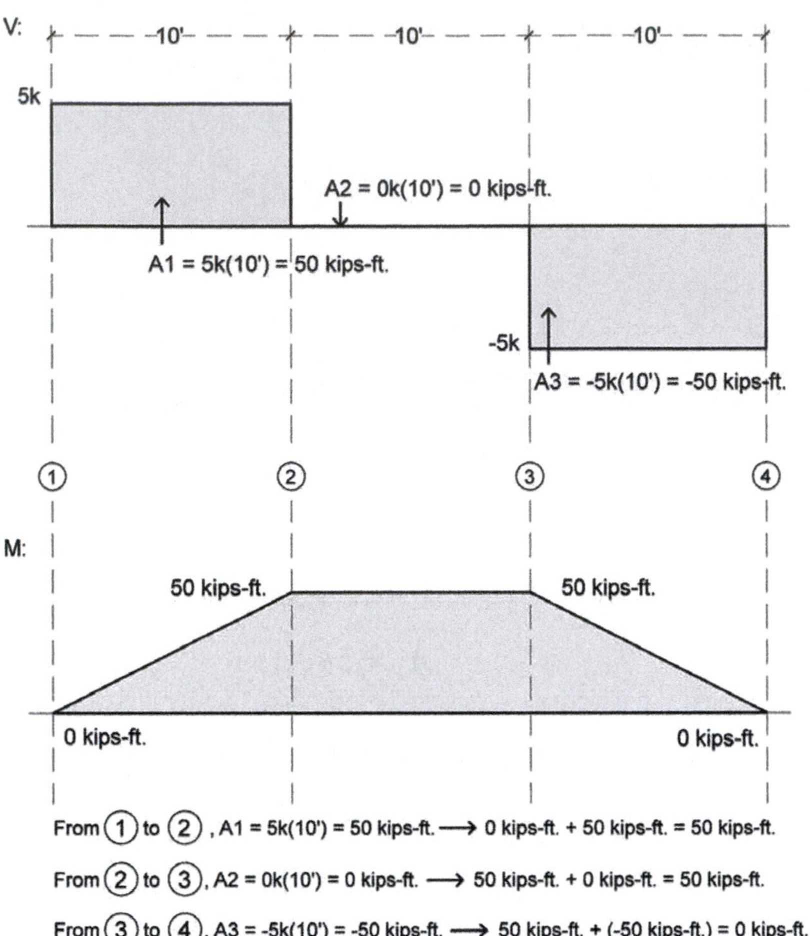

$$V_{Max} = 5\ k$$
$$M_{Max} = 50\ \text{k–ft}$$

Problem 11.2

1. Determine the loading and reactions of beam B & C:

The tributary width for each beam is = 6 ft, therefore, the beam loading is:

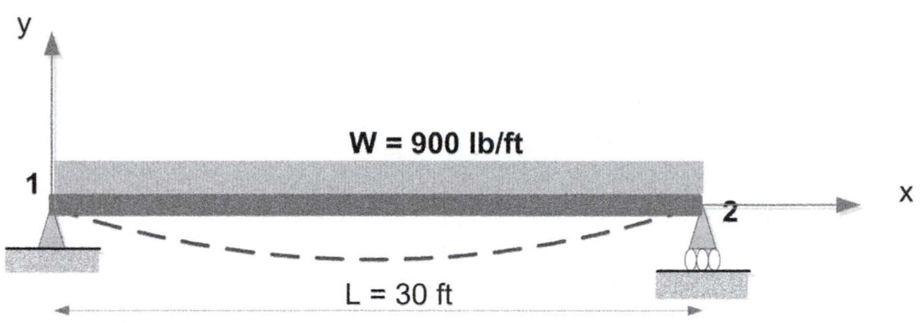

$w = 150$ psf x 6ft = 900 lb/ft
The reactions at 1 and 2 are = $R1 = R2 = wL/2$ = (900 lb/ft)(30 ft)/2 = 13,500 lb = 13.5 kips

2. Construct the shear diagram:

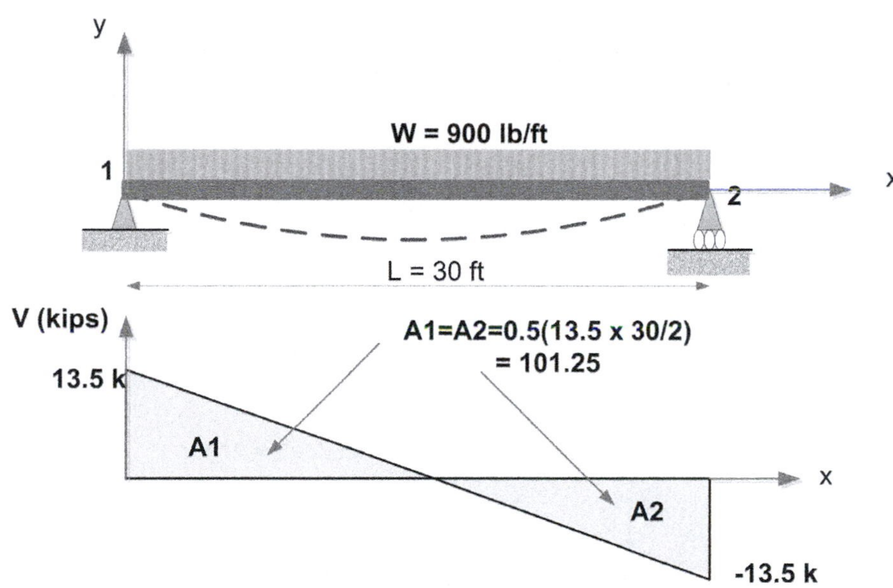

3. Determine the areas under the curves of the shear diagram in order to obtain the values of the moment diagram. Then, determine V_{Max} and M_{Max}:

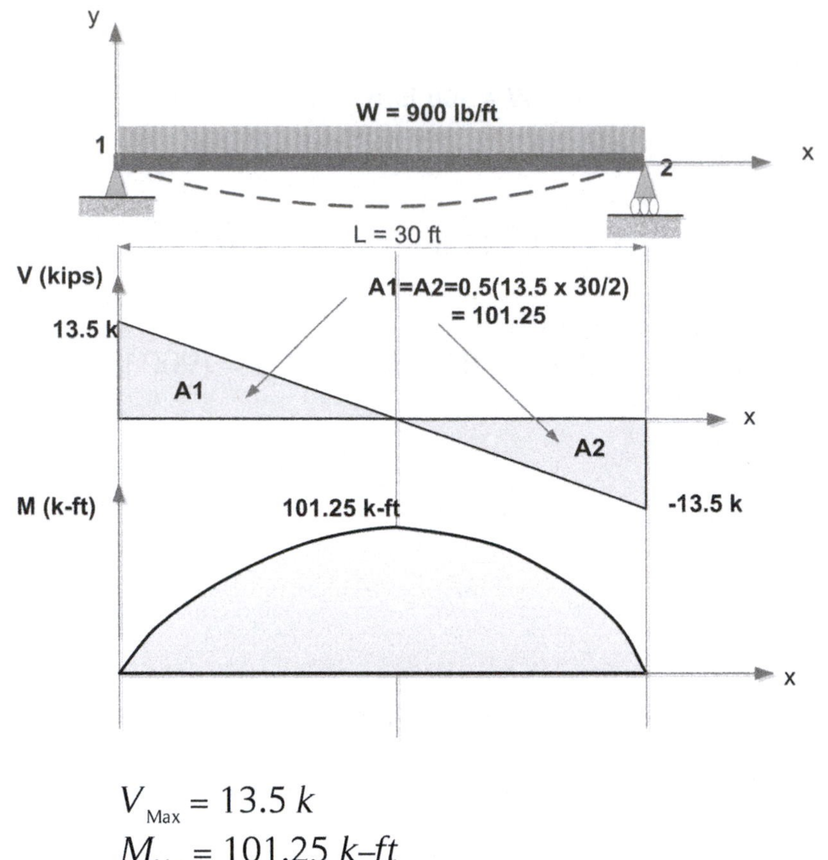

$V_{Max} = 13.5\ k$

$M_{Max} = 101.25\ k\text{–}ft$

4. Consider the girder *ABCD* and construct the loading diagram.

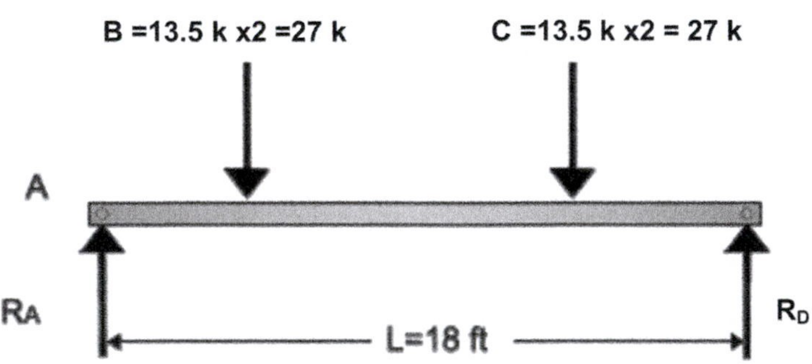

5. Determine the reactions at *A* and *B*, then draw the shear force diagram:

From the symmetry $R_A = R_B = 27$ kips

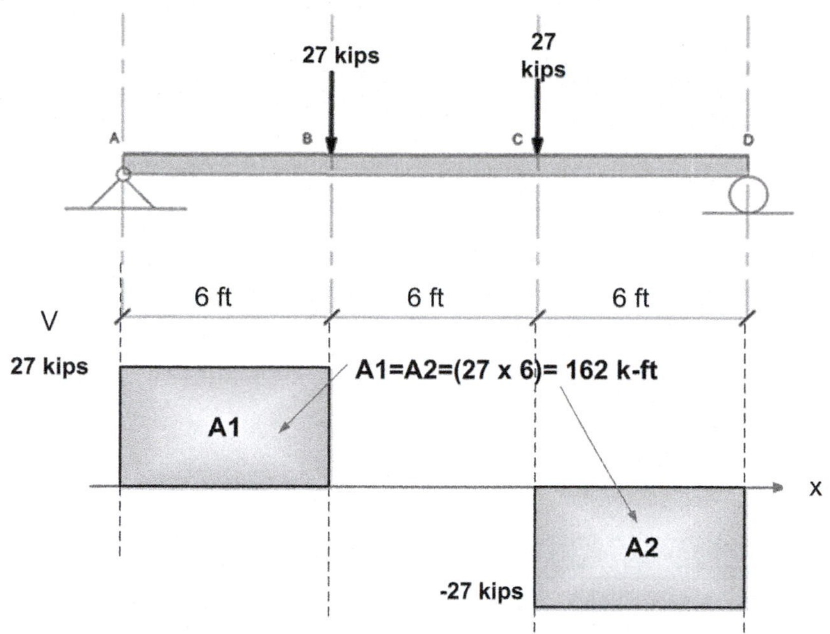

6. Determine the areas under the curves of the shear diagram in order to obtain the values of the moment diagram. Then, determine $V_{\text{Max and}} M_{\text{Max}}$:

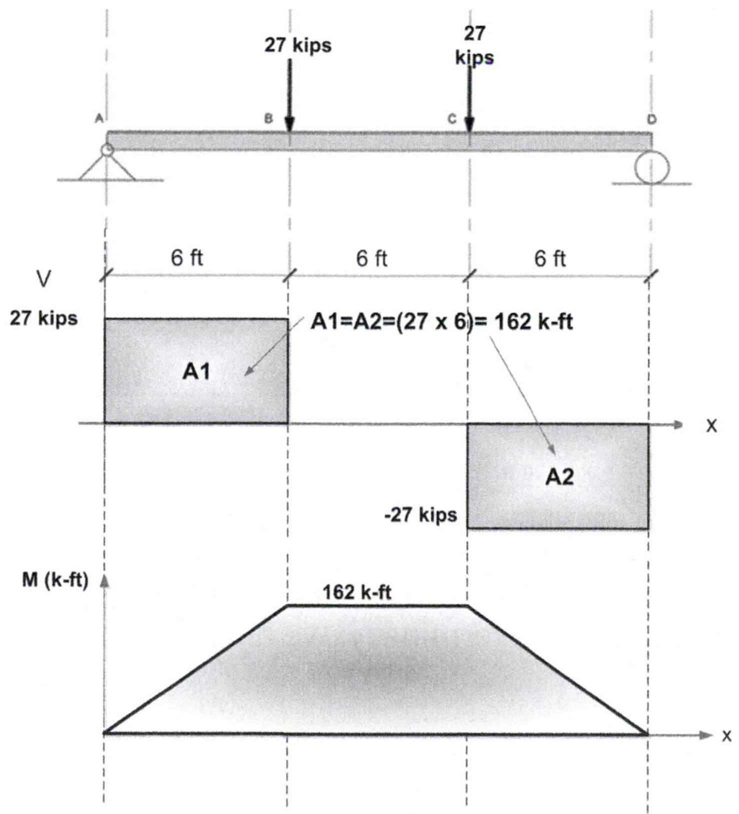

Therefore, the maximum shear force and bending moment are

$$V_{Max} = 27.0\,k$$
$$M_{Max} =$$

Problem 11.3

(a)
1. Draw the FBD:

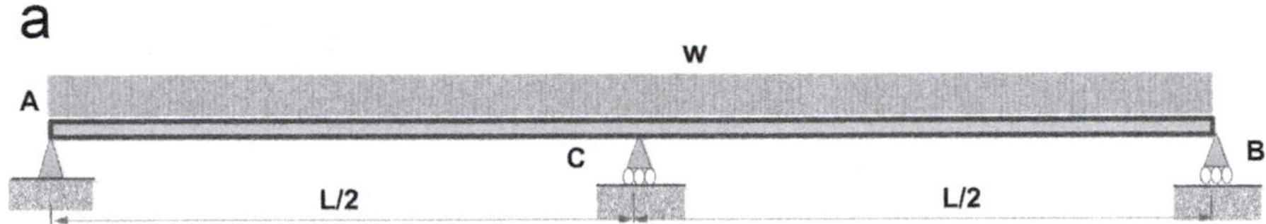

2. The FBD of beam (a) is given in figure 11.3d. Now applying the equation for indeterminacy, we have:

$$R - E = 4 - 3 = 1 \rightarrow 1^{st} \text{ Degree Indeterminacy.}$$

(b)
1. Draw FBD:

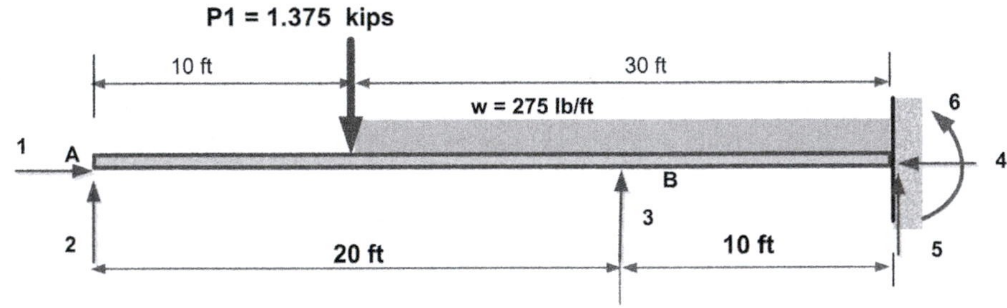

2. The FBD of beam (b) is given in figure 11.3e. Now applying the equation for indeterminacy, we have:

$$R - E =$$

(c)
Draw the FBD and determine the number of reactions required. In this case there are 5 reactions required. Now applying the equation for indeterminacy, we have:

$$R - E =$$

Problem 11.4

1. Determine the reactions at A and C:

$$[\Sigma M_A = 0]: \quad -10(10') - 2\,{}^{k}\!/_{ft}\,(30')(25') + C_y(40') = 0$$

$$C_y = 40\ k$$

$$[\Sigma F_y = 0]:$$

$$A_y =$$

2. Construct the shear diagram.

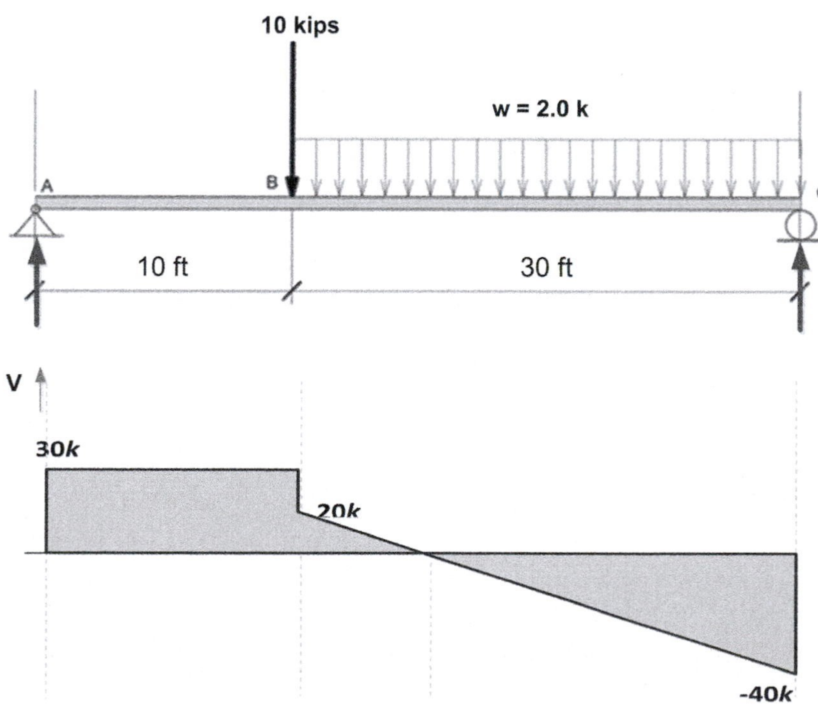

3. Determine the areas under the curves of the shear diagram in order to obtain the values of the moment diagram. Then, determine V_{Max} and M_{Max}:

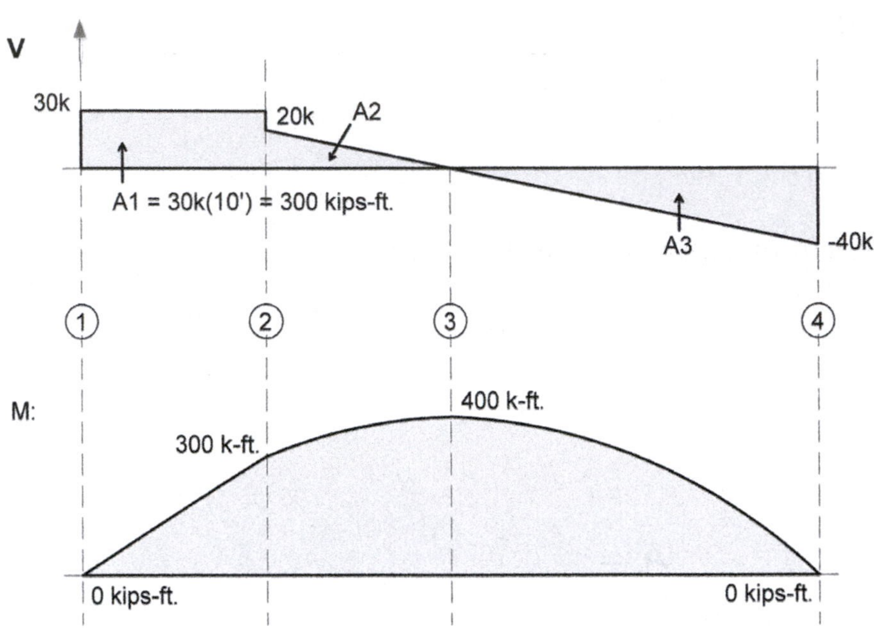

From (1) to (2), A1 = 30k(10') = 300 kips-ft. ⟶
0 kips-ft. + 300 kips-ft. = 300 kips-ft.

From (2) to (3) , A2 = Recognize similar triangles in order to obtain distance and area using proportions.

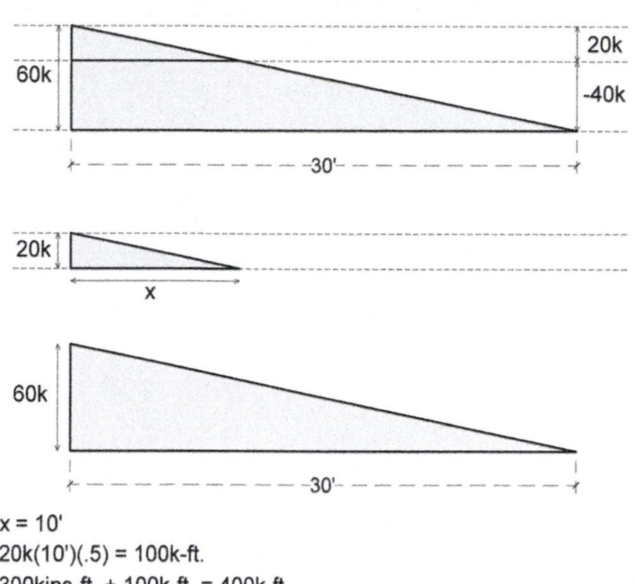

x = 10'
20k(10')(.5) = 100k-ft.
300kips-ft. + 100k-ft. = 400k-ft.

From (3) to (4), A3 = Use information found above to obtain distance.

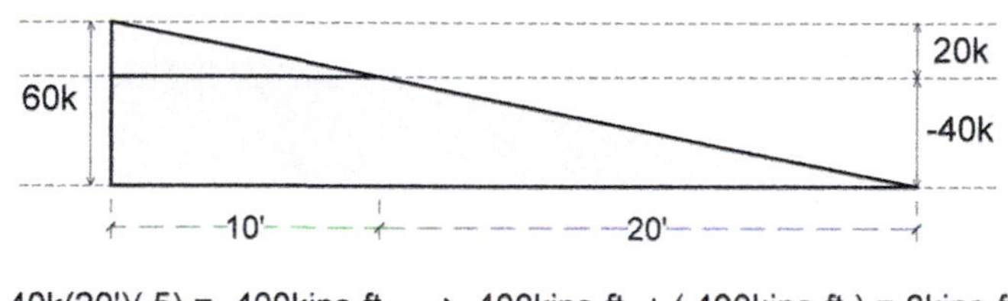

-40k(20')(.5) = -400kips-ft. ⟶ 400kips-ft. + (-400kips-ft.) = 0kips-ft.

Thus, maximum shear force and bending moment are

$$V_{Max} = -40\ k$$
$$M_{Max} =$$

Problem 11.5

1. Determine the reactions at A and B:

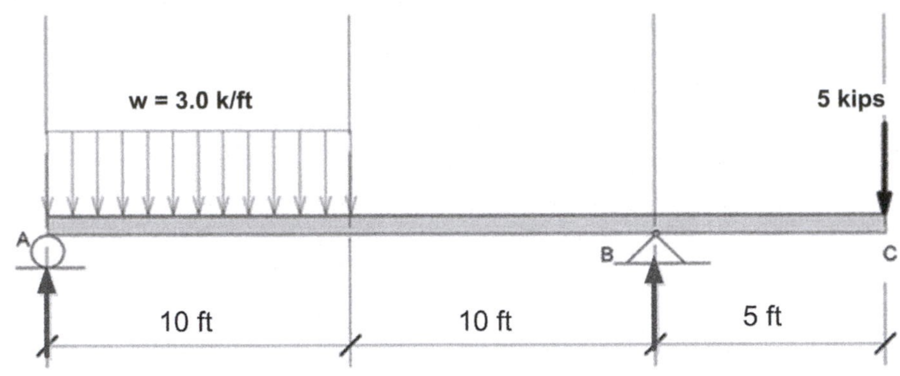

$$[\Sigma M_A = 0]: \; -30\,(5') + B_y(20') - 5\,k(25') = 0$$

$$B_y = 13.75\text{ k}$$

$$[\Sigma F_y = 0]:$$

$$A_y =$$

2. Construct the shear and moment diagrams. Determine V_{Max} and $M_{Max.}$

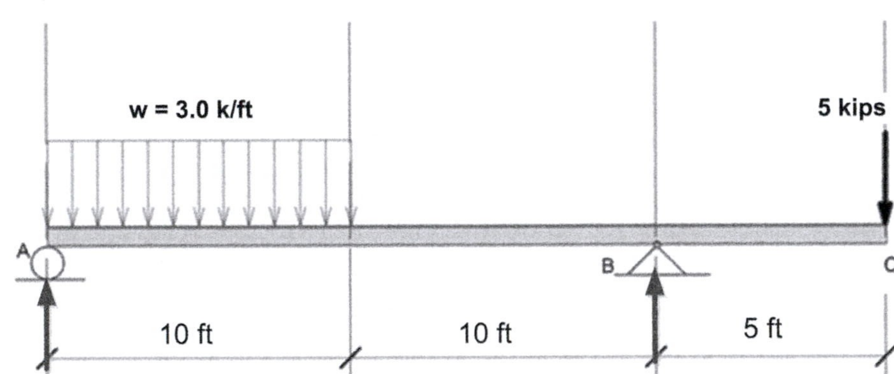

V:

3. Determine the areas under the curves of the shear diagram in order to obtain the values of the moment diagram:

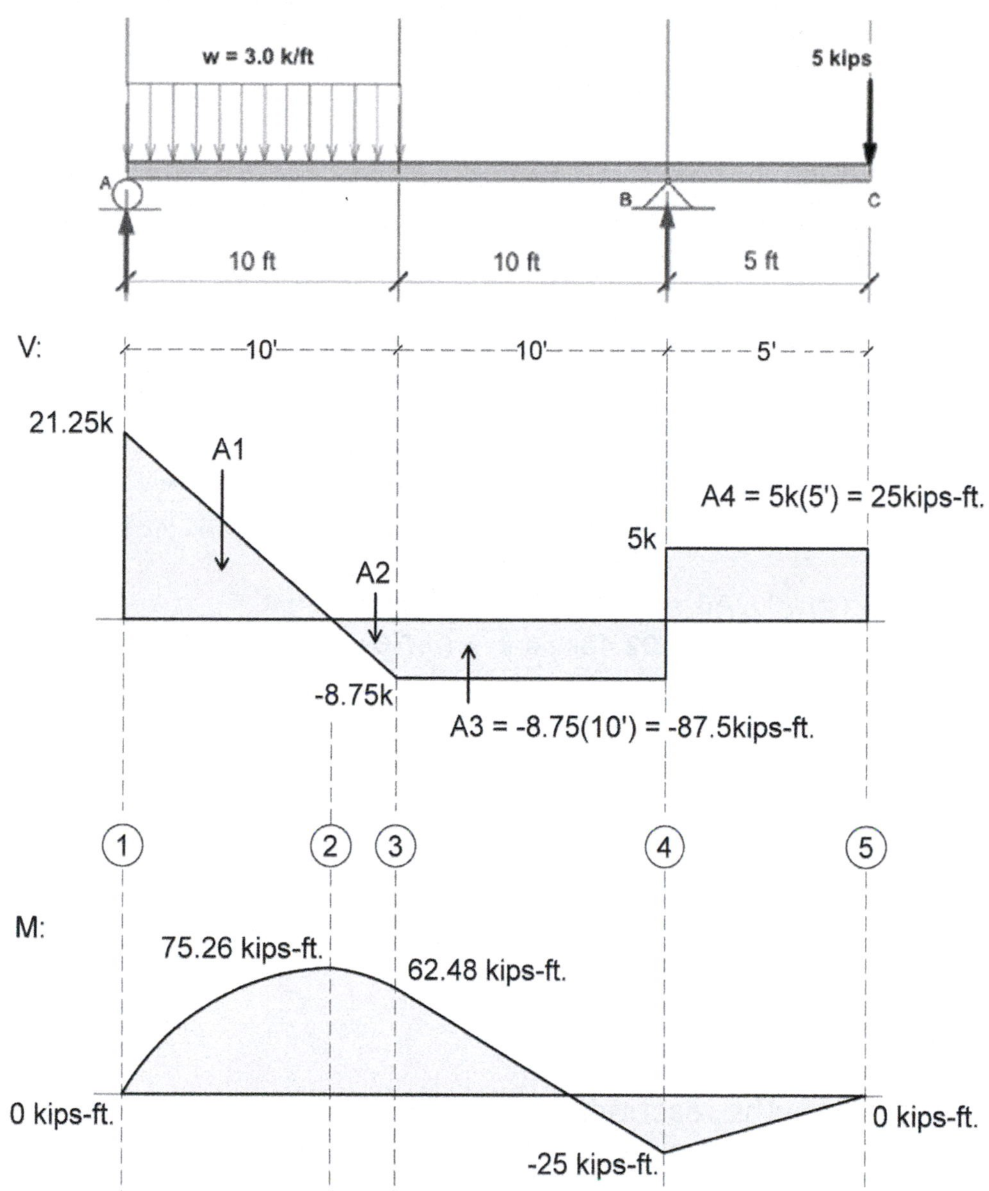

From (1) to (2), A1 = Recognize similar triangles in order to obtain distance and area using proportions.

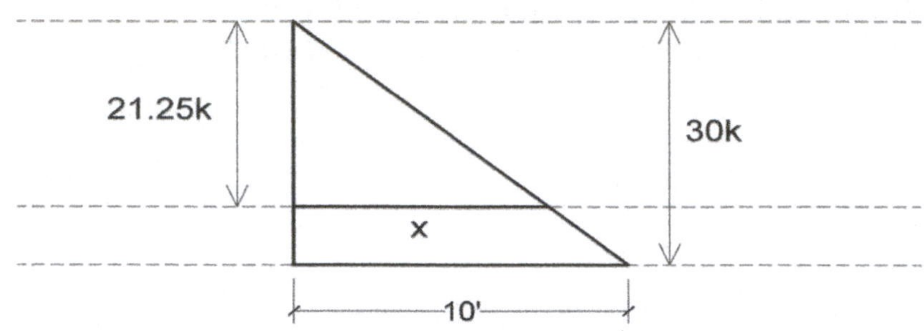

x = 7.08'

10'-7.08' = 2.92'

A1 = 21.25k(7.083')(.5) = 75.26kips-ft. ⟶

0k + 75.26kips-ft. = 75.26kips-ft.

From (2) to (3), A2 = -8.75k(2.92')(.5) = -12.78kips-ft. ⟶

75.26kips-ft. + (-12.78kips-ft.) = 62.48kips-ft.

From (3) to (4), A3 = -8.75(10') = -87.5kips-ft. ⟶

62.48kips-ft. + (-87.5kips-ft.) = -25kips-ft.

From (4) to (5), A4 = 5k(5') = 25kips-ft. ⟶

-25kips-ft. + 25kips-ft. = 0kips-ft.

$$V_{Max} = 21.5 \text{ k}$$
$$M_{Max} =$$

Problem 11.6

1. Determine the reactions at *A* and *B*:

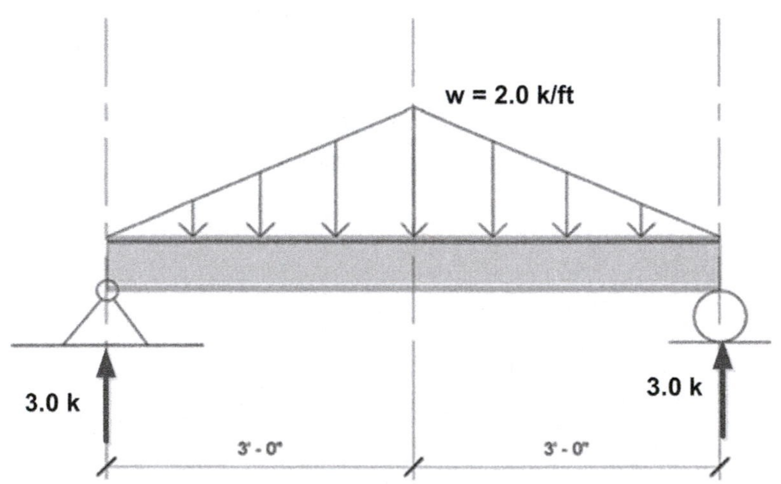

Total load = $2.0\,k\ 6'.5 = 6.0\,k$

$A_y =$

$B_y =$

2. Construct the shear force diagram:

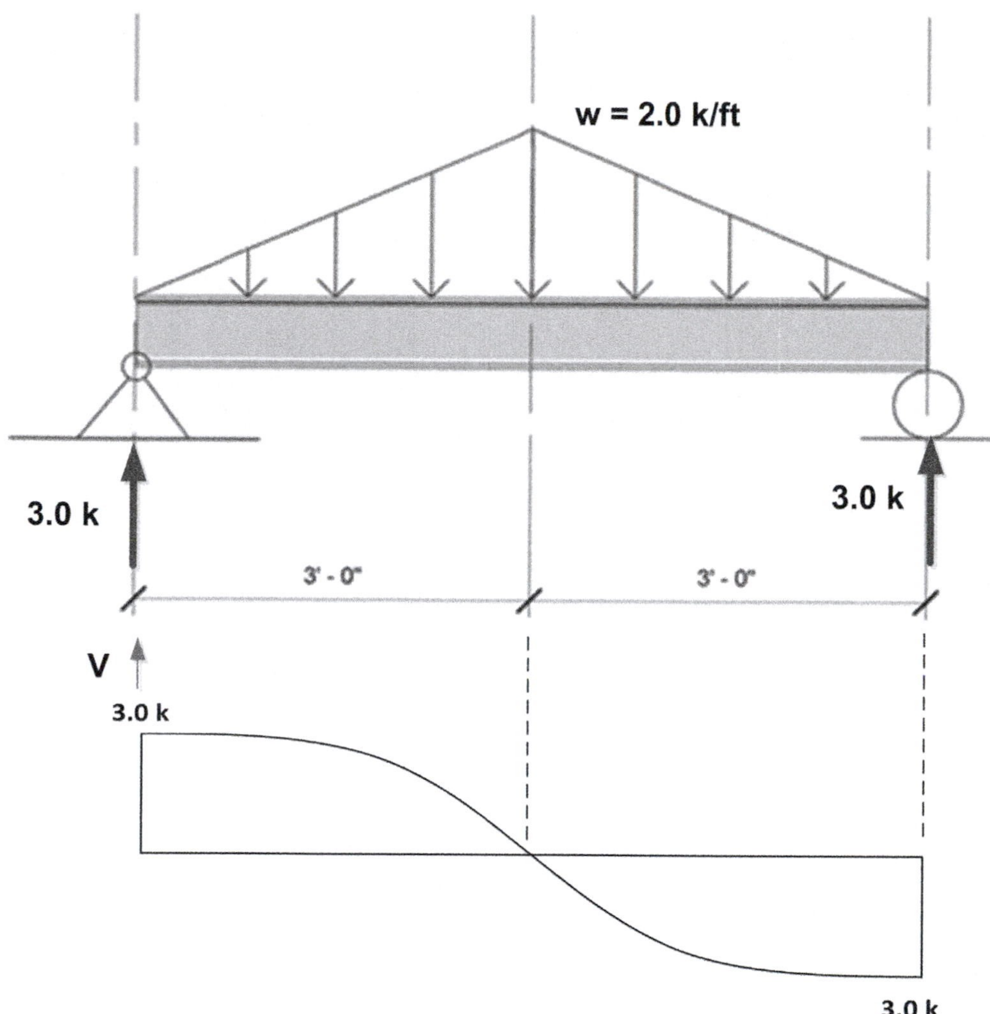

3. Determine the areas under the curves of the shear diagram in order to obtain the values of the moment diagram:

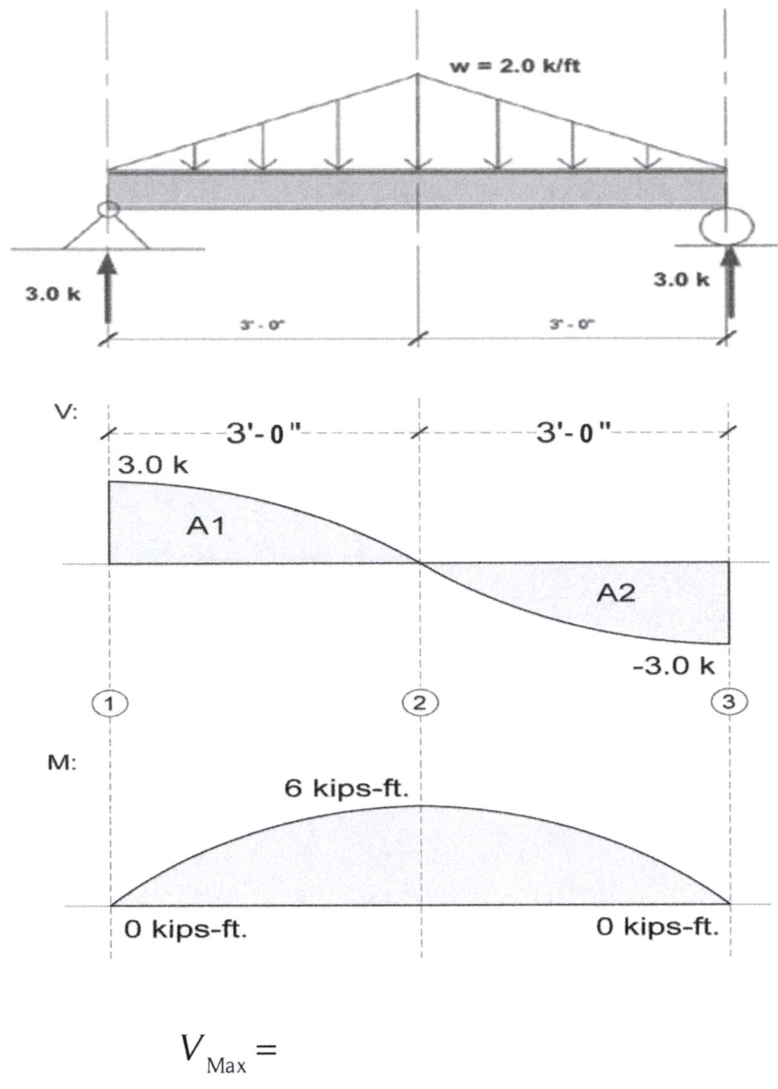

$$V_{Max} =$$
$$M_{Max} =$$

Problem 11.7

For the identical beams having spans in the ratio 1:2, the shorter beam carries eight-ninths of the load, whereas the longer beam carries one-ninth of the load (see textbook: *Building Structures* by N. Nawari and M. Kuenstle, page 359):

$$P_{AB} = 8P_{CD}$$
$$9k = P_{AB} + P_{CD}$$

Problem 11.8

In a beam grid system, two cantilever steel beams are crossed at 90° in plan as illustrated in figure 11.8 below. The two beams have the same cross-section and beam *AB* is twice as long as beam *BC*. Determine how much of the load is taken by each beam.

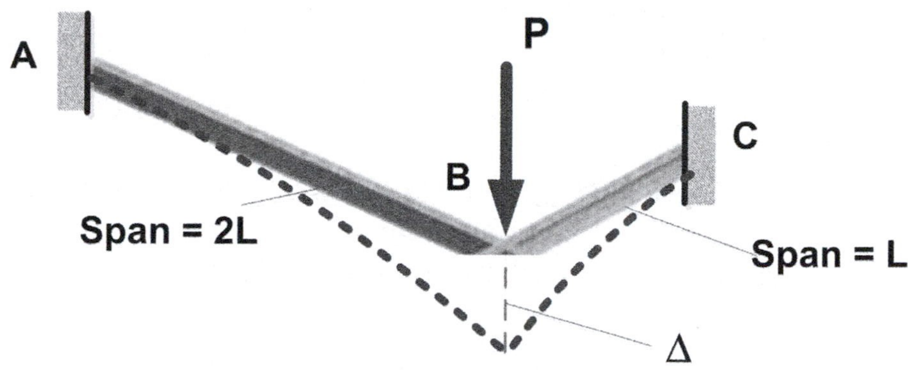

Assume that beams *AB* and *BC* will deflect the same amount at the intersection and deform independently. This is known as the compatibility condition of deformation, in which deflection at the beams' intersection point must be the same for both beams:

$$\Delta_{AB} = \Delta_{BC}$$

The deflection at mid-span for a cantilever beam subjected to a concentrated load, P, at the free end is (see table 11.2 in *Building Structures* by N. Nawari & M. Kuenstle)

$$\Delta_{max} = PL^3/3\,EI$$

Therefore, we have,

If in the above equation, the beams are made from the same material and have the same cross-section, then, $(EI)_{AB} = (EI)_{BC}$. The above equation simplifies to

Hence, the respective load that each beam carries is inversely proportional to the cube of its length.
For example, if the spans ration is 1:2 as depicted in figure 11.8, beam *AB* will carry the load:

Also for equilibrium,

$$P = P_{AB} + P_{BC}$$

Hence, for the identical beams having spans in the ratio 1:2, the shorter cantilever beam carries eight-ninths of the load, whereas the longer beam carries one-ninth of the load.

Problem 11.9

<u>Step 1</u>: Determine the total load

Problem 11.10

1. Reactions at *A* and *B*:

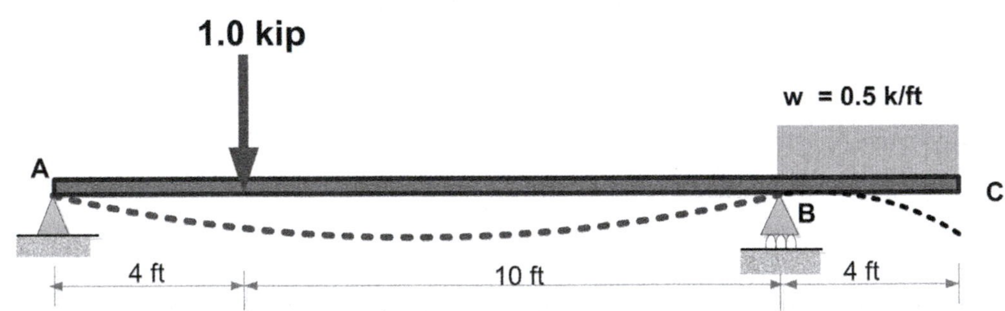

$\Sigma M_A = 0$: $\quad -1.0\text{ k }(4') + B(14') - (0.5\text{ k/ft})(4'(16') = 0$
$-4 + 14B - 32 = 0$
$B = 2.571\text{ k}$

$\Sigma F = 0$: $\quad 1.0\text{ k} + (0.5\text{ k/ft})(4') - A - 2.571\text{ k} = 0$
$A = 0.428\text{ k}$

1. Draw the shear force and bending moment diagrams:

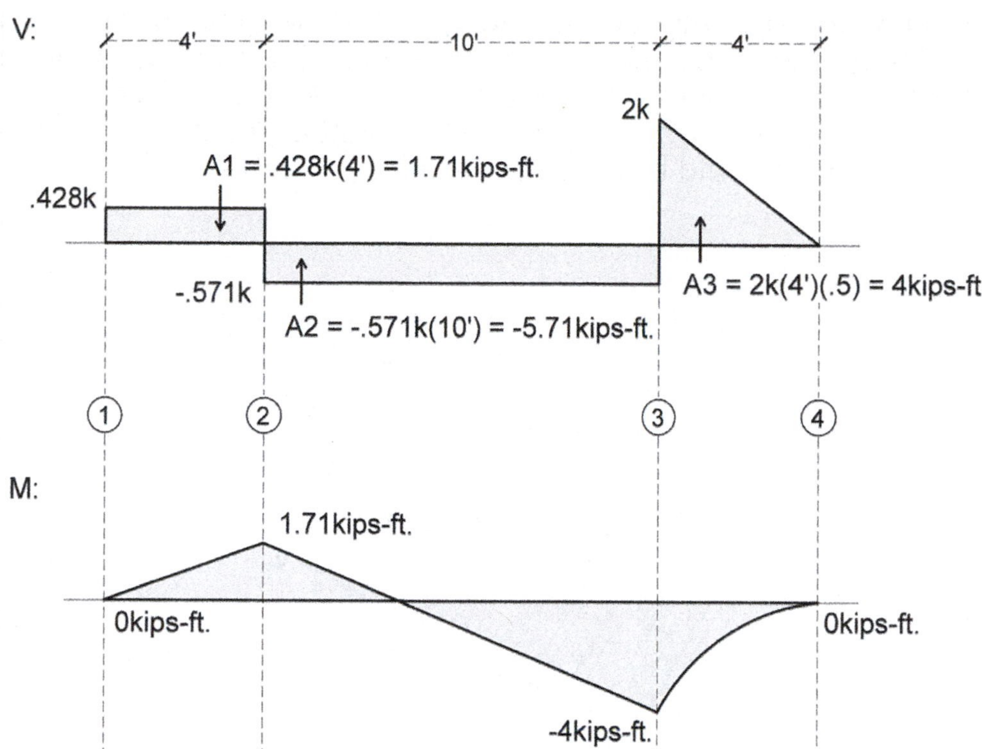

From ① to ②, A1 = .428k(4') = 1.71kips-ft. ⟶
0kips-ft. + 1.71kips-ft. = 1.71kips-ft.

From ② to ③, A2 = -.571k(10') = -5.71kips-ft. ⟶
1.71kips-ft. + (-5.71kips-ft.) = -4kips-ft.

From ③ to ④, A3 = 2k(4')(.5) = 4kips-ft. ⟶
-4kips-ft. + 4kips-ft. = 0kips-ft.

Section modulus, $S = 73.8 \text{ in}^3$

$$f = \frac{MC}{I} = \frac{M}{S} =$$

Problem 11.11

For the wood framing shown below, determine the maximum bending moment and deflection for a typical interior joist and the edge joist to the opening (see figure 11.11). Assume Dead Load = 12 psf, Live Load = 68 psf. Ignore self-weight of members. What size wood joist could be used for each if F_b = 1,500 psi?

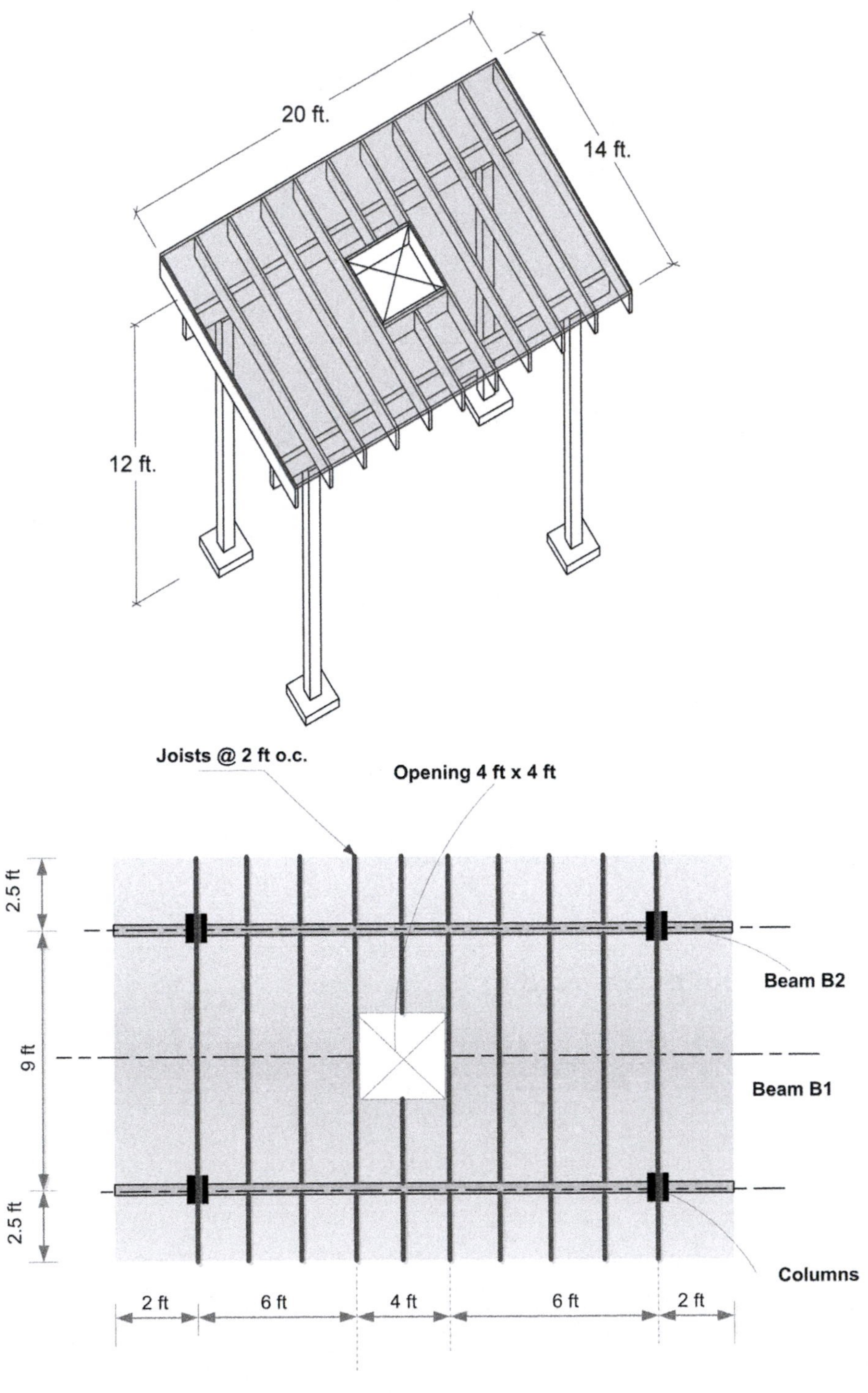

Interior Joists

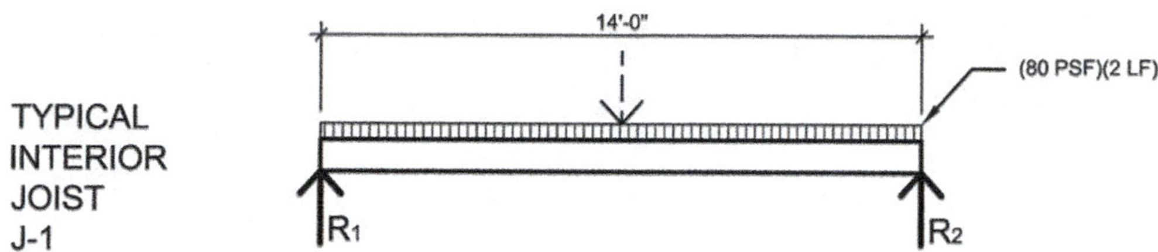

1. Calculate resultant uniform load:

   W = (80 psf)(2 ft)(14 ft) = 2,240 lb
   Load diagram is symmetrical, therefore $R_1 = R_2$ = 2,240 lb / 2 = 1,120 lb

2. Draw shear force and bending moment diagram.

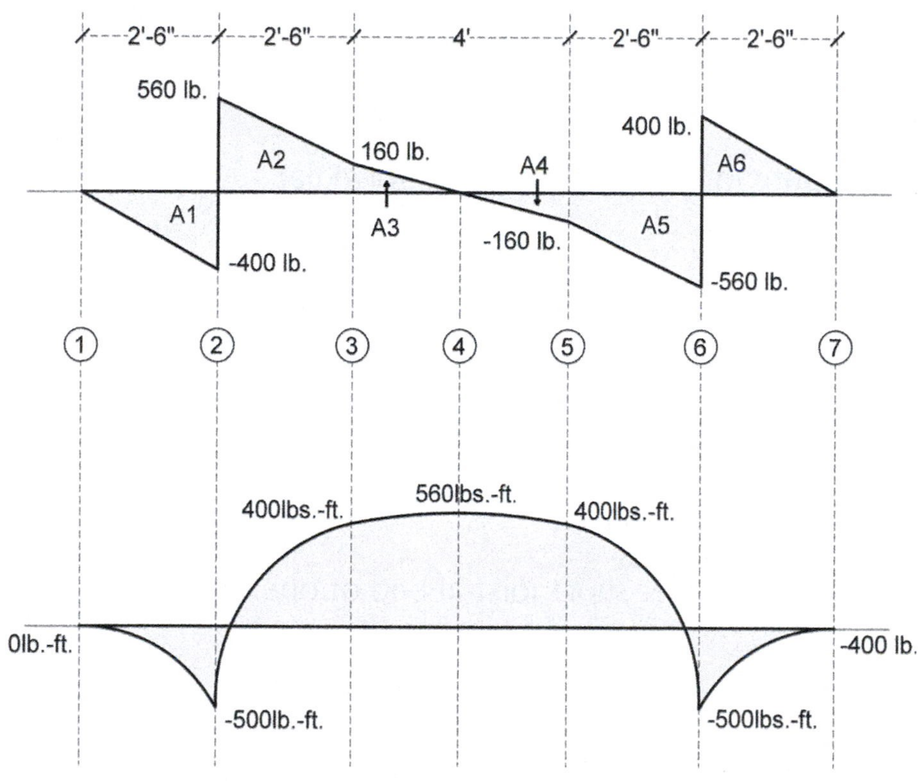

From ① to ②, A1 = -400lbs.(2.5')(.5) = -500lbs.-ft. ⟶
0lb.-ft. + (-500lbs.-ft.) = -500lbs.-ft.

From ② to ③, A2 = (560lbs.-160lbs.)(2.5')(.5) + (160lbs.)(2.5') = 900lbs.-ft. ⟶
500lbs.-ft. + 900lbs.-ft. = 400lbs.-ft.

3. Determine the section modulus (S):

$$M = F_b \times S$$

$$S_x = \frac{M}{F_b} =$$

From Appendix A, try 2x8 S4S where,

$$S_x = 13.14 in^3 > 8.96 in^3$$

$$A = 10.88 in^2$$

$$I_x = 47.63 in^4$$

4. Compute joist deflection using formula:

$$\Delta = \frac{5wL^4}{384EI}$$

$Where,$

$E = 1700 ksi$

<u>Joist at end of opening</u>

First consider short joist at end of opening:

SHORT
JOIST AT
EDGE OF
OPENING

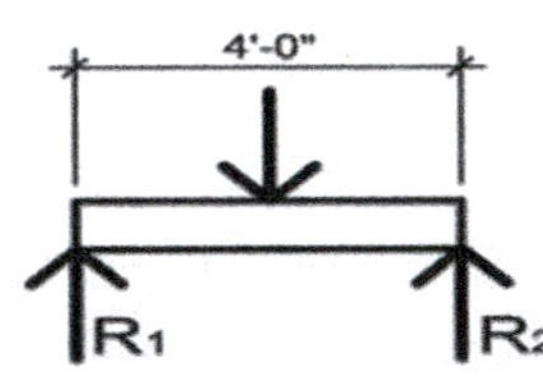

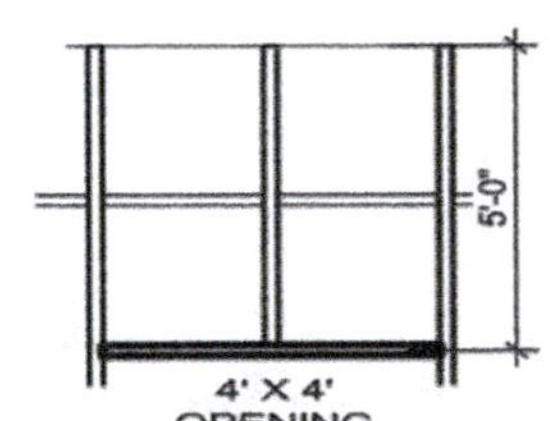

1. Calculate uniform load:

$W = (80 \text{ psf})(2 \text{ ft})(5 \text{ ft}) = 800 \text{ lb}$
Calculate the moment about the left support point:
$\Sigma M_{R1} =$

$R_2 =$ lb
$R_1 = 0$

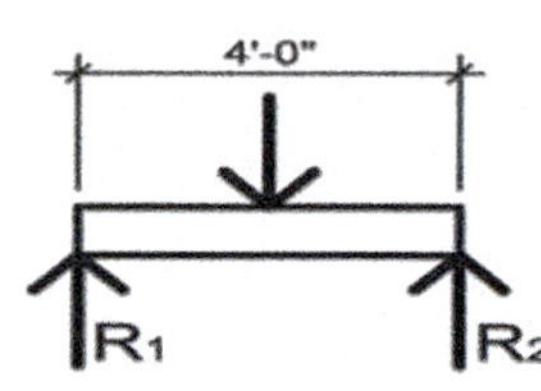

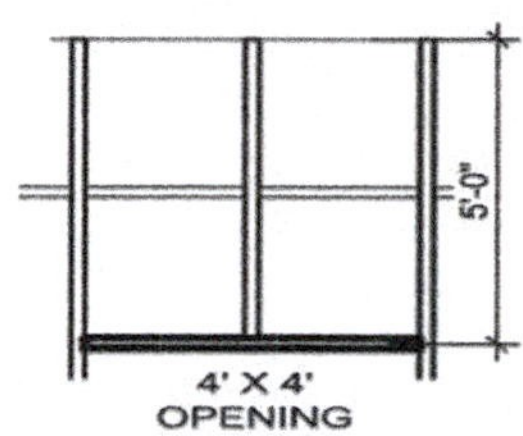

2. No reactions—point load is 0

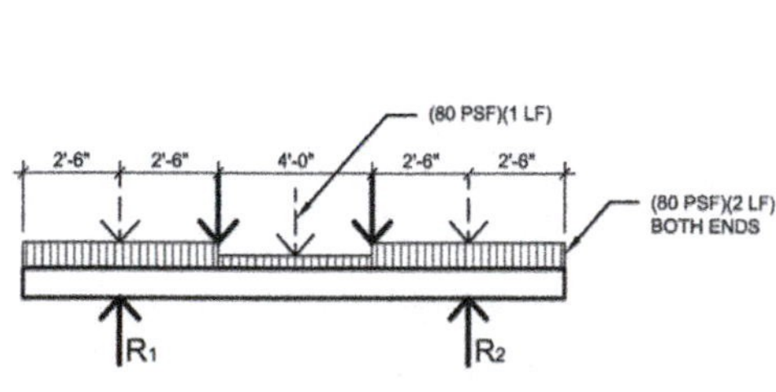

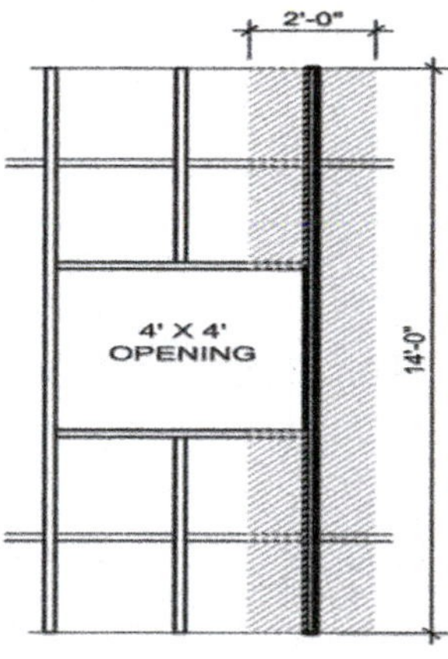

3. Total load = 800 lb + 320 lb + 800 lb = 1,920 lb

Load diagram is symmetrical, therefore $R_1 = R_2 =$

4. Draw shear force diagram and bending moment diagrams.

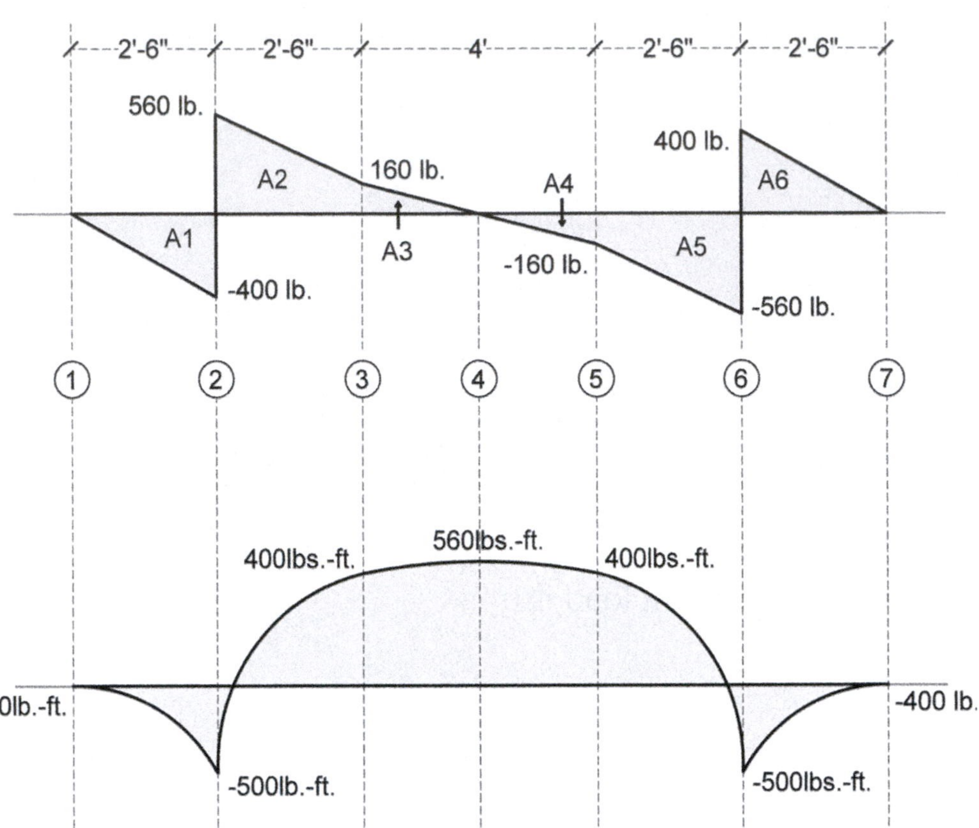

From ① to ②, A1 = -400lbs.(2.5')(.5) = -500lbs.-ft. →
0lb.-ft. + (-500lbs.-ft.) = -500lbs.-ft.

From ② to ③, A2 = (560lbs.-160lbs.)(2.5')(.5) + (160lbs.)(2.5') = 900lbs.-ft. →
500lbs.-ft. + 900lbs.-ft. = 400lbs.-ft.

From ③ to ④, A3 = 160lbs(2')(.5) = 160lbs.-ft. →
400lbs.-ft. + 160lbs.-ft. = 560lbs.-ft.

From ④ to ⑤, A4 = -160lbs(2')(.5) = -160lbs.-ft. →
560lbs-ft. + (-160lbs.-ft.) = 400lb.-ft.

From ⑤ to ⑥, A5 = [-560lbs. - (-160lbs.)](2.5')(.5) + (-160lbs.)(2.5') = -900lbs.-ft. →
400lbs.-ft. + (-900lbs.-ft.) = -500lbs.-ft.

From ⑥ to ⑦, A6 = 400lbs.(2.5')(.5) = 500lbs.-ft. →
-500lbs-ft. + 500lbs.-ft. = 0lb.-ft.

5. Determine the section modulus (S).

$$M = F_b \times S$$

$$S_x = \frac{M}{F_b} =$$

From Appendix A, try 2x8 S4S where,

$$S_x =$$

$$A = 10.88 in^2$$

$$I_x = 47.63 in^4$$

6. Compute joist deflection using formula:

$$\Delta = \frac{5wL^4}{384EI}$$

Where,

$$E = 1700 ksi$$

$$\Delta = \frac{5wL^4}{384EI} = \frac{(5)\left(\frac{160 \ ^{lb}/_{ft}}{12 \ ^{in}/_{ft}}\right)(9' \times 12 \ ^{in}/_{ft})}{384(1{,}700 psi \times 10^3)(47.63 in^4)} = .292 in$$

Problem 11.12

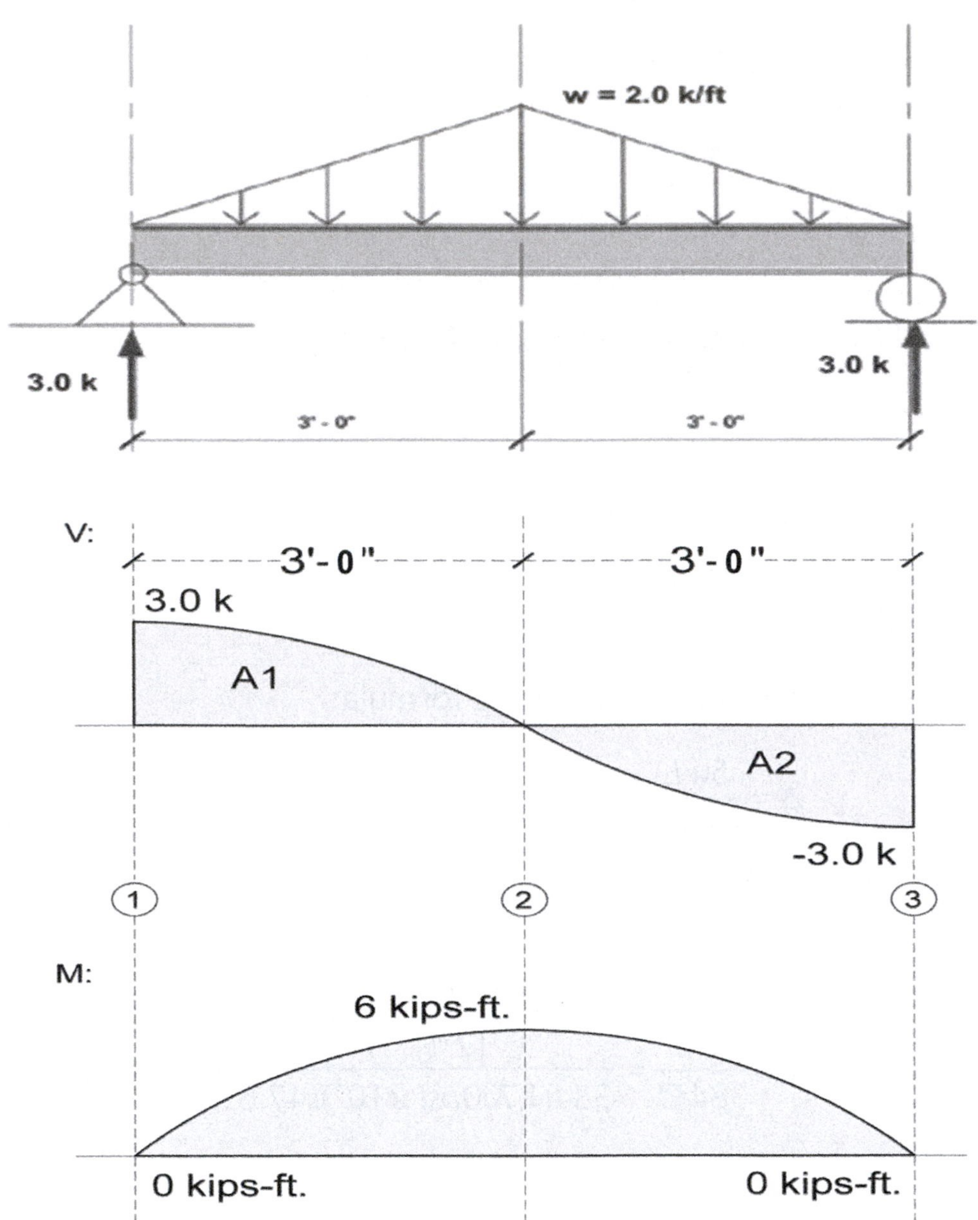

(a) $W10x19$

$$S_x = 18.8 in^3$$

$$f = \frac{M}{S} =$$

(b) Timber beam required:

$$S_{req'd} = \frac{M}{F_b}$$

From table:

Problem 11.13

1. Beam $B1$ is supporting Beams $B2$, $B3$, and $B4$. Therefore, an intital step is to determine the loads on these beams and compute their reactions.

Beams $B2$ and $B3$ are loaded in the same manner (figure 11.13b):

Total load = dead load + live load = 50 psf + 100 psf = 150 psf

Beam load, w = 150 psf x tributary width = 150 psf x 10 ft = 1,500 lb/ft = 1.5 k/ft

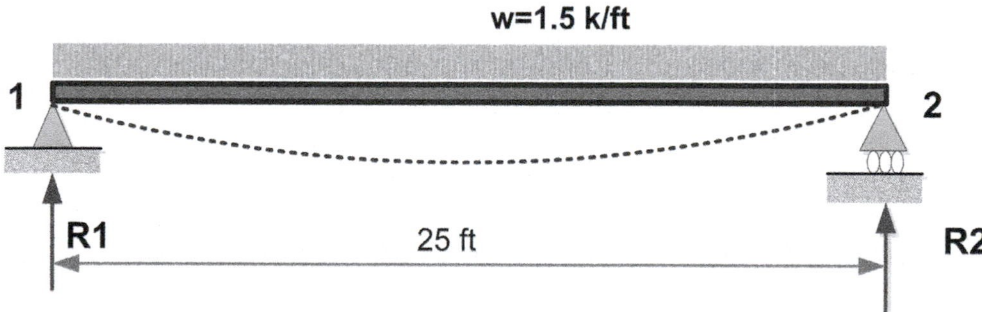

Figure 11.13b

Thus, reaction $R1 = R2 =$

On the other hand, beam $B4$ carries loads from only one side, and therefore the beam load is

w = 150 psf x tributary width = 150 psf x 5 ft = 750 lb/ft = 0.75 k/ft

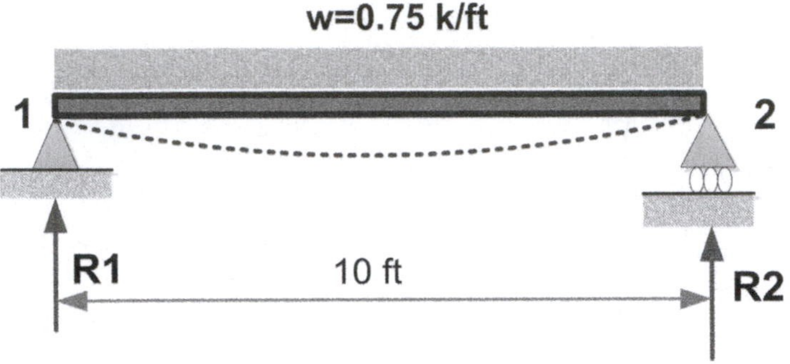

Therefore, the beam $B4$ reactions are
$R1 = R2 = wL/2 =$

2. Load on Beam $B1$:

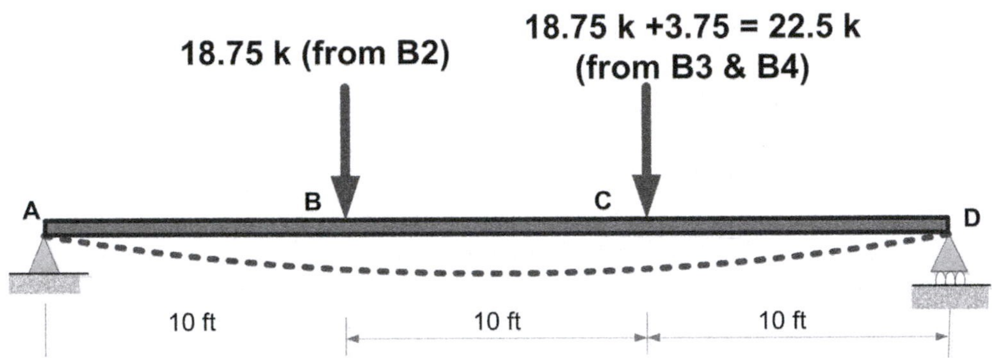

3. Draw shear force and bending moment diagram for beam $B1$:

4. Estimate the depth of the beam using rule of thumb:

Using the chart in figure 11.74d (*Building Structures* by N. Nawari and M. Kuenstle) to determine preliminary steel beam depth for a span of 30 ft. From the chart, beam depth $d = 18$ inches. Therefore, use W 18 beam section.

CHAPTER 12

Problem 12.1

See chapter 12 in *Building Structures: Fundamentals of Crossover Design* by Nawari & Kuentsle.

Problem 12.2

A *W* 10 x 49 steel column 20 ft long is pin supported at both ends. Determine the critical buckling load and stress developed in the column. E = 29 x 10^3 ksi.

1. Shape factors for column *W* 10 x49:

$A = 14.4 \text{ in}^2$; $r_x = 4.35$ in ; $r_y = 2.54$ in

2. Slenderness ratio (*kL/r*):

Effective length for the x-axis = $(KL)_x$ =
Effective length for the y-axis = $(KL)_y$ =

The corresponding slenderness ratios are

$$\left(\frac{KL}{r}\right)_x =$$

$$\left(\frac{KL}{r}\right)_y =$$

$$f_{critical} = \frac{\pi^2 E}{\left(\frac{KL}{r}\right)^2} =$$

The critical load = $f_{critical}$ x A

Problem 12.3

1. Shape factors for column W 8 x31:

   $A = 9.12\ \text{in}^2$; $\quad r_x = 3.47$ in ; $\quad r_y = 2.02$ in

2. Slenderness ratio (kL/r):

   Effective length for the x-axis = $(KL)_x = 1 \times L = L$
   Effective length for the y-axis = $(KL)_y = 1 \times L = L$

   The corresponding slenderness ratios are

   $$\left(\frac{KL}{r}\right)_x =$$

   $$\left(\frac{KL}{r}\right)_y =$$

The weak axis (y-axis) is critical; the critical buckling load is given by:

$$P_{critical} = \frac{\pi^2 AE}{\left(\frac{KL}{r}\right)^2} =$$

Solving for the critical column length (L) =

Problem 12.4

1. The section properties for the 4 x8 column are

   $A = 25.38\ \text{in}^2$; $\quad r_x = 2.09$ in ; $\quad r_y = 1.00$ in

2. Slenderness ratios (KL/r):

Effective length for the x-axis = $(KL)_x$ =

Effective length for the y-axis = $(KL)_y$ =

The corresponding slenderness ratios are

$$\left(\frac{KL}{r}\right)_x =$$

$$\left(\frac{KL}{r}\right)_y =$$

The weak axis (y-axis) is critical, but by a small amount in comparison to the x-axis.

The critical buckling stress is given by:

$$f_{critical} = \frac{\pi^2 E}{\left(\frac{KL}{r}\right)^2} =$$

The critical load = f_{critical} x A =

If the weaker axis was not strengthened, the critical slenderness ratio would have been 240, the column critical stress would have been 0.2 ksi, and the critical buckling load would have been 5.08 kips. In other words, bracing the weaker axis has increased the column's carrying capacity by four times.

Problem 12.5

1. Shape factors for column W 8 x24:

$A = 7.08\ \text{in}^2$; $r_x = 3.42$ in ; $r_y = 1.61$ in

2. Slenderness ratio (kL/r):

Effective length for the x-axis = $(KL)_x$ =
Effective length for the y-axis = $(KL)_y$ =

The corresponding slenderness ratios are

$$\left(\frac{KL}{r}\right)_x =$$

$$\left(\frac{KL}{r}\right)_y =$$

The weak axis (y-axis) is critical by a large amount in comparison to the x-axis.
The critical buckling stress is given by:

$$f_{critical} = \frac{\pi^2 E}{\left(\frac{KL}{r}\right)^2} =$$

The critical load = $f_{critical}$ x A =

Problem 12.6

1. Slenderness ratio (kL/r):

Effective length for the y-axis = $(KL)_y$ =

The corresponding slenderness ratios are

$$\left(\frac{KL}{r}\right)_y =$$

2. The critical buckling stress is given by:

$$f_{critical} = \frac{\pi^2 E}{\left(\frac{KL}{r}\right)^2} =$$

Try W 8 x 18 : $A = 5.26$ in^2; $r_y = 1.23$ in

The allowable load (safe load) = $f_{critical}$ x A / factor of safety

=

Problem 12.7

1. Section properties W 10 x 49:

$A = 14.4$ in^2; $r_x = 4.35$ in; $r_y = 2.54$ in

2. Slenderness ratio (KL/r):

The effects of end conditions on buckling are illustrated in figure 12.7b below. From this diagram, effective lengths in the x- and y-axis are different.

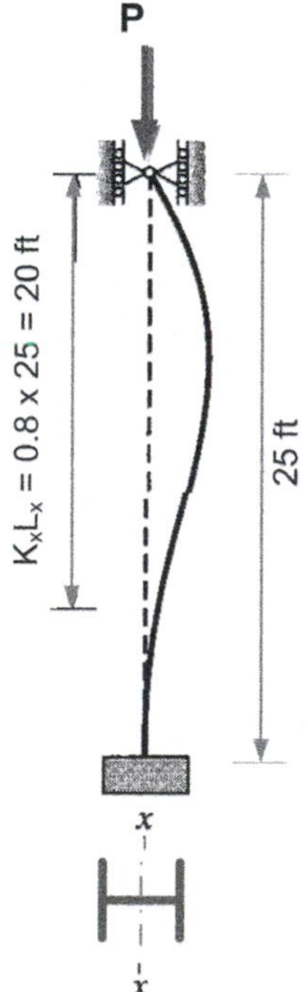

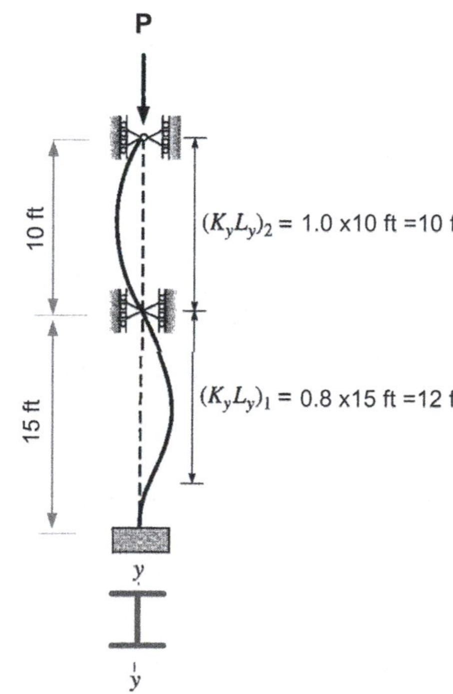

Figure 12.7b

Effective length for the x-axis = $(KL)_x$ =
Effective lengths for the y-axis are

$= (K_y L_y)_1 =$

$= (K_y L_y)_2 =$

The maximum value controls, i.e. $(K_y L_y) =$

The corresponding slenderness ratios are

$$\left(\frac{KL}{r}\right)_x =$$

$$\left(\frac{KL}{r}\right)_y =$$

The critical buckling stress is given by:

$$f_{critical} = \frac{\pi^2 E}{\left(\frac{KL}{r}\right)^2} =$$

The critical load = $f_{critical}$ x A =

Problem 12.8

1. Determine total loads on the roof and typical floor:

   Roof load = (Dead load + Snow load) x (tributary area)
   = (50 psf + 40 psf) x (30 ft x 10 ft) = 27,000 lb
   = 27 kips

   Floor load = (100 psf + 125 psf) x 300 ft^2 = 67,500 lb = 67.5 kips

2. Total load on the 1st floor column = floor load + roof load

   =

3. Slenderness ratio (kL/r):

   Effective length for the y-axis = $(KL)_y$ =
   The corresponding slenderness ratios are

   $$\left(\frac{KL}{r}\right)_y =$$

4. therefore, the critical buckling stress is given by:

   $$f_{critical} = \frac{\pi^2 E}{\left(\frac{KL}{r}\right)^2} =$$

The allowable load (safe load) = f_{critical} x A / factor of safety

=

Problem 12.9

1. Determine total loads on the roof and typical floor:

   Roof load = (Dead load + Live load) x (tributary area)
   = (80 psf + 20 psf) x 500 ft^2 = 50,000 lb = 50 kips
   Floor load = (100 psf + 150 psf) x 500 ft^2 = 125,000 lb = 125 kips

2. Total load on the third floor column = 4th floor load + roof load =

3. Effective length of the 3rd floor column = KL =

   Slenderness ratio (kL/r):

   $$\left(\frac{KL}{r}\right)_y = \frac{180}{r_y}$$

   The weak axis (y-axis) is critical for steel W-shapes.

The critical buckling stress is given by:

$$f_{critical} = \frac{\pi^2 E}{\left(\frac{KL}{r}\right)^2} =$$

Try W 10 x 39 with: $A = 11.5$ in^2 and $r_y = 1.98$ in
The allowable load $= f_{critical}$ x A / safety factor

=

4. Total load on the 1st floor column = roof load + 3 x typical

   Try W 10 x 54 with: $A = 15.8$ in^2 and $r_y = 2.58$ in
   The allowable compressive load $= f_{critical}$ x A / safety factor

   =

CPSIA information can be obtained at www.ICGtesting.com
Printed in the USA
LVOW02s0810250815

451018LV00002BB/2/P

9 781609 2758